A Soldier's Story of His Regiment (61st Georgia)

Seeing the Elephant: Southern Eyewitnesses to the Civil War

Series Editors

Gary W. Gallagher • Robert K. Krick

A Soldier's Story of His Regiment (61st Georgia)

And Incidentally of the Lawton-Gordon-Evans Brigade Army of Northern Virginia

George W. Nichols

Introduction by
Keith S. Bohannon

The University of Alabama Press
Tuscaloosa

The University of Alabama Press
Tuscaloosa, Alabama 35487-0380

Manufactured in the United States of America

∞

The paper on which this book is printed meets the minimum requirements of American National Standard for Information Sciences--Permanence of Paper for Printed Library Materials, ANSI Z39.48-1984.

Library of Congress Cataloging-in-Publication Data

Nichols, G. W. (George Washington), 1843–1916.
A soldier's story of his regiment (61st Georgia) : and incidentally of the Lawton-Gordon-Evans Brigade, Army of Northern Virginia / George W. Nichols ; introduction by Keith S. Bohannon
p. cm. — (Seeing the elephant : Southern eyewitnesses to the Civil War)
Originally published: Kennesaw, Ga. : Continental Book Co., 1961, c1898.
Includes index.
ISBN 978-0-8173-5646-0 (paper : alk. paper) — ISBN 978-0-8173-8523-1 (electronic) 1. Nichols, G. W. (George Washington), 1843–1916. 2. Confederate States of America. Army. Georgia Infantry Regiment, 61st. 3. United States—History—Civil War, 1861–1865—Personal narratives, Confederate. 4. United States—History—Civil War, 1861–1865—Regimental histories. 5. Confederate States of America. Army. Georgia Infantry Regiment, 61st—Registers. 6. Soldiers—Georgia—Registers. 7. Lawton, Alexander Robert, 1818–1896. 8. Gordon, John Brown, 1832–1904. 9. Evans, Clement A. (Clement Anselm), 1833–1911. 10. Confederate States of America. Army of Northern Virginia. I. Title.
E559.561st .N42 2011
973.7'82—dc22

2010047590

Contents

List of Illustrations

G. W. NICHOLS,
1898
AUTHOR.

G. W. NICHOLS,
1868.
AUTHOR.

Series Editor's Preface

"I have read a great many histories of the war," George W. Nichols wrote at the beginning of his memoir, "but have never read one that was correct." His aptly titled *A Soldier's Story of His Regiment (61st Georgia) and Incidentally of the Lawton-Gordon-Evans Brigade Army, Northern Virginia* set about telling his own story as accurately as possible. The result is one of the classic narratives of front-line infantry service in the army of Northern Virginia. Nichols's 61st Georgia fought in the renowned brigade commanded consecutively by generals Alexander R. Lawton, John B. Gordon, and Clement A. Evans. Nichols framed his account without any excess of sentimental hindsight. In addition to reporting on great battles and dramatic moments, he told the story of two cousins killing each other in a quarrel about cooking duties, and described maggot-infested corpses around Spotsylvania's Bloody Angle. An annotated roster of the 61st supplies details about Nichols's fellow veterans, some of it not available anywhere else.

Years of exhaustive research have made Professor K. S. Bohannon of the University of West Georgia the nonpareil leading authority on Georgia's Civil War troops. Bohannon's introduction adduces strong new evidence about George Nichols and his book. A thorough index also makes the work more accessible than earlier editions.

Robert K. Krick
Fredericksburg, Virginia

GEN. STONEWALL JACKSON.

Introductory Preface.

At the request of many of my old friends and comrades, and the youths of the country, I have written the pages of this history.

I wrote a part of it in 1887 and had it published in the *Pioneer and Eagle*, a newspaper, then published in Bulloch county, Ga. After its publication I was complimented highly by all of my old company, and at the request of my own children I have rewritten and enlarged it, and decided to publish it.

At the beginning of this introductory I will state that the history is incomplete.

I could not tell all the heroic deeds, even of what I saw, for it would fill a large volume. I have never seen a history like this one. All that I ever read tells what officers did. This gives its readers a faint idea of what officers and private soldiers did.

I have referred to my own company more than the other companies because I supposed it a fair average of what most all the companies in the brigade and the balance of Gen. Lee's army did and suffered in battles and marches, etc.

I have no recollection of seeing more than two brigades reduced more than ours was. That was Gen. Hays' and Gen. Taylor's Louisiana brigades.

I have read a great many histories of the war, but have never read one that was correct. I was an eye-witness to most of what I have written, especially the campaigns of 1863 and 1864. I know it is truth, and the survivors of the old brigade know it is truth.

I have tried hard to write it impartially, for I desire

that the present and the generations to follow us, may know the truth and what a struggle the Confederate soldiers had in fighting American soldiers, when they outnumbered us more than two to one.

It was a lamentable war, and one in which more than one million American soldiers received wounds or perished in battle or otherwise.

I am proud, in my old days, to see the nation as well united as it is, and I want to live to see every possible stain and ill-feeling removed, and I would love to see all old soldiers, Union and Confederate, labor to this end.

I do not think the world ever furnished better or braver soldiers than the Confederate States furnished, or better leaders to lead them. And again, I do not believe the world ever furnished or ever will furnish better or braver soldiers than we had to fight. I have often wondered how we held out as long as we did.

I have had occasion to refer to myself a great many times, not that I was braver or did more than other Confederate soldiers, and I do not want the readers of this history to think so, for such is not the case. I was not as brave as some were, and I did not do near as much as some did, for I was a sickly, weakly boy, and seldom ever voluntarily put myself in bad danger like a great many others.

If I was asked which of the regiments in the brigade was the bravest, I would answer: "We did not have a 'bravest.'" Again, if I were asked which was the poorest, I would answer: "We did not have a 'poorest.'" I don't think a better brigade could be furnished from any source, or better commanders than we had, who were Gens. A. R. Lawton, John B. Gordon and Clement A. Evans, and Cols. Marcellus Douglas, E. N. Atkinson and J. H. Baker, or a brigade that ever did more hard service than it while in the Virginias, Pennsylvania and Maryland.

I have one chapter about my hospital life and what I saw and suffered there. I did this that the present and coming generations may have some idea of what private soldiers had to suffer. I have also given the readers one chapter of W. H. Bland's prison life. He was one of our company and I can safely say that it is true.

I have also fixed up the muster rolls and casualties of the most of the companies of the Sixty-first Georgia Regiment, and would have fixed them all up, but the survivors of one of the companies failed to fix the muster roll and casualties for me. I am sure that all of the members of the different companies are not reported, for it has been to do from the memory of the survivors, thirty-three years after the struggle ended. And if there are any left out we hope you will excuse us and the members who fixed up the rolls and casualties for us, for none have been left out on purpose. I would also like to add in some future edition all the different companies and regiments of the brigade, and will do so if some of the surviving members of the companies and regiments will aid me.

AUTHOR.

What Others Say of the Book.

Notice what some of the brigade commanders and others say about the history.

"The book of which Mr. G. W. Nichols, of Georgia, is the author, is a simple recital of facts connected with our great civil war as those facts came under his own observation while serving as a private soldier in the armies of the Southern Confederacy. The author, who was an excellent soldier in war and has been an exemplary citizen since its close, has made no effort at mere verbal display, nor does he base his claim to public recognition upon any peculiaraties of style, nor upon any pretense to literary merit in composition. He does claim, however, for his book the merit of truth; of absolute fidelity in the record it makes of his personal experiences and of those of his comrades in the battles, on the marches and in the camps, as well as of their countless privations and sufferings. Such a book must prove of interest to many readers.

"J. B. GORDON."

"This work by a brother soldier, who tells the story of chivalry and suffering which his comrades endured, will meet with a welcome.

"It will recall many memories which are dear to a soldier's heart, and it will furnish to his children a picture of the scenes through which the Confederate soldiers proved in their valorous, though vain effort, to sustain their cause by arms.

"The book is a story of one most gallant regiment and incidentially, of the Lawton-Gordon-Evans brigade, (Army of Northern Va.) but it fairly represents the actions of all gallant regiments in every other brigade. The book is well worth the reading by all soldiers and their sons and daughters.

"CLEMENT A. EVANS."

[General Clement A. Evans commanded the brigade in many battles and was promoted to division commander. He was an excellent Christian gentleman and an excellent general and commander.—Author.]

"This history, written by a brother soldier of a most gallant regiment (Sixty-first Georgia)of the Lawton-Gordon-Evans Brigade, is well gotten up, and is a true history of the brigade, and is written different to any history I have ever seen written about the late war from 1861 to 1865. It is written in a fair and impartial way to the Union as well as to the Confederate soldier, and should be read by every old soldier, their sons and daughters, and all others that desire to know the truth about what the brigade saw, did, and suffered, which, I suppose, is a fair average of what other Confederate soldiers did and suffered in the Army of Northern Virginia.

"This history is mainly a history of the Sixty-first Georgia Regiment and incidentally of the brigade.

"JOHN H. BAKER."

Colonel Thirteenth Georgia Regiment, Army of Northern Virginia, from 1861 to 1865.

WAYCROSS, GA., Sept. 14th, 1898.

"*Mr. G. W. Nichols, Jesup, Ga.:*

"MY DEAR SIR:—I have carefully read from your manuscript, the history of the Sixty-first Georgia Regiment, and of the Lawton-Gordon-Evans brigade, and I take great pleasure in saying that I find it very interesting and instructive, and especially so was your accounts of the battles of the Wilderness and Spottsylvania.

"It is written a little different to any history I have

ever read about the war, in that it goes into more minor details of the subject matter and the results.

"I hope you will be successful in getting your manuscript put in book-form and put them on the market, as I think that every Confederate veteran and every Confederate veteran's son and daughter ought to read it. I was especially struck with the absolute fairness in which you wrote of the Union army as well as the Confederate army.

"Wishing you much success in your undertaking, I am

"Yours very truly,

"JOHN W. BENNETT,"

"Attorney-at-Law and Solicitor-General Brunswick Circuit."

"Every school-boy and girl should read this history, for I find it instructive and will give a better insight into a soldier's life and a clearer idea of the struggles of the Confederate soldiers than any history I have ever examined.

J. R. BENNETT,

"County School Commissioner Wayne county, Ga."

GEN. A. R. LAWTON.

General A. R. Lawton was a South Carolinian by birth, a graduate of West Point and served in the First Regiment of United States Artillery for eighteen months on the frontier of the British Provinces. Resigning, he became a lawyer, graduated at Harvard Law School, and settled in Savannah, Georgia.

He was colonel of the only volunteer regiment in Geor gia when the war begun, and seized Fort Pulaski under Governor Brown's orders in 1861. He retained command in Savannah under State commission until in April, 1861. He was commissioned brigadier general in the Confederate Army and assigned to the command of the Georgia coast until the latter part of May, 1862, when, at his own request, he went to Virginia with six of his best drilled Georgia Regiments, then stationed near Savannah. So with the Thirteenth, Twenty-sixth, Thirty-first, Thirty-eighth, Sixtieth and Sixty-first, which contained about 7,000 well drilled officers and men, he arrived in Richmond the first week in June, 1862, with the largest brigade in General Lee's army, and was assigned to General Stonewall Jackson's command, then operating in the great Shennandoah valley. He joined Jackson's command June 10th, 1862. In Virginia his service was brilliant and honorable.

He returned with General Jackson to make the flank movement against McClellan, and took in the Seven Days' battle around Richmond, and bore a conspicious part, losing heavily in the battles of Gaines' Mill, Cold Harbor and Malvern Hill. When General Ewell was wounded at the second battle of Manassas he took command of that officer's division, which he commanded at Chantilly, Harper's Ferry and Sharpsburg.

At Sharpsburg his horse was killed and General Lawton severely wounded. He was disabled until May,

1863, when, though still lame, he reported in person for duty to the adjutant general in Richmond.

Under General Lawton's command the Ewell division, as usual, made a glorious record.

The Richmond press declared it had covered itself with glory.

When General Lawton reported for duty in May, 1863, the president and secretary of war decided to assign him to the responsible position of quartermaster general of the Confederate States. He objected strenuously to the assignment, declaring that he had entered the service for duty in the field, that he had no experience whatever in bureau service. His objections were snch as to cause a delay of two months in ordering him to that duty. When it was pressed upon him the second time, President Davis said that he considered the position one of such importance to our success that there was no man, of any rank whatever in the Confederate army, save only the commanders of the two great armies, whom he would not withdraw from the field and assign to that duty, if he could find the person best fitted, to be assigned to that duty.

Under these circumstances General Lawton accepted and was ordered to the head of that bureau, and took charge of it in August 1863, and continued to perform its great and invaluable duties until the close of the war, to the satisfaction of the president.

Since the war he was one of the acknowledged leaders of the Georgia bar, conducting many of the most important cases in the supreme court of Georgia and the supreme court of the United States.

General Alexander Robert Lawton was born in Lawtonville, S. C., in 1818, and died July 2nd, 1896.

At the time of his death the leading newspapers of the State spoke of him "as the great warrior statesman, lawyer and orator." He was minister to Austria under Cleveland's first administration. He was at one time president of the American Bar Association.

Introduction

by Keith S. Bohannon

In his classic bibliography, *In Tall Cotton: The 200 Most Important Confederate Books for the Reader, Researcher, and Collector*, Richard B. Harwell wrote that *A Soldier's Story of His Regiment* (61st Georgia) and Incidentally of the Lawton-Gordon-Evans Brigade Army, Northern Virginia was primitive in its style, "but lively and refreshing." Since the 1978 publication of Harwell's assessment, the usage of *A Soldier's Story of His Regiment* in numerous campaign and battle studies suggests its value as one of the finer memoirs penned by an Army of Northern Virginia veteran.[1]

George Washington Nichols, the author of *A Soldier's Story of His Regiment*, was born January 22, 1843, in Bulloch County, Georgia. He was the son of Theophilus Nichols (1808–1881) and Rebecca Crumpton Nichols (1818–1869). Theophilus Nichols was "a large farmer, honored and esteemed by the community." Despite being listed as illiterate in the census, Theophilus "was successful in the management of his many acres" and "a master with tools." For labor, he relied on his large family and possibly hired hands, for neither Theophilus nor his children owned slaves.[2]

The Nichols family farm was near Bengal, a post office established in the early 1850s close to Lower Lotts Creek in Bulloch County. In 1860 the Nichols farm included 1,600 acres, one hundred of them improved for cultivation. Like many inhabitants of the wiregrass region of southeastern Georgia, the Nichols family raised livestock, including cattle, sheep, and hogs. They also cultivated Indian corn, oats, sweet potatoes, peas, and beans.[3]

On the eve of the Civil War, George Nichols, his older brother Absalom Jackson Nichols, and five younger siblings all attended a country school. They might have been under the tutelage of James C. Hodges, a well-respected man identified by George Nichols as "his old professor." Hodges was a twenty-one-year-old teacher in the Bengal community in 1860.[4]

The Nichols brothers did not rush to join the Confederate Army immediately upon the outbreak of the Civil War. Absalom Nichols waited until early September 1861 to enlist as a private in a company commanded by Captain Henry Tillman. According to a 1911 memoir, Colonel Charles A. L. Lamar swore Tillman's company into service in Bulloch County on September 1, 1861. The compiled service records state that Absalom Nichols enlisted for the duration of the war along with his company on September 9, 1861, at Eden Station, No. 2, on the Central Georgia Railroad. Tillman's men and several other South Georgia companies remained along the Central Railroad at the Eden and Guyton stations until late September, when they moved into Savannah. There the companies became part of the 7th Georgia Infantry Battalion.[5]

George W. Nichols joined his brother's company on May 10, 1862, at Camp Bethesda, ten miles south of Savannah. During the succeeding weeks, the 7th Battalion received three additional companies and became the 61st Georgia Infantry Regiment. Shortly thereafter, the 61st went to Virginia, where it joined "Stonewall" Jackson's command in the Shenandoah Valley in the second week of June 1862.

When the 61st Georgia marched into battle for the first time at Gaines Mill on June 27, 1862, George Nichols had a high fever. After collapsing during the engagement, the exhausted and ill youth awoke the next morning to discover the corpse of his brother Absalom. The sickly George, unable to rejoin his regiment, began an extended period in the Confederate hospital system.

After a stint in Richmond and Lynchburg hospitals and a failed attempt to rejoin his unit, Nichols entered the general hospital in Danville, Virginia, suffering from "debilitas" on August 23, 1862. After being discharged from the Danville hospital on October 31, 1862, Nichols entered General Hospital No. 19 in Richmond on November 5, where he stayed through February 1863. By the end of February, Nichols had rejoined the 61st, who were then encamped below Fredericksburg. The extended hospital stay apparently invigorated the youth, for one of his comrades wrote home from Hamilton's Crossing in late March 1863 that G.W. Nichols had been out washing in the cold weather and was "quite hearty."[6]

Nichols served with his regiment in the Chancellorsville Campaign, having bullets pass through his blanket and shoe during the fighting around Fredericksburg. In the subsequent march into Pennsylvania, the "sick and weakly boy" once again fell ill. Nichols spent the battle of Gettysburg in an ambulance, and on the retreat worked as a hospital steward for roughly a week before rejoining his regiment.

Throughout the rest of 1863 and 1864, Nichols served faithfully with the 61st. He passed unscathed through many engagements with two exceptions. The first was on July 6, 1864, when he received a bruise from an artillery shell fired by Union batteries on Maryland Heights. Then at the Third Battle of Winchester, Nichols endured a brief captivity before escaping back to his regiment. Later during the same battle, a spent ball struck him in the thigh and another pierced his hat, cutting his hair.[7]

On January 15, 1865, Nichols and several comrades left the 61st in the trenches at Petersburg to visit Georgia on twenty-four-day furloughs. When Nichols arrived nine days later at his parents' home, he found that Union General William T. Sherman's soldiers had ransacked the place, stealing horses and many other things. In his memoirs and pension, Nichols claimed that the passage of Sherman's Army into the Carolinas and the destruction of railroads made it impossible for him to rejoin his regiment before Lee's surrender.[8]

Two years after the end of the Civil War, George Nichols married on May 25, 1867, Jincy Parrish (1849–1923), the daughter of Absalom Parrish (1816–1865) and Rebecca Alderman Parrish (1819–1862). The ceremony took place in the home of the groom's father. Three years later, the census enumerator recorded that George's real estate was worth $500 and his personal estate worth $2,300. The couple also had a seven-month-old baby named John.[9]

The Nichols household grew steadily throughout the 1870s, so that by 1880 George and Jincy had five sons and a one-year-old daughter. Sarah Parrish, Jincy's sister, along with Sarah's daughter Jincy, also lived in the household. Eventually George and Jincy Nichols had eleven children, seven of whom became teachers—a testament to the importance that the family placed on education. A descendant noted that the Nichols household was "a center of learning" and that the Nichols clan was known "far and wide as both public school teachers and farmers."[10]

Nichols enjoyed moderate success as a farmer in the 1870s. The agricultural census in 1870 lists him as the owner of 180 improved acres and 4,082 acres of woodlot worth a total of $500. He raised livestock, including several cows and 35 hogs; he also grew corn, oats, and sweet potatoes. Nichols might also have been engaged in timber cutting or the production of naval stores, as his census entry lists $100 in forest products.

By 1879, the value of the Nichols farm had tripled. He now owned 100 tilled acres and 700 acres of woodland, having apparently sold off much of his woodland, perhaps due to declining timber prices. Nichols had also moved into cotton and rice production, devoting twenty acres to the former crop and five acres to the latter. The ability of Nichols to hire "colored labor" for twenty-five weeks of the year gives further evidence of his prosperity. Nichols appears to have been following the advice given by many country newspaper editors to move into commercial crops only after first raising enough to meet household needs.[11]

In 1887, George Nichols dictated his memoirs of Confederate service to his daughter, Jincy Parrish Nichols. He then sent the manuscript to the *Pioneer and Eagle*, a newspaper published in the Excelsior community of Bulloch County by the Reverend Jason A. Scarboro. The paper ran the memoir in installments.[12]

Three years after his recollections appeared in print, George Nichols became involved in a dispute that resulted in his family's departure from Bulloch County. When the Upper Lotts Creek Primitive Baptist Church burned, G.W. Nichols was one of the members instrumental in erecting a new building. When a member of the church apparently did not pay for building materials he had purchased in Statesboro, Nichols, a justice of the peace and the church secretary and treasurer, felt obligated to serve papers on the man. Nichols believed that either this church member or the entire congregation must pay the bill.

When the issue came before an open church conference, the minister's nephew accused Nichols of lying. Nichols responded by rising from his seat, advancing toward his accuser, and demanding that he retract the statement or be stomped "through the floor." "Four abled-bodied deacons" had to restrain Nichols, and the congregation immediately voted to remove his name from the membership rolls. Nichols and his older sons subsequently took five mules and three wagons south to the Empire community in Wayne County, where they settled on a new farm. Jincy and the balance of the family joined them shortly thereafter.[13]

Following the move to Wayne County, George Nichols rewrote and enlarged his war memoirs at the urging of his children. In doing so, he corresponded with veterans of his regiment and brigade. The expanded version, which included muster rolls of the 61st Georgia acquired "by memory," appeared in 1898 as *A Soldier's Story of His Regiment.*

According to descendant Troy Nichols, the veteran's children were not happy with the considerable expenses their father incurred in the book's publication and the subsequent disappointing sales.

No publisher is listed in the first edition of *A Soldier's Story*, but Troy Nichols surmised it might have been Benjamin Miliken, a Confederate veteran and newspaper editor in the Wayne County seat of Jesup. Inscriptions in several surviving copies suggest that Nichols sold them through the mail from his home. The author stated that he hoped to issue subsequent editions, but he apparently never did.[14]

George Nichols claims in his introduction that he attempted to write impartially and truthfully about the Civil War. He largely achieved this goal, even including in his book an 1885 lecture on the Chancellorsville Campaign written by Union General Theodore A. Dodge. In a letter written to Union veteran Benjamin Borton, Nichols claimed that "God has so blessed me with his love that I cherish no animosity against anyone, not even those Union commanders who burned so many of our beloved Southern homes." Nichols also gave Borton permission to use any part of *A Soldier's Story*. Borton did so, including in his memoir, *On the Parallels,* a lengthy quotation from Nichols describing the Confederate retreat from Gettysburg.[15]

The strongest chapters of *A Soldier's Story* are those that describe the Confederate hospitals where Nichols was a patient in 1862, and that discuss the campaigns of 1863 and 1864. Notes taken by the south Georgia soldier on a nearly daily basis in 1864 allowed him many years later to describe in detail, and often with a sense of immediacy, the various battles and marches he passed through. Earlier chapters, which relied largely on information relayed to Nichols by other veterans, are less valuable.[16]

George Nichols was deeply involved in the commemoration of the Lost Cause. In 1899, he became concerned about the neglected graves of approximately forty Confederate soldiers in Waynesville. Nichols and another man put up a fence around the cemetery and urged the local chapter of the United Daughters of the Confederacy to erect individual markers on the graves. Nichols was also a member of the United Confederate Veterans, Camp Harris, No. 1125, and received the U.C.V. Cross of Honor in 1903.[17]

In late 1910, George Nichols sold off 292 acres of his farm to a son and two other buyers in order to liquidate debts. Two years later, when the elder Nichols applied for a pension with the state of Georgia, he owned eleven acres of land, ten head of cattle, and household and kitchen furniture. The estate had a total value of $280.[18]

George W. Nichols died on October 5, 1916, and was buried

in the city cemetery in Screven, Wayne County, Georgia. The epitaph on Nichols' tombstone notes his membership in the Confederate Army and Primitive Baptist Church, both organizations to which he exhibited great loyalty.

Keith S. Bohannon
Department of History
University of West Georgia

Notes

[1] Richard Harwell, *In Tall Cotton, The 200 Most Important Confederate Books for the Reader, Researcher and Collector* (Austin: Jenkins Publishing Company, 1978), 47.

[2] George W. Nichols was the third oldest of ten children, including: Absalom Jackson, John Thomas, James M., Mary Jane; Sarah Elizabeth; Daniel N.; Levina Ann; Emeline Rebecca; and Loven M. "Descendants of Sarah Graves and Abraham Newton of MA and NC," unpublished ts. in author's possession; *Memoirs of Georgia, Volume II* (Atlanta: Southern Historical Association, 1895), 359, 360; Solomon Nichols, "Our Nichols Family," unpublished ts. provided to author by Lowell Berenguer, Montgomery, Alabama; Frances T. Ingmire, *Bulloch County, Georgia Marriage Records, 1796–1845* (privately printed by author, 1985), 10; U. S. Eighth Census, 1860 Schedule I, Free Inhabitants, Bulloch County, Georgia, 804.

[3] U.S. Eighth Census, 1860, Agricultural Schedule, Bulloch County, Georgia, 7; Dorothy Brannen, *Life in Old Bulloch: The Story of A Wiregrass County in Georgia* (Gainesville, GA: Magnolia Press, 1987), 14.

[4] U.S. Eighth Census, 1860 Schedule I, Free Inhabitants, Bulloch County, Georgia, 781, 804.

[5] Absalom Nichols, 61st Georgia Infantry Regiment, Compiled Service Records [cited hereafter as CSR], M266, National

Archives, Caleb W. Smith, "History of the First Company That Went From Tattnall To the Civil War," Mss. 1165, Georgia Historical Society, Savannah, Georgia.

[6] Absalom's parents or other family members erected a memorial stone to him in the family cemetery in Bulloch County. Solomon Nichols, "Our Nichols Family," 12; Absalom and George Nichols, 61st Georgia Infantry Regiment, CSR, M266, National Archives; *Confederate Reminiscences and Letters, 1861–1865*, vol. XVIII (Georgia Division, U.D.C., 2002), 240.

[7] Nichols, A Soldier's Story of His Regiment (61st Georgia) and Incidentally of the Lawton-Gordon-Evans Brigade Army, Northern Virginia, 120, 121, 170, 183–188, 210.

[8] George W. Nichols, Wayne County Pension Applications of Confederate Soldiers and Widows who applied from Georgia, Microfilm Drawer 276, Box 73, Georgia Department of Archives and History [cited hereafter as GDAH]; Nichols, A Soldier's Story of His Regiment (61st Georgia) and Incidentally of the Lawton-Gordon-Evans Brigade Army, Northern Virginia, 209, 210.

[9] U.S. Ninth Census, 1870, Bulloch County, Georgia, 234; Jincey Nichols, Wayne County Pension Applications of Confederate Soldiers and Widows who applied from Georgia, Microfilm Drawer 276, Box 73, GDAH.

[10] Jincey Parrish Nichols may have wished to provide her children with the education she never received, since the census and her pension record reveal that she was illiterate. Bobby M. Martin, ed., *Wayne County, Georgia, Its History and Its People* (Dallas, TX: Curtis Media Corp., 1990), 285.

[11] U.S. Ninth Census, 1870 Agricultural Schedule, Bulloch County, Georgia, 9; U.S. Tenth Census, 1880 Agricultural Schedule, Bulloch County, Georgia, 14.

[12] The editor has been unable to locate issues of the *Pioneer and Eagle*. Nichols,A Soldier's Story of His Regiment (61st Georgia) and Incidentally of the Lawton-Gordon-Evans Brigade Army, Northern Virginia, iii; Martin, *Wayne County, Georgia*, 284, 285; Brannen, *Life in Old Bulloch*, 45, 104.

[13] Nichols' accuser later retracted his accusation, and the Lotts Creek Church restored the veteran's membership. George Nichols appreciated that "old wounds were in [the] process of healing," but chose to stay in Wayne County. (Martin, ed., *Wayne County, Georgia*, 284; Personal conversation with Troy Nichols of Jesup, Georgia, notes in possession of editor; Solomon Nichols, "Our Nichols Family" 9–10).

[14] Surviving copies of the first edition are crudely bound with staples that have rusted over the years. The book's cover features three colored Confederate flags. Continental Book Company of Kennesaw, Georgia printed a second edition of A Soldier's Story of His Regiment (61st Georgia) and Incidentally of the Lawton-Gordon-Evans Brigade Army, Northern Virginia in 1961. Since that time, Nichols' descendants have reprinted the book in 1988, 1999, and 2002. Personal conversation with Troy Nichols of Jesup, Georgia, notes in possession of editor.

[15] Nichols, *A Soldier's Story of His Regiment (61st Georgia) and Incidentally of the Lawton-Gordon-Evans Brigade Army, Northern Virginia*, 87–111; Benjamin Borton, *On the Parallels: Or, Chapters of Inner History A Story of the Rappahannock*(Woodstown, NJ: Monitor-Register Print, 1903), 180.

[16] Nichols, A Soldier's Story of His Regiment (61st Georgia) and Incidentally of the Lawton-Gordon-Evans Brigade Army, Northern Virginia, 210.

[17] *Brantley County History and Preservation Society, The Story of Brantley County, Georgia Volume I*(Waynesville, NC: County Heritage, Inc., 1999), 49–50; Margaret C. Jordan, *Miscellany of Wayne County*(Jesup: Jesup Sentinel, 1976), 148.

[18] George W. Nichols, Wayne County Pension Applications, GDAH.

JOHN H. BAKER, COL. 13TH GA. REGT.

CHAPTER I.

FORMATION OF THE REGIMENTS OF GENERAL A. R. LAWTON'S BRIGADE.—THE THIRTEENTH GEORGIA REGIMENT.

The Thirteenth Georgia Regiment was formed and mustered into the Confederate service about the 8th of July, 1861, at Griffin, Ga., with Walter Ector elected colonel; Marcellus Douglas, lieutenant-colonel, and J. M. Smith, major.

Col. Ector died in the winter of 1861. Lieut.-Col. Douglas was then promoted to the rank of colonel, Major Smith to lieutenant-colonel, and Capt. J. H. Baker, of Company A, to major.

Col. Douglas was killed at Sharpsburg, Md., September 17th, 1862, while in command of Lawton's brigade. Lieut.-Col. Smith was then promoted to colonel, but was soon afterwards elected to the Confederate Congress. Lieut.-Col. J. H. Baker was then promoted to the office of colonel. He received eight wounds during the war, four of which were severe. He served through the war with credit to himself and his country. He commanded the brigade several months until near the time of the surrender, and would have been promoted to brigadier-general if the war had continued.

After the formation of the regiment at Griffin, it was ordered in a few days to Richmond, and from there it was ordered to join Gen. John B. Floyd's brigade in West Virginia. It remained there till the latter part of December, 1861.

During its stay in the mountains of West Virginia, the brigade suffered severely from hard marches and the rigor of that climate, it being continually on the march.

It had two engagements with the enemy, and lost a few men in each engagement. One was at Sewell Mountain, the other was at Laurel Hill, or, by some, called Colton Hill. The casualties of the regiment from the cold climate and exposure on the marches were very heavy. From Laurel Hill it fell back to Newburg, West Virginia, and was ordered from that point to Charleston, S. C, and from there to Savannah, Ga.

It arrived at Savannah the 1st day of January, 1862, and remained there till the latter part of May. During its stay in Georgia it had several skirmishes with the enemy, and captured a boat load of marines with several officers. It had an engagement with the enemy on Whitmarsh Island, where it had several men killed and wounded. It fought the Eighth Michigan Regiment, and in their own report, they had forty men killed and wounded.

The boat in which the marines were captured was used the rest of the war as a picket boat and was called "The Thirteenth Georgia." The regiment was ordered from Savannah the latter part of, May, 1862, with Gen. A. R. Lawton's brigade to Virginia, and was in every battle in which the brigade was engaged during the war. There were no better regiments in the Confederate service than the Thirteenth Georgia Regiment.

It went to Virginia in June, 1862, about eleven hundred strong, and after serving two years and ten months with the brigade, it surrendered at Appomattox C. H., April 9th, 1865, one hundred and sixty-one, rank and file, as shown by the war records at Washington, D. C.

I especially ask all the surviving officers and men in

all the different companies of the Thirteenth Georgia Regiment to fix me up a complete muster-roll and casualties of their companies, like the most of the companies of the Sixty-first Georgia Regiment are fixed up in the back part of this history, and I will publish it in the second edition of this history.

THE TWENTY-SIXTH GEORGIA REGIMENT.

The Twenty-Sixth Georgia Regiment was organized in Brunswick, Ga., October, 1861, for twelve months, with Carey W. Stiles elected colonel; ——— Lane, elected lieutenant-colonel, and ——— Gardner, major. E. N. Atkinson was appointed adjutant and W. B. Folks, M. D., regimental surgeon. The following counties furnished companies for the regiment: Charlton, Brooks, Berrien, Glynn, McIntosh, Twiggs, Clinch, Ware, Coffee and Wayne. It was armed with Enfield rifles and was soon ordered to St. Simon's Island, seven miles east of Brunswick. Here it had to work very hard, building a fort and other batteries, and fighting sand flies and mosquitos and drilling with its heavy siege-guns, and company and battalion drills with the small arms.

They had to do a lot of picketing.

After they finished the fort and other batteries, they were ordered to move all of their heavy guns back to Brunswick and the regiment was ordered to Savannah, Ga. From here it was ordered to Camp Beulah, twelve miles from Savannah, near Green Island Sound, and back to the shell road, where the regiment reorganized and re-enlisted for three years, or during the war.

It then elected Adjutant E. N. Atkinson, colonel; William A. McDonald, lieutenant-colonel E. Shorter Griffin, major; E. A. Jelks, M. D., regimental surgeon; A. J. Lials, adjutant.

About the 20th of May, 1862, the regiment was ordered to Charleston, S. C., and it stayed in Charleston about one week when it was ordered to Virginia with Lawton's brigade, and served in Stonewall Jackson's command till he was killed, after that, under Generals Ewell, Early, Gordon and Evans.

The Twenty-sixth Georgia Regiment was made up entirely with South Georgians, who were brought up in a thinly settled country where there were but few schools. The most of them were taught early how to handle and use a gun, and could kill the fleet-footed deer, panther, wolf, bear, wild-cat and fox running at break-neck speed or could take off a squirrel's head with the old plantation rifle.

When the Twenty-sixth had to fight the enemy, it al ways punished them severely. It always had tne ground well strewn with dead and wounded.

It went to Virginia more than eleven hundred strong and lost in killed, wounded, captured and died in hospitals and prisons till it only had seventy-eight at the surrender at Appomattox C. H.

Colonel E. N. Atkinson received his military education at the military academy near Marietta, Ga. He was wounded in the battle of Fredericksburg December 13th, 1862, and captured, but was exchanged within a short time and returned to his command when sufficiently recovered from his wounds.

He was captured in the valley in 1864—probably at Strasburg, and kept in prison at Fort Delaware until the war ended.

During the war he contracted sciatic rheumatism from which he never fully recovered. He died in Waycross, Ga., a few years ago.

Lieutenant Colonel McDonald did not remain in the war a great while. He was elected to the Georgia Legislature from Ware county, and returned home to fill that office.

He lived to a ripe old age and died as he had lived, a splendid citizen and a Christian gentleman.

MajorEli Shorter Griffin was severely wounded at the second battle of Manassas and returned home and was elected to the legislature from Twiggs county, Ga. He died a few years ago. The places of these two gentlemen and officers were filled by Captain J. S. Blaine, of Brunswick, and Captain B. F. Grace, of Darien. Lieutenant Colonel Blaine was an excellent officer and was wounded in the shoulder in a skirmish battle near Shepherdstown, W. Va.. 1864. From the effects of this wound he wasrendered totally unfit for military duty and retired. Major Grace was an excellent officer and yielded up his life at or near the enemy's breast-works at Hatchers' Run on the 5th of February, 1865, and left the regiment to mourn the loss of this good man and officer. Captain James Knox commanded the regiment until the bloody struggle ended.

Captain Knox is yet living in Waycross, Ga., but is getting old and feeble.

The noble surgeon, E. A. Jelks, was with the regiment through all the bloody struggles in the Virginias Maryland and Pennsylvania. He was seldom ever away from his post of duty and was an excellent physician and surgeon, and the Twenty-sixth Georgia Regiment and the brigade all loved him for his kindness to them and his efficiency in treating the sick and wounded. He is living in Quitman, Ga., and has the love and respect of the city and community in which he lives.

The history of the regiment from the first of June 1862, till the close of the war is consolidated with the history of the brigade. I especially ask all the surviving officers and men of every one of the different companies of the Twenty-sixth Georgia regiment to fix me up a complete muster roll and casualities of all the different companies of the regiment, and I will publish them in the next edition of this history. Fix it up like the different companies of the Sixty-first Georgia Regiment is in the back of this history and send them to me at Jesup, Ga.

THE THIRTY-FIRST GEORGIA REGIMENT.

This noble regiment was organized in October, 1861, and enlisted for twelve months, as very nearly all the others did at that time. P. J. Philips was elected colonel, Pike Hill lieutenant-colonel and C. A. Evans, major.

At the re-enlistment and re-organization of the regiment for three years, or during the war, in the spring of 1862, Major C. A. Evans was elected colonel, John T. Crowder, lieutenant-colonel, and Captain J. H. Lowe was elected major. At the battle of Sharpsburg Colonel Crowder was wounded and totally disabled, and he had o resign. Major Lowe was then promoted to lieut-colonel, and Captain Pride, of Company B, was promoted to major.

At the battle of the Wilderness, May 5th, 1864, Colonel C. A. Evans was promoted to brigadier-general, Lieut-Colonel Lowe was promoted to colonel, and Major Pride was promoted to lieutenant-colonel. Colonel Pride was wounded in the latter part of the war and did not return ; he being disabled for military service.

The regiment was thoroughly drilled and was assigned to Lawton's Brigade, and ordered with the brigade, in the latter part of May, 1862, to Virginia, and was assigned, with the brigade, to Stonewall Jackson's command, which was then in the Valley of Virginia.

The Thirty-first Georgia Regiment shared, in all the battles, skirmishes and marches that the brigade was in, ts full share of the hardships and privations.

At its organization there were more than 1,200 men

The regiment surrendered 112 men at Appomattox.

The regiment was second to none in the armies of the Confederate States. Its history from June 1st, 1862, till the close of the war, is consolidated with the brigade.

I most especially ask the surviving officers and men of all the different companies to furnish me with a complete muster roll and casualties, like the different companies of the Sixty-first Georgia Regiment, in the back of this history, and I will publish them in the second edition of this book.

General Clement A. Evans is a native Georgian. He began business life as a lawyer in his native county (Stewart) after gaaduation from the law school of W. T. Gould. After a short while he was invited to a partnership with his first law preceptor, Col. B. S. Worrell, which he accepted.

His election when only twenty-one to the judgeship of his county and his subsequent election as state senator when only twenty-five, shows the esteem in which he was held by his people.

His military bent appeared in boyhood when he organized a boy military company and later on by his membership in the volunteer company of his town. Through these connections he gained considerable military training.

On the certainty that war was at hand, he joined with other young men in December, 1860, while he was State senator. In organizing the Stewart Grey's officers he was elected first lieutenant, and subsequently resigned this position. He enlisted with the Bartow Guards and was chosen major of the Thirty-first Georgia Regiment. Afterwards, as appears in this work, he was promoted to colonel, brigadier-general and commander of a division.

General Evans was continually with the brigade from its organization until the war ended, sharing all its batties except when absent on account of wounds received.

His career since the war is well known in Georgia and it need not be here repeated.

Wright's Legion, Afterwards Known as the Thirty-eighth Georgia Regiment.

This regiment was formed in the summer of 1861. It consisted of thirteen full companies, and was stationed at Camp Kirkpatrick, two miles west of Decatur, Ga., and four miles east of Atlanta, on the Georgia railroad.

The Hon. Augustus R. Wright, of Rome, Ga., was elected colonel, G. W. Lee, of Atlanta, was elected lieut-colonel, L. J. Barr, of Atlanta, was elected major, John H. Sherrod, of Swainesboro, Ga., was adjutant, B. D. Lee, of Atlanta, was sergeant-major, W. J. Arrington, M. D., of Louisville, Ga., was regimental surgeon, John M. Quinn, of Rome, Ga., was commissary, W. J. Jernigan, Lexington, Ga., was quartermaster, and G. W. Mashburn was regimental chaplain.

The following companies composed the "Legion," as it was then called:

1. Company A, known as Murphey Guards, of DeKalb county. Captain, John T. Flowers; lieutenants Pool, Marabel and Miller.

2. Company B, "Milton Guards," Milton county. Captain, George McClasky; lieutenants, McMakin, Philips and Maddox.

3. Company C, "Ben Hill Guards," Emanuel county. Captain, W. L. McCloud; lieutenants, Wright, Williamson and Oughsley.

4. Company D, "McCullough Rifles," DeKalb county. Captain, John G. Rankin (Old Reliable); lieutenants, McCurdy, Wells and Baxter.

5. Company E, "Tom Cobb Infantry," Oglethorpe

county. Captain, J. D. Matthews; lieutenants, Lester, Daniels and Hawkins.

6. Company F, "Thornton Volunteers," Hart county. Captain, J. D. Thornton; lieutenants, Teaseley, Brown and Maxwell.

7. Company G, "Batley Guards," of Jefferson county. Captain, W. H. Batley; lieutenants, Brinson, Vaughn and Farmer.

8. Company H, "Goshen Blues," Elbert county. Captain, R. O. Eberhart; lieutenants, Hall, Oglesby and Andrews.

9. Company I, "Irwin Invincibles," Henry county, Ala. Captain, J. E. Jones; lieutenants, Irwin, Jones and Campbell.

10. Company K, "Bartow Avengers," DeKalb county. Captain, William Wright; Lieutenants, Gober, Goodwin and Stubbs.

11. Company L, "Joe Thompson Artillery," Fulton county. Captain, C. L. Hanleiter; lieutenants, Shaw, Craven and McDaniel.

12. Company M, "Chastatee Artillery," Forsyth county. Captain, Thomas H. Bower; lieutenants, Hendrix, McDaniel and Hendrix.

13. Company N, "Dawson Farmers," Dawson county. captain, W. M. Blackburn; lieutenants, Hill, Marshburn and Goswick.

The legion was armed with Enfleld rifles. It was ordered from Camp Kirkpatrick to Savannah, Ga., and was stationed first on the shell road, and was ordered from there to the Skidaway Island; from there to the Isle of Hope, and from there back to Savannah, where it camped in Forsyth Park.

Here it learned to drill almost to perfection, for this was all it had to do except camp guard duty until the latter part of May, 1862, when it was ordered to Richmond, Va., with Gen. A. R. Lawton's brigade, which was formed out of six of the best drilled regiments on the Georgia coast.

When we were ordered to Virginia, the artillery companies L and M were detached and left at Savannah, and Company I, the Alabama company, was transferred from the Thirty-eighth to the Sixtieth Georgia Regiment, much against its will and the will of the whole regiment, for they had all grown attached to each other.

From this time till the close of the war the history of the regiment is consolidated with that of the brigade. It was about 1,200 strong when it was organized; 105 surrendered at Appomattox. It was indeed a noble regiment.

I desire the surviving officers and men to fix up a complete muster roll and casualties of all the different companies of this noble regiment, and I will publish it in the next edition of this history.

The Fourth Georgia Battalion.

The Fourth Georgia Battalion was organized in the summer of 1861 at Dalton, Ga., with the following field officers:

William H. Stiles, lieutenant-colonel; Thomas J. Berry, major; Samuel H. Smith, chaplain.

The battalion was ordered to Savannah, Ga., and formed into the Sixtieth Georgia Regiment in the spring of 1862.

Lieutenant-Colonel Wm. H. Stiles was promoted to colonel, and served the regiment until 1864, when his health entirely broke down. Col. Stiles resigned and returned home, and died during or soon after the war. Major Berry was promoted to lieutenant-colonel and promoted to brigadier general of cavalry in 1864.

Capt. W. B. Jones was promoted to major August 17th,

1863, and to the full rank of colonel on the 18th day of January, 1865, and commanded the Sixtieth and Sixty-first Georgia Regiments until the surrender. Capt. Stephen H. Kenedy, of the Sixty-first Georgia Regiment, was promoted to lieutenant-colonel of the Sixtieth and Sixty-first Georgia Regiments on the 18th of January, 1865, and received a severe wound at Deep Run on the 6th of February, 1865, and was sent to the hospital at Richmond and received furlough on the 2d of April, the day Gen. Grant broke Gen. Lee's lines at Petersburg.

Captain John Y. Beddingfield, of the Sixtieth, was promoted to major January 18th, 1865, at the consolidation of the Sixtieth and Sixty-first Georgia Regiments, and this noble man and officer was killed on the 25th of March in the charge on Fort Steadman.

Samuel H. Smith, the Sixtieth Georgia Regiment's good chaplain, was one of the most devoted Christian chaplains of the army, and loved the Sixtieth Georgia Regiment dearly, and was dearly beloved by the regiment and brigade. Often when we were going into battle the men and officers would run to him and give them their pocket-books to keep for them. He was so kind to the wounded and dying until no one could help loving this devoted Christian man.

R. S. McFarlin was promoted to adjutant June 20th, 1863. This good officer was wounded at Kernstown 1864, and was again wounded twice at the battle of Winchester the 19th of September, again at Hatcher's Run, and was again severely wounded at Fort Steadman on the 25th of March, 1865. He is living in Atlanta, Ga.

Daniel N. Speer was appointed quarter master July 15th, 1862, and was soon promoted to brigade quartermaster. In 1863 he was promoted to the office of inspector general and transferred to the Army of the West, and was twice elected State Treasurer, and filled this high office with credit to himself and State.

Lieutenant Benjamin J. Keller was promoted to adjutant at the organization of the regiment, but declined to accept the office. In the spring of 1864 he was promoted to the command of the brigade's battalion of Sharpshooters, made up of choice select men for bravery. He was captured at the battle of Winchester on the 19th of September, 1864.

He died in Savannah, Ga., since the war.

This noble regiment went to Virginia in June, 1862, with Lawton's Brigade, and served with the brigade in all its hardships in battle, marches, etc.

It went to Virginia more than 1,000 strong, and after serving two years and ten months in the Army of Northern Virginia it only had eighty-five men and officers. When General Lee evacuated the ditches at Petersburg about fifty of this number were in line and armed at the surrender at Appotomax.

If the surviving officers and men will get up a complete muster roll, and casualties of all the different companies I will publish it in the next edition of this history. Brother comrades, please do this for references for the dead heroes' posterity.

The Seventh Georgia Battalion, Afterwards the Sixty-first Georgia Regiment.

The Seventh Georgia Battalion was formed about the 10th of September, 1861, at Eden, Ga., No. 2 C. R. R., with seven companies.

C. A. L. Lamar was elected lieutenant colonel and J. H. Lamar was elected major. C. C. Schley, M. D., was batallion surgeon, Dr. Lamar, assistant surgeon. Captain J. H. Oattis, of Company F, Quitman county, Ga., was appointed commissary, Captain George Hagan was appointed quartermaster, Sergeant F. N. Graves commissary sergeant, and Granville C. Conner adjutant.

The following companies were from the following counties:

1. Company A.—"Irwin Cowboys," from Irwin county, Georgia. Captain, J. Y. McDuffie; first lieutenant, J. J. Henderson; second lieutenant, J. D. Wilcox; third lieutenant —— ———.

2. Company B, "Tattnall Rangers," Tattnall county, Ga. Captain, A. P. McRae; first lieutenant, D. R. A. Johnson; second lieutenant, J. M. Dus; third lieutenant, William Partin.

3. Company C, "Brooks Rifles," Brooks county, Ga. Captain, James McDonald; first lieutenant. J. A. Edmondson; second lieutenant, Daniel McDonald, and third lieutenant, J. M. Harris.

4. Company D, "DeKalb Guards," Bulloch county, Ga. Captain, Henry Tillman; first lieutenant, Stephen H. Kennedy; second lieutenant, James H. Wilkinson, and third lieutenant, J. Hoyt DeLoach.

5. Company E, "Montgomery Sharpshooters," Montgomery county, Ga. Captain, C. W. McArthur; first lieutenant, J. W. Vaughan; second lieutenant, John J. McArthur; third lieutenant, Thomas M. McRae.

6. Company F, "Wiregrass Rifles," Quitman county, Ga. Captain, Peter Brannen; first lieutenant, R. T. Cochran; second lieutenant, R. A. Fountain, and third lieutenant, Joel Crawford.

7. Company G, "Wilkes Guards," Wilkes county, Ga. Captain, Henry F. Colley; second lieutenant, Zack Kendrick; second lieutenant, Webster Fanning, and third lieutenant, T. L. Moss.

CAPT. J. T. ERWIN, CO. G, 61ST GA. REG'T.

With those seven companies the Seventh Georgia Battalion was armed with the best Enfield rifles, and was ordered to Jekyl's Island, about one mile south of St. Simon's Island, about seven miles east of Brunswick, where it had to work very hard building a fort, and fighting sand flies and mosquitoes and drilling on our siege artillery, and company and battalion drill with small arms.

After completing the fort we were ordered to transfer our heavy guns to Brunswick and the battalion was ordered to Savannah, Ga., and camped ten miles below Savannah, at Camp Bethesda. Here the battalion was well drilled and had two companies added to the battalion:

8. Company H, "Tattnall Volunteers." Tattnall county. Captain, James B. Smith; first lieutenant, J. M. Dasher; second lieutenant, M. B. Brewton; and third lieutenant, W. F. M. Edwards.

9. Company I,. "Thompson Guards," from the city of Macon, Bibb county. Captain, James D. Van Valkinburg; first lieutenant, C. S. Virgin; second lieutenant, E. P. Lewis; and third lieutenant, Eugene Jeffers.

The battalion of nine companies was ordered to Charleston, S. C., about the 20th of May, 1862, and camped in the city one week. Here Company K. was formed by volunteers from the different companies of the battalion. Sergeant E. F. Sharpe, of Company B., was elected its captain; Sergeant J. J. Mobley, of Company E., was its first lieutenant; D. L. Gray, second lieutenant; and Sergeant J. E. C. Tillman, of Company D., was elected third lieutenant.

The company being formed and added to the Seventh Georgia battalion, it then had ten companies and was called the Sixty-first Georgia regiment.

Lieutenant-Colonel Lamar had resigned and Major J.

H. Lamar was promoted to the office of colonel. Captain J. Y. McDuffie, of Company A., was promoted to lieutenant-colonel and Captain A. P. McRae, of company B., was promoted to major.

The regiment was ordered, with the rest of Lawton's brigade, to Virginia. It arrived at Petersburg, Va., June 2nd, 1862. Its history from this time is consolidated with the brigade. The regiment went to Virginia more than 1,000 strong. Eighty-one left the ditches near Petersburg and had forty-nine armed and in line at the surrender at Appomatox. The names of all of the Sixty-first Georgia Regiment that left the ditches at Petersburg, April 2nd, 1865, are as follows:

CAPTAIN—T. M. McRae, Company E. Captain McRae killed before the surrender.

ORDNANCE SERGEANT—H. R. Mims.

HOSPITAL STEWART—Benjamin Goodger.

COMPANY A.

SERGEANTS:

J. McDuffie,
R. H. Henderson.

PRIVATES:

Wm. Branch,
J. Branch,
H. L. Paulk,
Wm. Vickers,
M. Hansel,

COMPANY B.

MUSICIAN:

S. W. W. Higgins.

PRIVATES:

Wm Higgs,
J. H. Odum.
John Powell,
J. T. Sharp,

COMPANY C.

SERGEANT:

N. M. Reddick.

PRIVATES:

C. K. Browning,
E. W. Burton,
W. Lewis,
J. L. Moone,
William Smith.
G. J. Welden,

COMPANY D.

CORPORAL:

Wm. Holloway.

PRIVATES:

Thomas Boyet,
Lemuel Davis,
Jackson Collins,

Remer Franklin,
Ivy Sumerlin,
Madison Warren,
Thomas Waters.

COMPANY E.

SERGEANT:

D. N. McRae.

PRIVATES:

J. Browning,
G. M. Burkhalter,
P. H. Clark,
J. L. Clark,
J. McSwain,
H. McSwain,
L. C. Marsh,
R. T. Vaughn,
J. Watson,
F. G. Williiams.

COMPANY F.

SERGEANTS:

John E. Wade,
John M. Wade.

CORPORAL:

George F. Rice.

PRIVATES:

S. Barton,
G. W. Brown,
Levi Bridges,
H. L. Causey,
B. W. Forrest,
E. D. Harrell,
G. W. Harrell,
John A. Jordan,
Thomas Lindsey,
Irwin Nesbet,
Samuel Nesbet,
J. Mercer.

COMPANY G.

CORPORALS:

G. Colley.
E. A. Booker.

PRIVATES:

J. C. Agee,
W. B. Armmer,
D. B. Conner,
J. Hanson,
G. W. Hopkins,
J. E. Lunceford,
J. Spout,
G. B. Smith,
A. Wolf,

COMPANY H.

PRIVATES:

E. L. Bacon,
R. H. Lynn.
First seargent, Alfred Kenedy was captured at breast works.

COMPANY I.

PRIVATES:

W. B. Arnold,
Robert Burket,
William Booth,
McKinsie Blair,
J. A. Defoor,
J. B. Boyton,
C. Rainey,
W. Williams.

COMPANY K.

1ST. SERGEANT:

H. R. Sharp.

2ND SERGEANT:

J. M. Waters.

PRIVATES:

H. H. Blalock,
H. Sikes,
H. H. Sharp.

This was taken from the records of General Lee's surrender from the archives of the war department, Washington, D. C. Forty-nine of this number was in line and armed at the surrender.

Twelfth Georgia Battalion of Artillery.

This splendid command was composed of the flowers of Georgia's young manhood. It was recruited from the First Georgia Regiment after their term of enlistment for twelve months had expired. From its ranks the Twelfth Georgia Battalion of Artillery was formed by Major Henry D. Capers under special orders from the war department.

After a short furlough from their arduous service in the Cheat mountains of West Virginia in 1861, the following companies reported to Major Capers, at Augusta, Ga. on the 10th day of April, 1862:

1. Company A, "Newnan Guards." Captain George M. Hanvey, commanding; first lieutenant, William Beadlass; second lieutenant, Drew Brown; orderly sergeant, —— Freeman.

2. Company B, "Oglethorpe Infantry," Augusta, Ga. Captain George Allen, commanding; first lieutenant, Wilberforce Daniel; second lieutenant, I. I. Doughtry; orderly sergernt, Louis Piquet.

3. Company C, "Clarke Light Infantry," of Augusta, Ga. Captain Samuel Crump, commanding; first lieutenant, Joseph Taliaferro; second lieutenant, George M. Hood.

4. Company D, "Washington Rifles," of Sandersville, Washington county, Ga. Captain John Rudisill, commanding; first lieutenant, George W. Peacock; second lieutenant, Hanse Robson.

5. Company E, "DeKalb Riflemen," of Stone Mountain, DeKalb county, Ga. Captain George W. Johnson,

commanding; first lieutenant, Thomas Willingham; second lieutenant, —— Head; orderly sergeant, — ——

Under special orders from the adjutant general's office at Richmond, Va., these five companies were organized into a battalion of light artillery, and went into a camp of instruction in the vicinity of Augusta, Ga.

Major Capers received his appointment as major of artillery, in the provisional army of the Confederate States directly from the Secretary of War, so he was not elected. On his recommendation the following staff officers were appointed by the War Department and assigned to duty with him: First Lieutenant of Artillery Frank W. Baker, of Tallahassee, Fla., appointed adjutant; sergeant major, Ed. M. Clayton, of Augusta, Ga.; ordnance officer, Joseph M. Derry, Augusta, Ga.; assistant quartermaster, Capt. Kerr Boyce; quartermaster sergeant, Josiah Sibley; assistant commissary, Captain Geo. Crane, of Augusta, Ga.; commissary sergeant, Thomas Alexander, of Newnan, Ga.; assistant surgeon, Ben. Frank Rudisille, M. D.; hospital steward, —— Cummings.

The battalion remained in camp under strict discipline and regular drill till the 4th of July, 1862, when the rapid advance of the Federal General Buell on Chattanooga, Tenn., caused the Secretary of War to order Major Capers to report with his command to Gen. E. Kirby Smith, who was in command around Chattanooga.

The urgency of the occasion caused General Smith to use the command of Major Capers as infantry. He was ordered to report for duty to Major General Harry Heath, then with a small force confronting the advance of General Buell at and near Bridgeport, on the Tennessee river.

On the retreat of Buell General Smith advanced his

corps through Big Creek Gap, his rear guard being Heath's division.

On the march the Twelfth Georgia Battalion and Thirty-first Alabama regiment were detached and sent on a forced march at night to surprise a garrison of Federals who were strongly fortified at Huntsville, on the Kentucky line. The march was long and a toilsome climb and decent of the Cumberland mountains in the enemy's country, and with only two days' cooked rations in their havre-sacks.

The expedition was a complete success.

With the utmost gallantry the Twelfth Georgia Battalion assaulted the strongly built stockade on the crest of a high hill, carried the fort by storm, and in a very short time were masters of an immense depot of army supplies.

The colors of the fort were cut down by Captain Talliaferro, of Company C, who. under the general regulations of the service, was sent to deliver them to the adjutant general at Richmond, Va.

For this handsome and brilliant achievement the Twelfth Georgia Battalion was complimented in general orders by Gen. E. Kirby Smith. Two companies of the Twelfth Georgia Battalion (A and E) were detached and left with Heath's Division and served through the campaign in Kentucky as artillery with honor to themselves and country.

The remainder of the command with Major Capers were ordered to garrison Big Creek Gap and complete the investment of the Federal force at Cumberland Gap.

At the close of this campaign and on the recommendations of Gen. E. Kirby Smith, Major Capers was promoted in general orders from the war department to lieulenant-colonel of artillery, and his command was ordered to report to General Beauregard at Charleston, S. C.

In this department the Twelfth Georgia Battalion rendered efficient and gallant service at Fort Wagner, on Morris Island, and at Fort Sumter. At Fort Sumter, Lieut. Drew Brown, of Company A, was killed.

The soldiers' cemetery at Magnolia, near Charleston, preserves the names and is the burial place of a score or more of these gallant Georgians.

During the service at Charleston, Colonel Capers was ordered on special engineering service at Savannah, Ga., and transferred the command of his splendid battalion to Major Hanvey, a most excellent officer.

During the campaign of 1864, the Twelfth Georgia Battalion, on the voluntary motion of the men, joined the army of Northern Virginia and was assigned to the brigade, then commanded by Brig.-Gen. Clement A. Evans.

The rich standard of this command was placed in the line of General Gordon's division on the 20th of May, 1864, just after General Lee crossed the South Anna river and in time to share with the heroes of Lee's army in the second battle of Cold Harbor.

No Georgia command, or any command from any other state, so soon won the respect of the old veterans of the army of Northern Virginia, especially Evans' brigade and Gordon's division.

On the 2nd day of June they showed us for the first time their intrepid bravery. This was in an assault made by Gordon's division on Warren's corps, near Bethesda church.

Alas! that so many noble sons of our great mother State should have fallen in this battle. Among the killed was Adjutant Baker, and among the severely wounded was Colonel Capers, who fell near the enemy's line while leading the advance of his brave comrades.

This noble battalion again fought at Monocacy, Md., at Shenandoah River, Winchester, New Tow, Cedar Creek, Fisher's Hill, and a great many other places.

Whether on the march, at the bivouac or in battle, the Twelfth Georgia Battalion preserved, unsullied, the glory and honor of a Confederate soldier.

At Cedar Creek, when the gallant General Gordon was doing all that mortal bravery and cool generalship could do to retrieve disaster, he exclaimed: "Give me ten thousand such men and I will defy the legions of Sheridan."

After his wound at Cold Harbor, Colonel Capers was so disabled that he did not rejoin his command.

Major Hanvey remained in command till the bitter ending of Appomattox.

Before closing this sketch of one of the best and most representative commands, it will be proper for me to state that so popular were the officers of this battalion among the young men at home, and there were so many recruits coming to it, that Colonel Capers found it necessary to divide two or three of his companies. The "Washington Rifles" were made into two companies, and commanded by Captain John Rudisill, the other commanded by Captain Geo. Peacock. The "Clarke Rifles" were also divided into two companies; one commanded by Captain Samuel Crump, the other by Captain Geo. Hood, of Augusta, Ga.

During the siege at Petersburg, the Twelfth Georgia Battalion with Evans' Brigade was distinguished for the cool bravery and gallantry that they displayed. Especially was this evidenced at the assault on Fort Steadman and in the battle of Hatcher's Run.

Captain George Johnson, of Company E, was killed in the battle at Fort Steadman.

The colors of the battalion was a splendid combina tion of the confederate battle flag It was presented to the battalion by Miss Pinkney Evans, of Augusta, Ga., and was made of the rich silk of her mother's wedding dress and trimmed with ribbons from the fair ladies of Augusta, Ga.

At the close of the war the "standard," covered with honorable inscriptions, and beneath which seven color bearers had been shot down, was not surrendered at Appomattox with the army ot Lee. It was safely conveyed to Augusta and returned to the fair donor, who, we are informed, has it now as an heir-loom.

The author regrets that he cannot obtain a full and complete list of the killed and wounded of this noble battalion and the rest of the brigade. The list would be a long one, as the cemeteries of the country from Florida to the Ohio river and from the Chesapeake Bay to the Chattahoochee river plainly show.

If from memory our surviving comrades will aid us, we hope in another edition to make this record complete, like some of the companies of the Sixty-first Georgia Regiment are in this edition.

Of the field and staff officers the following list of casualities has been furnished to us of a few from some of the companies:

Lieutenant Colonel Henry D. Capers, severely wounded at Cold Harbor, Va., 2nd of June 1864 ; permanently disabled.

Adjutant Frank W. Baker, killed at Cold Harbor, 2nd of June, 1864.

Sergeant Major Ed. M. Clayton, promoted to adjutant, killed at Hatcher's Run, near Petersburg, Feb. 6th, 1865.

Major G. M. Hanvey, wounded slightly one time and severely wounded one time.

Lieutenant J. J. Doughtry, severely wounded at Monocacy, Md., July 9th, 1864.

Lieutenant Charles Doughtry, severely wounded at Cold Harbor, June 2nd, 1864.

Lieutenant Thomas Sessions, of "Washington Rifles," of Company A, killed at Monocacy, Md., 1864.

Lieutenant Thos. Tutt, killed at Cedar Creek, Oct. 19th, 1864.

Lieutenant William Beadlass, of company A, severely wounded at Hatcher's Run, (lost his leg), Feb. 6th, 1865.

Sergeant Hopps, color bearer, killed.

Sergeant Snead, color guard, wounded.

Sergeant Jesse Robson, color guard, severely wounded (lost his leg).

CHAPTER II.

Lawton's Brigade's Trip to Virginia—Joins Stonewall Jackson's Command—Seven Days' Battle Before Richmond.

The brigade being formed, we were ordered to Richmond, Virginia. The brigade was composed principally of young men and was nearly 7,000 strong, and was the flower of Georgia, and, I suppose, did as much hard and effectual service as was done in the war, and, I suppose, had as fine commanders.

Our first commander was General A. R. Lawton, who was assigned to the command of a division after the second battle of Manassas. Colonel Marcellus Douglas, of the Thirteenth Georgia Regiment, commanded the brigade. Colonel Douglas was killed at the battle of Sharpsburg, Md., and was succeeded by Colonel E. N. Atkinson of the Twenty-sixth Georgia Regiment, and remained in command until the battle of Fredericksburg, December 13th, 1862, where he was severely wounded, and Colonel C. A. Evans succeeded him in command and commanded until April, 1863. The famous General John B. Gordon was then assigned to the command of the brigade. He commanded until May, 1864, when he was promoted to the rank of major-general. Colonel C. A. Evans of the Thirty-first Georgia Regiment, was promoted to the rank of brigadier general and was assigned the command of Gordon's Brigade. He commanded the brigade until the fall of 1864, and was then assigned to the command of a division. And the noble Colonel John H. Baker, of the Thirteenth Georgia Regiment, was assigned the command of Evans' Brigade, and commanded it till near the close of the war. Colonel Jno. T. Lowe was the last commander, and surrendered the brigade at Appomatox.

We all loved, respected and obeyed these dear commanders. We private soldiers were never ordered to go where our commanders would not go. They often went where they would not order us. They always led in battle, and made the old brigade famous, and was second to none in the armies of the Confederacy.

We received orders in Charleston, S. C., about 9 o'clock one beautiful Sunday morning, while the church bells were ringing all over the city for divine services, to cook and prepare four days rations, and to strike (take down) our tents, pack our baggage, and be ready to leave Charleston at sundown. We hurried up all day and had everything ready and on the train, on the Northeastern Railroad, on open dirt cars, and started when the sun was about a half hour high. We traveled day and night and a great deal of the way in a very cold rain.

At Goldsboro, N. C., we met a great many Yankee prisoners, who were captured at the battle of Fair Oaks or Seven Pines, which was fought on the last day of May, 1862.

On the way to Richmond on those open cars and in the cold rain a great many of the boys got sick. Some died from the exposure.

When we got to Petersburg, Va., we were formed in line and our officers came around with whisky and gave us all a "treat."

The writer was used to but very little of strong drink and drank but very little. I decided I wanted a good drink for my benefit. So I backed out of my place in the line and went further down the line, and when Capt. Tillman got there I drank again. It took the "shakes" out of me and warmed me up, and I felt much better. Then we drew about two pounds of boiled bacon and about a dozen hard tacks apiece, went into a large house out of the rain and stayed all night, and left next morning for Richmond. We stayed in Richmond about two days until the brigade arrived. We were then ordered to the great Shenandoah valley to join the famous "Stonewall" Jackson, and was assigned to Jackson's old division. We got on the Southside Railroad and went by way of Lynchburg, then to Charlottsville, where we could see the Blue Ridge mountains. We then got on the Virginia Central Railroad and soon crossed the Blue Ridge mountains, through a great tunnel, which was a mile and a quarter long, into the valley. and went on to Staunton. We remained here bnt a short while, and marched toward Port Republic. We arrived at this place on the 10th of June, 1862. The battle of Port Republic was fought on the 9th of June, where the famous Stonewall Jackson routed the Union army commanded by General Shields. Here we saw a great many dead Union soldiers before they were buried.

We stayed here about two days, crossed the mountain and started on a long force march. We did not know where we were going. We soon found that our faces were turned towards Richmond. We had to march very hard, sometimes almost night and day, across mountains, creeks and rivers. We had to march from Port Republic to Richmond, except that we went by rail about fifty miles.

On this march we rested one Sunday and had religious service near our camp, where the famous General Stonewall Jackson met to worship God. It was the first time some of us had ever seen him. We started very early next morning and marched very hard till late in the afternoon. We stopped to camp and cook rations. Our tents were all left behind. The clouds began to collect and thunder very heavily, and the rain began to pour down in torrents, with a heavy gale of wind. It rained for very nearly two hours, and we all got as wet as we could be. Our fires were about all out. Ive Summerlin, of Company D, wrapped in his blankets, was lying down with the water ponded around him. He raised up a little and said, "Boys, it rains very well to-night." It created a big laugh. When it quit raining we renewed our fires, dried off the best we could, and finished our cooking.

We started about day next morning on a forced march, with full creeks and branches to cross. The roads were so cut up with the wagons and artillery until we could hardly get along. Some of the boys would bog so deep into the mud till when they got out their shoes would remain often ten and twelve inches below the surface. Every man had to carry his own haversack, knapsack, gun and cartridge-box. Some of the boys had white sheets, and I believe a few had feather pillows. Jackson's old soldiers, who had been following Jackson in his campaigns, made sport of us.

They would ask us what command we were wagoning for, and what train that was. Some of "our boys" cursed out the war, others shed tears (for there were a lot of *young* boys in the brigade), and said but little, while others, I suppose, prayed. We were being initiated and taking the first degree in war. We had been mustered into the Confederate service eight months, and had learned but little about the the rough life of a soldier.

One evening on this march we stopped to camp for the night. We had kindlèd our fires, and had begun to cook, when we witnessed a very sad sight. It happened in one of the companies of another regiment in the brigade. Two fine-looking young men had a dispute about their cooking. One of them had a large butcher-knife that he was cutting meat with. He stabbed it in the other's breast to the handle, and left it sticking there. The young man in death's agony said, "You have killed me." He then took hold of the handle and, after several efforts, succeeded in getting it out, and threw it at the other and stuck it to the handle near his collar bone. He then replied, "Yes, and you have killed me." They both looked faintly at each other for a moment, seemingly with deep regret, reeled and fell helpless to the ground. The doctors ran to them, but could do nothing for them. Both were dead in a few minutes. We were told that they were first cousins, reared near each other; had been great chums; had attended the same school, and that it was the first difficulty they had ever had. Such horrible news to go to their parents!

We had to leave our baggage near Hanover Junction.

We piled it up and left a guard over it. We have never seen it since.

Stonewall Jackson put his old soldiers that were used to marching and fighting in the front, for they could get along better than we could.

He secretly moved around to the right flank of McClellan's army near Mechanicsville. On the 26th of June General Lee crossed a portion of his army over the Chickahominy river and fought the terrible battle of Gaines' Mill on June 27th. We were in the rear of Jackson's column, and marched at quick step for about four hours. We could hear the cannons booming very fast. We finally got near enough to hear the small arms, and could hear the rebel yell, and meet the wounded who were coming out of battle. We were ordered to double quick (run) for about three miles, with a few shells being thrown at us. We were all doing our best. The writer had a high fever. As we passed an old gentleman's house, one of our company said: "Old man, how far is it to hell." The old man looked like a preacher, and he replied, "My dear sir, I am afraid you will find out pretty soon." The young man was shot dead in about thirty minutes. We got up and were hurriedly formed in line and ordered to advance in a storm of grape-shot and shells.

One grap-eshot broke Joe Nevill's gun and came very near breaking his neck. One shell exploded so close to Jack Collins until it addled him and partly paralyzed him for several days. We went on in line through a very thick, boggy branch where we found a great many dead and wounded yankees. Some of them were lying in the water. I was so thirsty from fever and a long march and run to the battle till my tongue was swollen. I stopped, dipped up and drank water which I knew had yankee blood in it. I am sure it was the best water to me that I ever drank. I have often thought it saved my life. We forwarded across the branch and up a little hill, stopped a minute and reformed our line. There was a terrible battle raging about three hundred yards in our front. Our line advanced in an open field, which was very smoky. We could see both the Confederate and Yankee lines. We were about two hundred yards from the Confederate line and they mistook us for Yankees coming up in the rear and fired a volley at us, and I suppose the yankees shot at us too, for we were about three hundred yards from their line.

We forwarded one hundred yards in a storm of minnie balls. We were ordered to fall back over the hill. We did so, and lay down. We only fired one volley. In the little advance of one hundred yards and back we lost about one hundred men killed and wounded in the Sixty-first Georgia Regiment. The brigade suffered severely. Our company lost three men killed and eight wounded. The killed in Company D were A. J. Nichols, Joshua Kirkland and Wesley Hodges. A. J. Nichols was a dear brother of the writer. Nichols and Hodges were both brave and noble young men. The company mourned their loss. The wounded were : Lieutenant John Brannen, R. J. Williams (now Rev. R. J. Williams), Daniel Parrish, John R. Beasley, F. M. Warren and A. M. Rimes. All of these were seriously wounded. T. B. Jones had one toe shot off. Joe Nevill and Jack Collins were slightly wounded.

The noble captain, Henry F. Colley, of Company G, was mortally wounded, and died a few days afterwards in Richmond, Va.

We heard a terrible rebel yell, and heard firing at some distance to our left for a few minutes, and then it all ceased. It was other troops at our left charging and routing the Yankees on their part of the line.

We were ordered to the right. I made several efforts to get up, but could not, for I was exhausted. I had marched all day with a high fever, and at double quick for three miles. Jim Hendrix, of our company, was nearly as bad off as I was. We were obliged to lie there all night. Just before dark Jim Hendrix gathered up a few "Yankee" blankets, made a bed out of them and got me on it. He then lay down with me. We slept some. The next morning we got up and made some coffee, which we drank, and ate a little of our cold rations. Our breakfast somewhat revived us. We then went to look on the battlefield. Three of the dead wore our company's uniform, and we went to see who they were. The first one was my brother. I had been too sick the evening before to pay any attention, and did not know who was hurt. My finding my brother, with a minnie-ball shot through his heart, and he cold in death, was a *terrible* shock to me ; but *such is war.*

The litter corps had taken care of all the wounded the night before, friend and foe alike. They came around gathering up the sick and carrying them to the doctors, and caring for them the best they could under the circumstances. There were so many wounded to haul and look after until we were looked after but little. I, with two or three more of our company, and a great many of the sick of our regiment and brigade, was sent to Richmond to the hospital. The distance was nine miles, and it took us two days to walk it.

(I will give the readers a chapter of hospital life and the surgeons' table after the close of the campaign of 1862.)

I must continue about the battle. It has since been told me by members of Company D and others, which I know is true. When we were ordered to the right and Hendrix and I left, as just stated, the brigade went a short distance and advanced, over the dead and wounded friends and foes, and charged the enemy, and took their battery and captured their guns and some prisoners and horses before the "Yankees" could kill the horses. The battery we captured was the Hoboken Battery, and the troops we charged was Porter's Division United States regulars, (then the flowers of the United States army), whom we routed and drove from the field. We had cause to be proud, for we were complimented by the famous "Stonewall" Jackson for the splendid charge we had made. Our regiment was on the right of the brigade, and was engaged but little in the action. Thus ended the battle of Gaines' Mill. Though we lost *many* brave, noble lives, it was a Confederate victory. We were well initiated and had taken the first degree in *war*.

Some of the wounded were Lieutenant Colonel L. J. Barr, Major J. D. Matthews, of the Thirty-eighth Georgia Regiment, the gallant Colonel Celement A. Evans, Thirty-first Georgia Regiment; Captain McKlasky, of company B, and Captain Jones, of company I, were both killed. Lieutenants Marable, Phillips, Stubbs, Oglesby and Andrews were all severely wounded. The Thirty-eighth Georgia Regiment carried 700 men into action and had fifty-four killed and 118 wounded on the field. Company K carried fifty seven men into this action, had ten killed and twenty-three wounded. Company G carried ninety-eight men into action, lost ten killed and thirty wounded. All the other companies suffered severely. The Thirty-eighth Georgia Regiment was the most exposed to the fire of the Hoboken battery, that they afterwards captured, of any of the brigade.

The enemy left our front as soon as we routed them. We remained in line all night, and what little sleep we got we slept with gun in hand, with a heavy skirmish line in front. Next morning everything was quiet for a while. We drew plenty of provisions but did not have a single thing to cook in.

Our noble Lieutenant S. H. Kennedy said, "Boys, I have read about how General Washington's men baked bread on their ram-rods," so we got some poplar bark and used it for "kneading pans" and prepared our flour for baking. We rolled it out in little long rolls, wrapped it around our ramrods, and held it close to the fire and baked real nice bread. We broiled our meat on forked sticks and soon had plenty of breakfast cooked.

We pursued and soon found the enemy, and they were very well fortified at and near Savage station. After some very heavy skirmishing and cannonading, the Confederates charged their works, with a yell, and carried them, and captured some prisoners and artillery. Our brigade was not specially engaged in this, but were exposed to heavy shelling.

On the night of the 28th of June we again had to lie with gun in hand, and had very strict orders to obey. The Yankees were certainly doing all in their power to make good, and cover their retreat, and get under shelter of their gun-boats on the James river.

On the 29th we pressed them hard and overtook them at Frazier's Farm and Whiteoak Swamp, and routed them badly.

On the 30th the Yankees made a successful stand at Malvern Hill, near the James river, where their gunboats were, and they were well fortified.

We had desperate fighting, which lasted until late in the night. The Yankees got the best of us here. We were exposed to the most teriffic shelling and dislodged, after nightfall, the right wing of McClelland's army. Our loss was small.

The next morning the Yankees had left all our frnot,

and had gotten under shelter of their gun-boats, with their wagon train backed up in the Horseshoe Bend of James river, on Hackle's farm. This ended the "seven days' battle before Richmond."

CHAPTER III.

FROM THE SEVEN DAYS' BATTLE TO THE BATTLE OF SHARPSBURG OR ANTIETAM, INCLUDING THE BATTLES OF CEDAR MOUNTAIN, SECOND BATTLE OF MANASSAS, CAPTURE OF HARPER'S FERRY AND THE BATTLE OF SHARPSBURG.

After the Seven Days' Battle we rested a few days, then Jackson's corps was ordered to Gordonsville, Va., and camped around Gordonsville, Orange C. H. and Liberty Mills to watch a new army, made up and styled "The Army of Virginia," which was composed of four Union forces, which had been commanded by Generals Fremont, Banks, Shields and McDowell, and put in command of Major-General John Pope. Our brigade camped four miles above Gordonsville till the first week in August.

Our (Lawton's) brigade was transferred from Jackson's old division to Ewel's division. On the 7th of August we were ordered to cook two days' rations. On the 8th we marched in the direction of Culpepper C. H. Pope's army was guarding the line of the Rapidan river. Pope's plan was to attack Richmond on a different line and different plans from those which McClellan had used. 'Twas said that his headquarters was in the saddle, and his policy to guard and press the front and let the rear take care of itself. I suppose he would have gotten to Richmond in a few days if he had not met the Confederates. Jackson's corps met him at Cedar Mountain, August 9th, and gave him a terrible defeat. Generals Jackson and Stuart taught Pope a grand lesson, which was: "Guard the rear as well as the front."

General Stuart went around and captured a lot of his wagons and reserve artillery in the rear of his army, and went to General Pope's headquarter's at night. Just as he had undressed to retire, General Stuart walked into his tent. Pope blew out the candle, pulled up one of the tent pins and crawled out into the dark in a drenching rain and made good his escape. General Stuart captured his horse, headquarter wagon, tent, order book, uniform, and in fact all but his dear self in his night attire.

After this defeat his front was changed to the rear. He found it was to his interest to guard front, rear and flanks. General McClellan, the "over courteous" general, as he was called by the Union authorities, was ordered to hastily transfer his army from the Peninsular and the James river to Acquia Creek and Washington, and send it to Pope. Our loss in this engagement was very light.

We drove Pope across the Rappahannock. He was then receiving reinforcements from McClellan's army almost every day. He had about fifty thousand men before he received these reinforcements. Jackson had less than twenty-five thousand. Lee, learning the state of affairs, hurried up, with his veteran army to assist Jackson. Lee's and Jackson's armies being consolidated; Lee sent Jackson on a long circuit flank movement up the Rappahannock river. He crossed the Rappahannock at a rocky ford near Henson's mill; then commenced a series of night marches, for which old "Stonewall" was so famous, across fields and woods almost discarding roads. He made these night marches in order to avoid being seen by Pope's balloon spies. He moved around by Warrenton, Salem and through Thoroughfare Gap. This march of Jackson's was terrible; it was very dry, the roads were very dusty and the weather was desperately hot. We had a great many sun-strokes, and men so exhausted until a great many died by the roadside. On this march General Jackson caught a spy and treated him to six feet of rope and left him dangling from the limb of a tree not many paces from the road. We were often very short of provisions, because the supply trains could not catch up, and our "pot wagons" were often behind, so we had to use our bark trays and ramrods for cooking our bread and forked sticks for frying our meat. We cooked and ate after the ancient style.

We finally got through Thoroughfare Gap and swooped down on Pope's supplies and captured them at Bristow Station, and at Manassas. On Lawton's Brigade's part of the line there came two heavy supply trains loaded with bacon, hard-tacks and almost everything that we needed to eat. Our artillery had not caught up and we had not had time to tear up any railroad track, so the engineer pulled his throttle wide open and let his engine fly by while he and the fireman lay down in the tender. Many shots were fired but to no effect. Doubtless they would have gone on to Pope's army, for we were then away in the rear, but Lieutenant John Brannen, of our company, threw a heavy oak cross tie across the track in a curve and ditched the front engine. The other engine crushed into the rear of the first train and made a terrible wreck of both trains with some of the cars completely smashed to pieces.

We were not scarce of supplies then, for every one

took all he wanted. Some of the men carried off a whole side of bacon.

We fell back near the old battle field of Bull Run, where Pope had an immense amount of supplies. General Pope was completely flanked, his supplies captured and his communication with Washington was completely cut off. He was doing all he could to head Jackson off, and I suppose he was mad, or at least fretted with Jackson for such treatment.

General Lee was following Pope, and was two days behind him. Pope got up, formed his lines, and it seemed to us, threw his whole force on Jackson's corps, which was reduced by long hard marches to about twenty thousand men. It appeared once or twice that we would be crushed, and all be killed or wounded. At one time our brigade was almost surrounded by Yankees, and we had a dreadful struggle in cutting our way out. Our losses were very heavy. On one occasion two brigades (Thomas' of Georgia and Taylor's of Louisiana), of Hill's division, held their lines solidly for a long while after they had used up their ammunition. They were in a railroad cut and were protected. The railroad bed was covered with broken rocks which weighed from one to four pounds. The boys said they would pile up rocks and have them handy, so that when the Yankees got close enough they would hurl the rocks over the banks with such force that the enemy could not come up close enough to shoot them.

There were some Yankees killed and many knocked down and severely wounded. Our boys finally received more ammunition and held their part of the line like true heroes. They promised Jackson they would hold the line at all hazards and they did it admirably well.

Jackson was so pressed for men till he had all the able-bodied teamsters armed and sent into battle. Jackson held the field all day the 29th. Lee arrived that night and they pressed Pope so heavily the next day on the front and rear until he was completely routed and demoralized and retreated towards Washington in great confusion. The enemy's lines seemed to be in the shape of the letter "V." Our artillery was arranged at the point and shelled down their lines. Some Yankee prisoners told us that they lost nine major generals. The Union Army fought bravely and nobly.

The loss was very great on both sides. This was called the Second Battle of Manassas.

Some of the killed in the Sixty-first Georgia Regiment were as follows:

The noble lieutenant, John Brannen, of Company D, who was a perfect idol in our company and regiment. His hat-band was shot through in front and back, the ball passing through his brains.

The reader will recollect that he was the man who threw the cross-tie across the railroad that ditched the front engine and wrecked both trains, where we got so much provisions.

The privates killed were as follows: S. H. Kennedy, Jr., Frank Butts, Jackson Turner, G. A. Collins, Berrien Collins and James Williams.

The wounded officers were as follows: Captain S. H. Kennedy, Lieutenant James Mincy, Sergeant Joshua Ellis. Privates: Thos. Waters, Joshua Holloway, G. F. Hendrix, John L. Jerrill, and, perhaps, others. Several others were missing and we do not know what became of them. We would be proud to know just what became of all the dear boys, but we will never know.

The wounded were carried to Middleburg, twelve miles from Manassas.

For further casualties of the Sixty-first Georgia Regiment, I refer you to the different companies muster rolls, and their casualties, in the back part of this book.

Something over half of the men of the Sixty-first Georgia Regiment that were carried into the battle were either killed, wounded or missing. The Thirty-eighth Georgia Regiment carried about two hundred and sixty men in the battle, and they lost forty-eight killed, and one hundred and twelve wounded. Some of the killed were as follows: Captain Geo. Goodwin, Lieutenant Morris, both of Company K; Lieutenant G. R. Wells, of Company D, was severely wounded.

I suppose all the different regiments of the brigade suffered about like the Thirty-eighth and Sixty-first Georgia Regiments. After this battle General Lawton was promoted to the rank of major-general. The gallant Colonel Marcellus Douglas, of the Thirteenth Georgia Regiment, was assigned the command of the brigade.

After the second battle of Manassas the march was again taken up toward Washington City. At Chantilly we overtook Pope and had a small engagement on September 1st. Our loss was slight. After resting two days we marched toward the Potomac river by way of Leesburg, crossing at Edwards' Ferry. We entered Maryland and marched to Monocacy Junction, on the Baltimore and Ohio Railroad, forty miles west of Baltimore. We rested a short while here, and then marched on toward Frederick City, where we had a small engagement, the Yankees retreating at once. Corporal W. A. Woods, of our company, was wounded and left at Frederick City. We were again put on a forced march by way of Middletown, Boonesboro and Sharpsburg. We recrossed the Potomac at Williamsport and marched to Martinsburg, W. Va., on the Baltimore and Ohio Railroad. We were then put on a forced march to Harper's Ferry. Jackson had made this long circuit, flank movement around Harper's Ferry and had it surrounded while General Hill held the passes in South Mountain and kept McClellan cut off.

Jackson planted his batteries and shelled the garrison around Harper's Ferry and put his storming columns in motion. The garrison hauled down their United States flag and raised a white flag and surrendered the fort with thirty-four siege guns and other light batteries, with a lot of commissary and ordnance stores and about twelve thousand prisoners of war, with about fifteen thousand stands of small arms and many stands of colors. We hardly had time to rejoice over our splendid achievements before we were again on a forced march. We left Harper's Ferry on the evening of the 16th of September. We had to march all night, crossed the Potomac at Shepherdstown at midnight, and rejoined Lee and were in line of battle at daylight at Sharpsburg or Antietam Creek.

McClellan attacked Lee with his massed forces. He had Pope's and his own armies combined, which made over 120,000 men. Pope had been relieved of the command and the cautious little "Mc." put in command of both armies.

The battle raged all day with fearful loss of life on both sides. At one time the Union army broke Lee's lines, but it was soon retaken and established, and was held the remainder of the day. It was all General Lee could do to hold the lines with Jackson's corps added to his own forces.

If Jackson had not come, with lightning-like speed, from Harper's Ferry and joined Lee, it looked like Lee would have been crushed by General McClellan's powerful army, which was as large as two of Lee's and Jackson's combined. Here our brigade lost its commander, the brave Colonel Marcellus Douglas, of the Thirteenth

Georgia Regiment, was killed, and our good Major A. P. McRae. Lieutenant Colonel Crowder, of the Thirty-first Georgia Regiment, was severely wounded. Major W. H. Battey, of the Thirty-eighth Georgia Regiment, and probably other field officers were killed. Lieutenant T. L. Moss, of company G, Sixty-first Georgia Regiment, was also killed. Captain Daniel McDonald was severely wounded.

The Thirty-eighth Georgia Regiment carried only 123 men into the battle. After fighting hard all day their losses were forty killed and fifty-five wounded. At night they had only twenty-eight men and three officers left. Lieutenants Wells, Baxter and Matthews were the officers left. Company K carried eleven men into the battle, commanded by Corporal James E. Chandler. He and four of the men were killed. In this battle company D, of the Sixty-first Georgia Regiment, was in a very good position, among some large rochs. Our casualties were not as great as some other companies.

Sergeant James C. Hodges was mortally wounded, his brains being shot out. He lived eleven days before death came to his relief. He was one of the best boys I ever saw, and an excellent school teacher. (He was my old professor.) He was almost an idol in his company and regiment, and the community in which he lived before the war, and with his pupils in school. Our officers left his uncle, William Alderman, to take care of him and the other wounded of our regiment. Alderman composed some verses on "Jimmie," which you will find at the close of this chapter.

The battle ceased before dark, with both armies holding about the same position that they held before the battle began. Next day both armies buried their dead. General Lee leisurely crossed the Potomac river at Shepherdstown ford, (with Jackson bringing up the rear), back into the Shenandoah valley. A part of McClellan's forces followed the retreating Confederates. Jackson backed off a mile or two and formed some of his men in line (Hill's Division), and permitted a few thousand Yankees to cross the river. He then made a dash on them and drove them panic-stricken back. Some of the Union army fell off the bluff, fifty or sixty feet, into the river and were killed. When the Union army was passing through the old Sharpsburg battlefield one little Dutchman went by the hospital tents, where our hospital nurse (Alderman) was cooking for the sick and wounded. He asked Alderman for some of his bread. Alderman gave him some bread, and asked him where he was going. The Dutchman replied, "We dosh be going to hunt Shockson." Alderman said the little Dutchman was gone about three hours and returned, wet all over and his hat and gun gone. He had been churning the Potomac river trying to get back. He called on Alderman again on his return, who asked him if he found Jackson. The Dutchman replied, "Vel, yas, and he dosh give us *hell* dish day."

The Finding of a Wounded and Dying Soldier Boy.

Oh! in this land so far from home,
My mother's son was bound to roam
In search of one whom I did love,
Who in this bloody war has served.

But oh! Alas! my friend I found,
All in blood upon the ground.
No cheering friend to raise his head,
Or comfort with a tender word.

Now to my knees I did fall and say:
"Dear Jimmie, how are you to-day."
His mind was so deranged with pain,
He could not say, though I asked again.

I washed and dressed his broken head,
Which was too badly to have said.
His broken head and skull and brain
Was all exposed to sun and rain.

I closely watched him night and day—
Obeyed his calls in every way—
With hope that he'd get well again,
Although his wound was in the brain.

But, oh! Alas! he had to die,
And leave me here to mourn and cry.
My heart did tremble, ache and smart,
To see my friend from me depart.

Dear James is gone and here I stay,
In trouble and toil from day to day.
His soul to the world of bliss is gone,
His mother and brother there to join.

But if like James, my life I yield,
While here on this bloody battle-field,
I hope to meet him 'round the throne
Where wars and sorrows are unknown.

Now, in Maryland, I am
And as a prisoner I am bound.
No cheering friend nor kindred nigh
Which brings on me the deepest sigh.

Now, to his father, who loved him dear,
And watched his steps with tender care,
While raising him to be a man,
Not knowing he'd die in a foreign land.

Now, to his brothers, I will say,
Whatever you intend, you may,
Perhaps, like James, may soon die,
Then all your works you must lay by.

And to the sisters of this youth
Pray seek and love the holy truth,
And pray to meet your brother where
There are no wars to interfere.

Now, to the circle of his friends
That monster, death, that God will send,
For he will lay your bodies cold
And to himself will take your soul.

To hear the cannons loudly roar
And men all standing in a row,
To face the balls and grapeshot too—
Some must be killed—no telling who.

To see young men torn up with bombs,
And knowing they are some mother's sons.
How would it make a mother feel
To see her son dead on the field?

In battles fought, and wars of old,
As I have read, and oft been told,
But never viewed such awful scenes,
Until this awful war has been.

Now, to his pupils, young and fair,
Your kind teacher is done with care,
While you are left to weep and cry,
Your teacher dwells above the sky.

J. W. ALDERMAN'S FAREWELL TO HIS MOTHER.

O, mother! mother! fare you well,
If I no more with you can dwell.
I hope we'll meet in heaven above,
And there be crowned with grace and love.

For years I've lived at home with you
With sister dear and brother, too.
Your tender love did melt my heart
When you and I did have to part.

So happy were my youthful days,
There with my brother's tender ways.
My mind on Christ did not seem to run,
Although my age was very young.

My sister, dear, seems near to me,
Though many miles apart we be,
But let us strive all sin to shun,
And to improve what God has done.

And when I left my home, you see,
And those dear friends that left with me
Are dead, and gone to worlds unknown,
And I'm like one that's left alone.

But when I'm done with troubles here,
About your son shed not a tear.
When I am in the cold, cold grave
I hope the Lord my soul will save.

And that this war will then be o'er,
And I shall hear the drums no more;
But with the God of love to dwell.
O, mother, hear my last farewell.

CHAPTER IV.

From the Battle of Sharpsburg to the Close of the Year 1862, Including the First Fredericksburg Battle.

After the Sharpsburg battle, General Lee retreated about twenty-five miles up the Shenandoah valley.

Jackson's corps was stationed near Whitepost, Berryville and Front Royal. We rested here, reorganized and recruited up the best we could. There had been a great many officers killed, wounded and resigned. Lieutenant S. H. Kennedy was promoted to captain soon after the Seven-day's battle before Richmond. Captain Tillman having resigned, Lieutenant S. L. Williams had been promoted from third to first lieutenant. Sergeant James Mincy was elected to second lieutenant and Hiram Franklin was elected to third lieutenant.

A great many of the other companies elected new officers in the different regiments of the brigade. It was an easy matter to get men to take the place of the officers, killed and resigned; but the places of the dear boys with guns could not be filled. We had none to take their places.

It was now about the first of November. A great many of the sick and wounded had returned to the army and we were much stronger than we were after the battle of Sharpsburg. The spirit of the army was excellent, for success had crowned our arms on every battlefield, except Sharpsburg, and while we did not gain anything there, we were not beaten.

Ewell's division was sent away up the valley to near New Market. It was then late in November. We were ordered to move, hurriedly, across the mountains on down to Fredericksburg.

In November McClellan crossed the Potomac and marched down on the east side of the Blue Ridge mountains to Warrenton. He was relieved of the command at Warrenton and General Burnside took his place as commander of the army of the Potomac. We were all glad of the exchange in the commanders of the Union Army, for whenever we struck "Little Mc," we always got hurt. We could never take him by surprise.

Burnside immediately began active operations. His plan was to attack Richmond by way of Fredericksburg. The weather had grown very cold and instead of sunstrokes, we had to march on frozen ground, over ice and snow, wade rivers and creeks and some of the boys were without shoes. M. J. Green was shoeless and could have been tracked in the snow by the blood from his feet, with many others in the same condition. He hardly murmured at his misfortune and did not waver. He was always at his post of duty. There were no better men in Lee's army. He was then a beardless boy, but as good a soldier as was ever marshaled into a battlefield, and was one of the vanguards in the first Fredericksburg battle.

Burnside's army marched to the Stafford Heights, on the north side of the Rappahannock river, opposite Fredericksburg.

General Lee threw his army in the front of Burnside's army and occupied Fredericksburg. He made Marye's Heights and Lee's hills on the south side of the the Rappahannock, strong with earthworks and batteries of artillery. It looked to us private soldiers like it would be very rash for any general to try to whip such an army and such generals as Lee and Jackson were with such a strong position.

When Ewell's division arrived we were ordered down the river, about fifteen miles below Fredericksburg, near the old historic town of Port Royal. We camped here a short while to watch the enemy from this direction. Burnside had his cannons planted on Stafford Heights in order to guard the river.

He put his pontoon bridges across the river and crossed on the 11th and 12th of December and arranged his lines ready for action.

Colonel Atkinson, of the Twenty-sixth Georgia Regiment, was then commanding Lawton's brigade. Ewell' division was ordered back from Port Royal to Hamiltons Crossing. Lawton's brigade, commanded by Colonel Atkinson, took a position as reserves near the eastern end of the range of hills. Here the heights reach out about one mile from the Rappahannock river and is almost a level plain from the foot of the heights to within about two hundred yards of the river. The Richmond. Fredericksburg & Alexandria railroad is situated at the foot of the heights.

On the 13th of December General Burnsides advanced and the battle began near Fredericksburg. I do not know what troops were in our front, but when the Yankees advanced on them they gave way.

The Yankees were near our brigade before we knew it. We raised a yell and gave them a well directed volley, which they returned with a storm of "huzzas." Our brigade had never been driven from any position, and the Yankees stood firm. After exchanging one or two volleys we charged them with a terrible yell and drove them back towards the river without much trouble.

We were on the extreme right of all the fighting that was going on between the two armies.

We drove the ones that were in our front back to the old turnpike road.

The Yankees had a heavy battery at our right which played havoc with some of our lines while they were forming. A little, light cavalry battery, of four guns, ran out from our rear into an open place, on a low elevation, under a perfect storm of shells and opened fire on the Union battery.

The first shot struck one of the enemy's caisson boxes of cap shells and exploded it, killing, wounding and demoralizing the officers and men of the Union battery so badly until they did not fire another gun. So the Union battery did us no more damage. Our part of the line had done its duty well and heroically. We had the ground strewn with dead and wounded Yankees. Here we also lost some brave, noble boys. The Union line was much longer than ours, so the enemy at our right begun to swing aronnd us and advance, which caused considerable confusion in our ranks. They were so close to us that they began to order us to halt and throw down our guns and surrender. We were ordered to retreat which we had to do in a galling fire. Our losses were much greater on the retreat from the fire of the flanking column than the ones we had been driving. In this retreat one of our company got severely wounded (Madison Warren). He was totally disabled in one of his legs, and almost any one else would have surrendered. He picked up another gun and used it and his own for crutches, aud ran out and got away. The balance of the brigade did not suffer like our regiment did, we being on the extreme right. If the Confederate line of battle on the right had moved up and carried the rest of the enemy's line like we did ours, we would have run them into the river, or would have captured all the Union army on our part of the line, for we had driven them to within four hundred yards of the river, and had them completely routed. The casualties of Company D were as follows: Killed, Isaac Barrow and Wyley Lewis; mortally wounded, Sergeant Silas E. Jones ; wounded, Lieutenant Hiram Franklin and Private Madison Warren. Lieutenant Franklin was wounded in the leg and has never been able to walk with ease since.

Some of the other companies in the Sixty-first Georgia Regiment suffered much worse than we did. For their casualties I refer you to their muster rolls and casualties in the back part of this book.

Some of the good officers of the Thirty-eighth Georgia Regiment have been kind enough to furnish me with the casualties of that noble regiment. I would gladly furnish the readers of this history with all the casualties of the different regiments, but I have failed to get them. I suppose the Thirty-eighth is a fair average of the different regiments of the brigade.

The Thirty-eighth carried about four hundred and fifty men into action. Thirty-seven men were killed and ninety-two wounded. Among the number were Lieutenants Farmer and Thornton, Oglesby, Wiggins, Henry, Goswick, Pughley and Eberhart. Capt. J. N. Jones, of Company I, was killed. In the battle of Fredericksburg the adjuntant-general, Captain Lawton, was mortally wounded. The Union army lost eleven thousand men. The Confederates lost about four thousand. It was a decided Confederate victory.

On the night of the 13th of December Burnside recrossed the Rappahannock, leaving his dead and wounded on the field. We took care of his wounded the best we could, for it was a very cold night, and buried the dead Union soldiers. I am sure some of his wounded froze to death, and probably some of our own.

General Lee's army remained in and around Fredericksburg during the rest of the winter, and Burnside took up a position on the north side of the Rappahannock. Both armies went into winter quarters.

Ewell's Division returned to nearPort Royal and went into winter quarters and rested quietly all the rest of the winter, doing picket duty on the Rappahannock river.

CHAPTER V.

I Will Devote This Chapter to the Hospitals, Among the Sick and Wounded, of 1862.

On the morning of the 28th of June, I and a great many others of my company, regiment and brigade, left the army at Gaines' Mill, very sick, and were sent to Richmond to the hospitals for treatment. It was only nine miles, but it took a great many of us two days to get there. We were so sick. We had to walk awhile and rest awhile on the road. Some of the poor boys died before they got to Richmond. When we arrived we were sent to Camp Winder hospital.

There were about two hundred rough houses built of sawed boards about thirty feet wide and fifty feet long, well covered and nicely arranged in rows. There were good "bunks" with straw beds. Here the sick and wounded were taken care of very well, everything considered. The wounded enemy were about as well cared for as we were. We had left all our clothing, except what we had on, near Hanover Junction while on the march. Our clothing was very dirty, and we had been in old camps until they had become filled with body lice, which tormented us nearly to death.

Nearly all the sick had fever and chronic diarrhœa.

Six of our company died, to wit: Irwin Warren, Reuben Carter, Mallichi Carter, Hezekiel Parrish, Henry Jones and Benjamin F. Bowen. Several others came very near dying. A great many of our regiment and brigade also died.

I will tell the readers what I witnessed in the death of a little North Carolinian. He was just a mere boy and his name was Frick. He was very sick—had a high fever. His nurse seemed to be a very wicked man. Frick was very religious He raised up on his bed one day and got off on the floor on his feet; his nurse ran to him and I have never heard such talk, such admonition as he gave the nurse. He asked him to do better and to quit cursing and repent of his sins and to try to prepare to meet him in the glory world.

The nurse melted into a flood of tears. Frick began to shout and praise God, and wrung his hands. He died on his feet with his arms around the nurse's neck, the nurse holding him in his arms. Frick died shouting and praising God in the strongest triumphs of a living faith I have ever seen, and with a pleasant smile on his face. The nurse tenderly laid him down on the bed, with a deep feeling of emotion, in a flood of tears, and said to the crowd—for all in the house that were able had gathered around them: "Boys, Frick is dead, and if he's not gone to the glory world, none of us will ever get there." I never heard that nurse use another profane word.

Here I witnessed another very sad event. I saw a little beardless youth from Georgia, who had had a long spell of typhoid fever, but was then convalescent. He was able to sit up and walk some and the doctor had promised him a sixty-days furlough to go home, which he seemed to be very proud of.

One day his nose began to bleed very freely and the nurse ran and brought in the doctor, but he failed to stop the blood, so he called in two or three of the finest surgeons that he could get, but none of them could stop the blood. He bled to death in less than twenty-four hours.

Here hundreds of the good women of Richmond and the country around, would come in every day about 9 o'clock A. M., and about 4 P. M., with the finest kind of nourishments and sweet milk for the poor sick and wounded soldiers, and with such motherly treatment and such good admonition to the poor fellows until it would revive them. They would bring in nice clean under-clothing, and would have the nurses bring them basins of warm water and would wash and dress some of the wounds and would wash the faces, hands and necks of some of the worst cases, and have the nurses put the clean cloths on the poor dirty fellows. It looked like these women, with their good, motherly treatment, would revive them so much till they could not die. They would get well, when I am sure if it had not been for such nursing many would have died.

They would often give the soldiers little pocket testaments and tell them to read them, for they told about *Jesus being the Saviour* of sinners.

Our regular hospital nurses were soldiers detailed for that purpose, and only a few knew anything about it—some did not *care* to know anything about it. These good women taught them how to nurse.

I can say this for the *good women* of Virginia: There are no *better women* on this globe. They seemed like angels of mercy, and I am sure all they like of being *white winged angels* is *death*, and I feel *sure* that death will have *no* sting, and that the grave, with them, will have *no* victory; for Christ will come after them and call them up *higher* and *seat them* near to *Him* in the paradise of the great God of Heaven. It fills my heart full of praise to God for raising up such good women. I fully believe that such women are the salt of the earth and the light of the world. But these good women are not all in Richmond and the vicinity; but are scattered all over the State, and indeed, all over these, our still United States.

In the hospitals the fare was very common except that which those good women furnished. We generally got boiled beef, baker's bread and beef soup, and it did not suit our complaints, (chronic diarrhoea and high fevers). But I suppose it was the best that could be done under the circumstances. The most of us were without money; for we had disposed of all that we had when we left Georgia, and we had not received any pay from the government.

We should have had sweet milk, but we had failed to get any. Some of us boys thought of a plan to get some: There were a great many fine dairy cows that came to the hospital kitchen to drink the dishwater and eat waste bread that was put out in large tubs. I was an excellent hand at milking, so the other boys would get around the cows while they were eating the bread and drinking the dish water to keep them from walking off, and I would milk all of our canteens full every day, and we were all much better in one week's time. We decided to return to the army, for we heard that it was resting quietly in camps near Gordonsville; so we reported to the doctor and he let us off.

We went, expecting to get our clothes that we had left six weeks before at Hanover Junction. We left Richmond on August 6, by way of the Virginia Central Railroad. We arrived in Gordonsville about 11 o'clock A. M. and marched out to the camps, which were four miles from Gordonsville, to where our brigade was stationed. We soon made inquiries about our clothes but the boys told us they had neither seen nor heard from them.

We had not changed our clothes in six weeks, and we had none to put on until we could wash those that we had on, so we got a camp kettle and some soap and went about four hundred yards to a little creek, pulled off our clothes and gave them a good washing, and boiled them to kill the body lice, and hung them out to dry. We lay around in the shade till they dried off some. When we put them on and returned to camp we found we had orders to cook two days rations and be ready to leave at daylight the next morning.

The next morning very early the drum beat the sick call. Captain Kennedy came to me and told me to go to the doctor, for he knew that I was not able to march, so I went with the orderly sergeant to Doctor Schley's quarters. When my name was called the doctor said: "Nichols, what are you here for?" I told him that I fared so badly at the hospital, and that I came expecting to get my clothes. He used some very rough language and told me to go back to the hospital and stay there till I got well, or I would die like a great many others had done trying to follow the army when they were not able. He told me not to expect hotel fare or mother's care, and for me not to let him see me again till I was well. I knew he was giving me good advice and that I would take it.

We were sent back to Gordonsville where we found very nearly one thousand sick who were sent there from Jackson's corps. It was two days before I could leave for Lynchburg, Va., which is up near the mountains and a very healthy place. I had relapsed and was as sick or worse than I had been.

The doctors in Lynchburg were very good and gave me some relief, but it was not permanent. Our fare here was about the same that it had been in Richmond, and I was reduced from 120 to about eighty pounds.

One morning I walked down to the business part of the city and sat down in a store-house to rest, for I was very feeble. Soon a fine looking old gentleman of about seventy years of age came to me and asked what was the matter with me. I told him that I had chronic diarrhœa. He called a fine looking old lady of about his age, and they commenced to ask me questions. "Where was my home?" and "how was I faring in the hospital?" I told them. The good lady said that it was not suitable diet for me with my complaint. The old man said, "No, he should have sweet milk." The old lady said, "Yes, that is what he should have, and it boiled." I told them that I did not get any at the hospital, and that I did not have any money with which to buy any, that I had not heard from my parents since the 1st of May, and that I could get the money from home if my parents knew that I was needing it and knew where to send it.

The old gentleman gave me one dollar and the good lady gave me fifty cents, and they told me to buy plenty of sweet milk, and when that money was gone to come back and they would help me again.

I took it and thanked them from the bottom of my heart. I was so rejoiced till I could not refrain from tears to find such God-sent friends in such a time of need. I looked at them with tearful eyes, and both of them had to wipe big tears from their own eyes, seeing me so overcome with joy and gratitude.

When I left the store and started back to the hospital I met an old man with some extra fine peaches. I bought about half a bushel for one dollar, and took them to the hospital and sold them, making about one dollar clear.

I felt delighted with two dollars and fifty cents in my pocket.

I went to a lady who lived near the hospital and who owned a fine cow, and contracted with her for a quart of sweet milk every day, getting a pint morning and evening. I received it regularly and soon began to mend. I speculated with my money until I had something over four dollars.

Here the good women treated the extremely sick soldiers like they did in Richmond. I did not receive any of their charities, for I was never so sick till I could not walk about and take exercise.

The Georgia Relief Association, headed by Governor Joseph E. Brown, had sent some of its noble women to the hospitals with clothing for destitute Georgia soldiers marked "Georgia Relief Association." One of the ladies gave me a new pair of drawers and a shirt. The hospital authorities had washing done every week, so the sick fared well on this line.

The Georgia Relief Association did not confine its charities especially to the Georgia soldiers, for the lady in charge would give any destitute Confederate soldier a shirt and a pair of drawers. I stayed in Lynchburg until after the second battle of Manassas, and was mending finely, but I was then transferred to Danville, Va., with all other convalescent soldiers of the Lynchburg hospitals. I hated to have to go, for I was expecting to be able to return to the army in another month.

When I arrived at Danville I found it quite different to what Richmond and Lynchburg were. It had about 1,000 inhabitants, the hospitals were new, and had one of the poorest doctors I ever saw. It seemed like every dose of medicine that he gave me would do me more harm than good. I could not get any milk, and the hospital diet was very poor. Beef, boiled about half done, baker's bread and beef soup, made with flour, and often with flies in it, for they had negro cooks, and the white man in charge did not care. It was to eat that or nothing, and I generally took nothing rather than that soup. I would take the bread and beef and re-cook the beef by broiling it, which made it so it could be eaten. The doctor was a young man and had the worst kind of a case of "big-head." He could curse like a demon, and I soon saw that I could not stay there and live. About this time the small-pox broke out there, and every case would be sent to the small-pox hospital, which was some distance from the town.

Major Payne, who had lost one leg in battle, was placed in command of the town. He had a guard of about one hundred men, detailed to do guard duty around the town, on account of the smallpox, and to keep down some regular hard cases, which were, I am sorry to say, men who had slight wounds and would not let them get well. They would put something on them to keep them from healing. They were perfect "hospital rats"—regular toughs. Some were so mean they prevented the good women from coming there.

I went to Sergeant Roberson, the commander of the guard, and gave him my name, for I wished to be one of the guards. He told me to go to the hospital, get my clothes and report at the tents, which were about half a mile from the hospital, in a beautiful grove with a nice spring of water.

When I went to get them the doctor said that I could not go, for he knew that I was not able. I told him that I would mend faster than I could there, for I could do my own cooking and would fare a great deal better; but he swore that I should not go. Both of us got very mad. The nurse seemed to get mad too, and helped the doctor to heap curses on me.

They said that if I went, they would report me to my officers as a deserter. I knew that would not do, so I sat down and studied what to do. I soon decided to go to Major Payne and tell him that I wanted to be one of the guards. Major Payne looked at me for a minute, when I went to him, and said: "My dear sir, you are not able to do guard duty." It made me feel bad. I then put in to plead my own case. I told him that I had had chronic diarrhœa ever since I had been in Virginia and with the fare that I was getting I would never get well, and that if he would let me go on the guard, where I could do my own cooking, fry my beef and get some corn bread to eat, that I would get better; for all the medicine that I had taken did me no good.

He said, "Well, my dear sir, you can go and try it."

About that time Sergeant Roberson came in and the noble hearted major told him not to have me stand guard more than two hours each day and not to put me on duty at night. I then felt rejoiced and thanked the good major.

I told him what the little pop-skulled doctor and nurse said about reporting me to my officers as a deserter. He turned to his desk and gave me a written detail as one of the guards. I took it and went after my clothes. I got them and told the doctor and nurse that I was going on the guard. They both cursed me again. I felt gratified to have the pleasure of telling them what I thought of them.

I told them that neither of them were fit for *buzzard's bait* and that if the Confederate States were as destitute of *gentlemen* doctors and hospital nurses as that hospital was of a doctor and hospital nurse, it would be in a terrible condition.

I did not curse them like they did me; but I abused them for about five minutes, as badly as I knew how, to not curse. I then showed them my authority to go. They turned off apparently defeated, and remarked: "You must be pretty d—d sharp."

I stayed on the guard two months and mended some without taking any medicine. I am now right sure that hundreds of good soldiers died in the Danville hospitals for want of proper diet; for very nearly all the guards got well when probably many of them would have relapsed and died in the hospitals.

About the first of November we received orders to go to the army: I knew that I was not able to go, and Sergeant Roberson told me so; but I was certainly going to leave Danville, so I started to the army. On the way to Richmond two of our regiment who had been on guard with me, (William Booth and William Jackson) told me that I was not able to go to the army and for me to stop in Richmond and go to the Third Georgia Hospital and let Dr. Green, of Milledgeville, Georgia, treat me, and I would get well. They said that I would get diet to suit my disease, and that Dr. Green would give me medicine that would cure me; for they said that Dr. Green had cured them of the same disease. They said that it would not do for me so try to go to the army.

These were noble boys and had treated me like a brother. I wished to go on with them; but I had promised Dr. Schley, our regimental surgeon, and myself, that I would not return to the army until I got well; so I reported sick—at the Wayside Home in Richmond, as Booth and Jackson had advised me.

The doctor in charge examined me and pronounced me "not able for service." I told him that I wanted to go to the Third Georgia Hospital; for I wanted Dr. Green to treat me, for I thought that he could cure me. The doctor gave me an order to go to that hospital, with two others of my regiment—Curry and Carpenter. The doctor asked us if we had drawn any money in two months; we told him we had not. He said "well, you can draw, for the army has been paid off." He took us to the door and showed us where to go to draw our money, and how to go to the Third Georgia Hospital.

We all went and soon received our money. I drew one hundred and sixty-five dollars, and went on to the hospital. We were assigned to our "bunks" just before dinner.

The dinner was just simply fine; everything in good condition, plenty to eat, it cooked nice and of the right kind for our diseases. Charles Goodwin, from Augusta, Ga., was the ward master, and a good one he was. He had the cooking done right and everything kept clean and nice in the hospital.

I am sure that no mother could take better care of their sick or wounded boy than they received in this hospital. All in it were Georgians. When Dr. Green came around he examined me and asked me how long I had been in Virginia. I told him ever since the 1st of June, and that I had been sick most of the time. He said I should have had a discharge from the army, and should have been sent home, and that he would give me one, but he had received orders to not give any then. He said that if he could not cure me and there was any chance he would give me a discharge.

He treated me as kindly as my own parents could, and prescribed what I should eat and gave me good medical treatment.

I have never seen any one mend like I did. In one month I really felt well. He put me to nursing in the place of one of his nurses that he discharged for getting drunk. He said he wanted me to get well before I returned to the army.

After the Fredericksburg battle, fought December

13th, 1862, many wounded soldiers came to the hospital.

I wish to tell the readers about two wounded soldiers that came to the hospital. One was a lad from Georgia whose name was Stanford. He had his foot cut off by a grape-shot, and the doctors had amputated his foot near the ankle. Our doctors had to amputate it again, higher up. He had a serious struggle between life and death for several days with cold and fever.

The nurses all petted him, and he soon got well enough to start home.

The other one came in nearly dead. He was an Alabamian, and his name was David A. Tibbs. His thigh was amputated near his body, and he took a severe case of pneumonia, for which we blistered him severely all over his breast. He subsisted several days on milk-punch and egg-nog, made of the best brandy. He was delirious most of the time during several days and we all thought he would die.

I became interested in him and the rest of the nurses saw it and would not do much for him, which made me more attentive to him.

I had to dress his wound every day, which smelt very offensive. After a hard struggle with him by the doctors and his nurse (myself), he began to rally, came to his senses and got so he could eat a little.

The doctors had us to feed him on very light diet, and he soon began to rally and got so he could eat more, and mended very fast.

After a few days he got to having a ravenous appetite. He would lie there and beg and cry for more to eat, but the doctors charged us to not give it to him. I would give him more than the doctors said.

Tibbs got very saucy and told me that if I did not give him more to eat he would tell the doctor that I was perishing him to death. I told him that if he did I would only give him just what the doctor said give him.

When the doctor came in again Tibbs told him that I was perishing him. The doctor seemed very sympathetic and asked Tibbs what I gave him, and how much. Tibbs told him the truth about it, and the doctor said: "My dear sir, that is twice as much as I told him to give you, and it is a wonder that he has not killed you." Tibbs went to crying. The doctor came to me and said: "Have you been giving him as much as he says?" I told the doctor that what I gave him was very light and I only gave him but a little at a time, and it all seemed to do him good, and I *could not* stand to hear him beg so pleadingly and cry so pitiful and not give him some. The doctor said: "Well you *must not* give him any more than you have given him, and if you find that he is the least sick with fever or colic, you come after me *at once.*"

Soon after the doctor left Tibbs motioned for me to go to him. I pretended to be angry with him, but I was very sorry for him. He kept on calling for me till I went to him. He then began to beg me not to be angry with him. I told him that I would forgive him. He then asked me if I was going to do like the doctor said—to give him only half of what I had been giving him. I told him, "Yes, that is what the doctor said." He cried and begged me, for God's sake, to give him as much as I had been giving him. I did so.

In about three or four weeks the doctors gave him a ninety-days furlough.

Tibbs gave me the furlough and told me to go and draw all the money the government was due him and get his transportation to his home in Alabama. I did so, and brought it all to him. We got a good litter, spread blankets on it and made him a comfortable bed, took more blankets and covered him up. We then put him in an ambulance and I got in with him and went to the cars and got him on and told him good bye. He cried and held on to my hand and said: "You have been as good to me as my own dear mother could have been, and I hope God will bless you to get through the war and to get home safe."

I have never seen or heard from David A. Tibbs since.

If this history should ever fall into the hands of anyone who knows anything of him or what become of him, they will confer a great favor on me by writing to me at Jesup, Ga. I hope he is yet living and doing well, and that I may some day have the pleasure of meeting him.

By the last of February, 1863, I had gotten well, weighed ten pounds more than I had ever weighed, and was able to return to the army. I went to them at Port Royal, fifteen miles below Fredericksburg. I found the few of the boys who were left in good winter quarters. They had drawn blankets, shoes and plenty of clothing, and were getting plenty to eat and were full of life.

The snow was about two or three feet deep all over the ground. They soon initiated me with snow-balls and wallowed me in the snow.

About half the company had been killed, wounded or had died in hospitals the year before. Some had just returned from northern prisons. Henry Oliff was the only man who had the same gun that he first drew in Brunswick before we went to Jekyl Island, where we were first ordered. He had not been sick, had not straggled, was up every night on all the marches, was in every battle and skirmish and had not been hurt. There were no braver man than Henry Oliff.

CHAPTER VI.

EARLY'S DIVISION—CAMP LIFE—SNOW BATTLES—GENERAL JOHN B. GORDON ASSIGNED TO THE COMMAND OF LAWTON'S BRIGADE—BATTLE OF MARY'S HEIGHTS AND THE SAD NEWS OF STONEWALL JACKSON'S BEING MORTALLY WOUNDED.

In the winter of 1862 and 1863 our brigade was transferred from General Ewell's division to General Jubal A. Early's division and was composed of Lawton's Georgia brigade, Hays' Louisiana brigade, Pegram's Virginia brigade and Hoke's North Carolina brigade. We were in winter quarters near Port Royal, Va., fifteen miles below Fredericksburg, on the Rappahannock river.

We fared well, had a great deal of sport in having company, regimental and brigade snow battles. One day the officers of Hoke's brigade formed a line of battle and charged our brigade before we knew it. We turned out and fought them. It was very amusing, for we got into a hand to hand battle, and a great many of our boys and the North Carolinians had friendly tussles. We wallowed each other in the snow and filled each other's bosoms full, and rubbed it in each others faces. A few days after this snow battle we charged the North Carolinians and drove them through and out of their camps.

In the camps we could see Hooker's balloon spies go up. They would stay up for hours, looking over our camps.

About the first of March we moved up near Hamilton's Crossing, built more winter quarters and did picket duty at what we called "the old brick house," on the Rappahannock river. This picket post was near where Burnsides had one of his pontoon bridges during the Fredericksburg battle.

In April the balloons went up every day and we could hear the Yankees drilling and having sham battles. They were teaching their fresh troops how to fight Confederate soldiers. We could hear them charge, one line would try to yell like the Confederate soldiers and the other would "huzza! huzza! huzza!" like the Union army.

One day our regiment was on picket and none of our officers or the Yankee officers were near the picket post, so we swapped newspapers, knives and traded tobacco for coffee, etc. We did this little traffic with a little sail boat, which I suppose would have carried about four pounds.

We were on one side of the river and the Yankees were on the other, and we were all friendly. At another time while we were on picket, M. J. Green and I were at the same post. We had very strict orders to not say a word to the Yankees, and they said they had the same orders. One Yankee said: "Hello, Johnnie, we will come over to see you before long." Green said,—"Yes, and you'll get a h—l of a whipping when you come." (This was before Green joined the church).

Here while we were in this camp the famous, energetic, gallant General John B. Gordon was assigned to the command of Lawton's old brigade. (Captains W. T. Mitchell and J. M. Pace were his staff officers, Beasley and Kidd couriers). We were soon all acquainted with him. He put the company and regimental commanders to drilling the boys. We often had three drills daily; first, company drill; then, battalion drill; and in the afternoon brigade drill. Gordon would ride along the

GEN. J. B. GORDON.

line, talk very kind, yet very positive, and the officers and men were soon liking him very much.

One day Company D. was well amused. We had a hard fight in the company. John Smith borrowed Harrison Rushing's pot to boil some peas. About the time Smith got his peas to cooking, Rushing wanted his pot, but Smith told him to wait till he got his peas cooked. Rushing said,—"No, I must have it now." Smith told him that he should not have it until he got his peas cooked. Rushing started to the fire where the pot was boiling. Smith got between Rushing and the pot. They then went together and to fighting. They fought about five minutes and Captain Kennedy had them parted. They were both very tired. Smith ran to the pot and took it in his arms,—his thick clothes preventing it from burning him—and swore that he meant to have it till he got his peas cooked. Rushing must have believed him, for he let him alone.

On the morning of April 29th I was on camp-guard, while the Thirteenth Georgia regiment was on picket and was guarding the river crossing. We heard a few guns fire at the picket post, and soon a heavy volley. This was just at day break. It was the Thirteenth Georgia regiment firing at the enemy across the river, who were trying to drive them away from the crossing.

This shooting immediately put the whole command in a stir. The drum was beating the long roll and the officers were shouting "fall in line." I and the rest of the guards around the line received orders to go to our tents, pack up and follow the brigade. We caught up with them while they were forming in line at the foot of Mary's heights, on the R. & F. R. R.

The Thirteenth Georgia Regiment had continued to fire at the enemy across the river till our line was formed, when they received orders to fall back to the line of battle. This gave the enemy the opportunity of putting down their pontoon bridge. Prisoners afterwards told us that there were twenty-nine of Company K killed in one of the Michigan regiments in this skirmish battle across the river.

Almost as soon as our brigade had formed in line, as stated above, we heard cheering of regiments on our left. It was rumored that they were cheering Stonewall Jackson. He was soon passing Gordon's brigade, and I am, oh, so sorry to tell you, we never cheered him again.

A heavy skirmish line was now thrown in front of the old Turnpike road leading from Fredericksburg to Port Royal.

We built breastworks nearly all day. Late in the afternoon we saw General Early ride up to our battery on the heights, which was about one hundred yards to our right and rear. Early rode off a short distance to the left of the battery, and with his field-glass looked towards the enemy's batteries.

We saw our cannoneers busily loading their guns, and they were soon firing at a rapid rate. The enemy made a spirited reply. 'Twas a regular battery duel for about thirty minutes, but there was more noise than blood. I do not think we got a man hurt. One of the enemies solid shot struck right in the muzzle of one of guns. It split our gun about six inches, the ball being some larger than the gun. It stuck fast and dismounted the gun, which, I think, was all the damage we received. There was some skirmishing in our front during the day.

We lay quiet next day with but little skirmishing in our front. Late in the afternoon we found out, from the skirmish line, that the enemy in our front was leaving.

We could hear heavy firing in the direction of Chancellorsville. Before dark the Yankees in our front were all back across the river. At dark we all moved out of our works and took the road leading to Chancellorsville. I suppose we had gone three or four miles when we heard an order come up the line, "Halt! Halt! about face! forward march!" and away we went back in a hurry.

We were afraid that the enemy had gotten our works and the heights by strategy, so we marched back as fast as we could. We had not gone far when we heard an excited commotion come up the line. Every man dodged to one side or the other of the road. We stopped about half a minute and all moved on quietly. We marched about half a mile and found an old crippled horse by the side of the road on a steep hillside. We could see him, for the moon was rising. The old horse was what caused the commotion. He was falling down the hill and the boys thought it was a cavalry charge. The commotion went through the brigade and probably through the division.

We were hurried back to our old line with orders for every regiment to take its old place in the line, and for every company to detail three men and send them to the skirmish line. They advanced to our old skirmish line. (The writer was one who went).

We advanced, expecting, when we got to the road, the Yankees to rise up and shoot at us at short range.

The moon had risen and was shining very clearly. When we got to the road we did not find a Yankee.

When the commanding officer came along the line to see if every thing was all right and the line well formed, he sent me and others out on vidette, about two hundred yards in front, to listen and find out what the Yankees were doing. I crawled to near their works and found them trying to get in their old places in the line as we had.

The next day all was quiet except some connonading

and skirmishing and some firing on our left about Fredericksburg.

We could also hear heavy cannonading up about Chancellorsville. We could hear the small arms and some times hear the Rebel yell when the wind was blowing from that direction. It was said that we were ten miles from Chancellorsville.

Hooker had left three of his army corps in command of General Sedgwick at Hamilton's Crossing and Fredricksburg, while he had gone up the river about twenty miles and had driven our cavalry pickets from the ford, crossed his army over, hurried it across the Rapidan and on to Chancellorsville.

Generals Lee and Jackson met him with the most of their army, leaving Early's division and Barksdale's brigade of McLaw's division.

Barksdale was charged with the protection of the heights in the rear of Fredericksburg, including Marye's hill, and the stone wall made famous by the Burnside campaign. His brigade consisted of about 1,400 men. It was disposed as follows (so history informs us): Seven companies of the Twenty-first Mississippi were posted between the Marye house and the plank road; the three remaining companies were posted on the telegraph road at the foot of the Marye hill; his other two regiments were on the hills farther to the right. Batteries were set up at Lee's hill and the Harrison house, while our pieces of artillery were stationed at the Marye house.

As soon as Early was made aware of Sedgwick's movement he sent Hays' brigade to reinforce Barksdale.

On Sunday, May 3rd, Sedgwick, in a dense fog, advanced on Barksdale's little brigade and a terrible battle opened for the amount of troops engaged; Hay's Louisiana brigade was soon on hand and both fought bravely, but Sedgwick succeeded in capturing Marye's heights with his much superior force, because he could flank the Confederates out of their positions.

Sedgwick captured the heights about noon. Gordon's brigade had not left its position in the front of the heights at the crossing, and when Sedgwick captured the heights we heard three huzzas from the Federals, although we were three miles away. Later in the day the enemy left our front and marched up the river to Fredericksburg. Early followed and formed his lines.

We remained in line all night, and just at day-break we advanced, Gordon's brigade being on Early's right and nearest the river. We advanced in excellent line through woods, brush, over hills and valleys, with the Thirty-first Georgia regiment, commanded by Colonel Evans, on skirmish. We had advanced about two miles when the skirmish line struck the Yankee skirmish line, and drove it in at once, and pushed on to the heights. Our line of battle forwarded and re-took the heights with but very little loss to us. In this little battle of only a few minutes, there were eight holes shot through my blanket; my shoe-sole was shot intwain and my foot stunned.

Captain Kennedy had his sword strap shot in twain and Corporal William Holloway had his canteen bursted open with a ball. There were not over fifteen or twenty of the Sixty-first Georgia killed and wounded. This happened early on the morning of May 4th.

We lay around all day till about night. General Lee had sent Generals McLaws, Mahone and Wilcox with their commands to Early's assistance. They were on one side of the enemy and Early on the other. Late in the afternoon we were ordered to see that our guns were all right and to take a full supply of ammunition. We could see the generals moving around, apparently deeply interested, and the couriers riding at a rapid rate, carrying orders to regimental commanders.

It was near 6 o'clock in the afternoon and we knew that something was going to happen. We heard a big signal gun and our regimental commanders commanded attention. We were all on our feet at once and ordered to move forward.

The enemy opened on us generally with their artillery; we advanced in excellent order and went some distance before we struck the enemy. There was heavy firing and a severe battle just to our left; so we hurried up. When we struck the enemy they had their batteries massed right in front of the Sixty-first Georgia Regiment.

They seemed to open fire at our regiment with every gun (about twenty), almost at the same time, loaded with grape and cannister shot. They were about two hundred yards from us. When we saw the smoke puff from the mouths of their cannons it looked like every man fell at once. It seemed that the air was full of grape and canister shot. I think they must have had double charges. Luckily for us we had not gotten to the top of the hill; and when we fell, which was almost automatically, the ground was about twelve or fifteen inches higher in our front than it was where we were, and the deadly missles passed harmlessly over us.

The rest of the brigade that was not exposed to this battery moved around on our lett and put the enemy to flight. We did not get a man hurt in Company D, and I don't think we lost more than twenty, killed and wounded, in the regiment, and I don't think there were over one hundred killed and wounded in the brigade.

While we were doing this Generals McLaws, Mahone, Wilcox and others pressed the enemy on the other side and caused a perfect route and stampede in Sedgwick's command.

It was now after sundown, very near dark, and we could not follow up our success. We lay quiet on the field of battle all night. Next morning the Yankees were all back across the river and the battle of Chancellorsville and Marye's heights was over.

We had reasons to thank God, for we had not gotten a man seriously hurt in company D. We stayed on the field until about 9 o'clock, when we were ordered back to our old camps. We went with very sad hearts, for we had heard what a sad calamity had befallen our beloved Stonewall Jackson—one of the greatest military men that had ever lived. His death was a terrible blow to the Confederate cause. It was almost equal to a Union victory. His name will go down in history as the hero of Chancellorsville.

General "Stonewall" Jackson was the most dashing and daring general in Lee's army, and his place could never be filled.

After this battle the Thirty-eighth Georgia Regiment was detailed to carry 1,700 prisoners that we had captured to Richmond. They were gone several days.

CHAPTER VII.

Union Account of the Battle of Chancellorsville, by Colonel Theodore A. Dodge, of the United States Army.

In the "Lowell Institute" course of lectures in Boston last winter (this lecture was delivered in 1885—Author.) the following lecture was delivered by Colonel Theodore A. Dodge, author of the admirable book on Chancellorsville, which we had occasion to notice so favorably.

In order that our readers may see clearly who it is that gives this able, clear and very fair account of this great battle, we insert the following brief sketch of Colonel Dodge, given by the Boston *Herald:*

"Colonel Theodore A. Dodge is one of the best known men in Boston military circles. He is now in his fifty-seventh year (1898), having been born in Pittsfield, Mass., in 1842. When quite young he went to Berlin, Prussia, where he received his military education under General Van Froneich, of the Prussian army.

"When the civil war cloud burst in the United States, he promptly returned home, enlisted and went to the front.

"He served constantly in the army of the Potomac (in every volunteer regimental rank up to that of colonel) from the Peninsular, where he was with Kearney through Pope's and Burnside's campaigns, and at Chancellorsville and Gettysburg, in which latter engagement he was with Howard. He was thrice brevetted for gallantry. After Gettysburg, where he lost a leg, he was ordered to duty in the war department. While there Secretary Stanton offered him a regular commission, which he accepted.

"Colonel Dodge remained in the war department until 1875, when he was, by reason of wounds, received in line of duty and placed on the retired list of the army, where he now is."

We insert with great pleasure the lecture, without note or comment of our own, except to say that while possibly we might find some statements in it with which we might not fully concur, yet we hail it as a happy omen when a gallant soldier who wore the blue can give to a Boston audience so candid and truthful an account of a great battle in which the Federal army suffered so severe a disaster.

COLONEL DODGE'S LECTURE.

Ladies and Gentlemen: You have listened to an eloquent and able presentation of the main issues and events of our civil war by one of our most distinguished fellow-citizens, a man upright in peace and zealous in war.

You have heard a graphic narrative of a great Southern victory from one of our late antagonists, whose record, as one of Stonewall Jackson's staff officers, stamps him honest and brave, as his presence and bearing among us have stamped him thoroughly reconstructed. You have had spread before you an elaborate and brilliant view of our glorious victories by a gallant soldier of two wars, who has beaten into a plough-shear the sword he wielded to such good purpose in Mexico and Virginia.

It has fallen my lot to tell you about one of our most lamentable defeats. To tell the truth about Chancellorsville is an invidious task. Less than the truth no one to-day would like to hear.

Under Burnsides the army of the Potomac suffered an equal disaster. But Burnsides blamed himself alone. No word but praise for his lieutenants passed his lips.

After Chancellorsville, on the contrary, Hooker sought

to shift all the blame upon his subordinates, even to the extent of intimating that they were braggarts, who would not fight. Particularly Howard and Sedgwick were his scapegoats, and for some years Hooker's views gained credence.

His course renders necessary a critical examination of the campaign. But be it remembered that every word of censure is uttered with the consciousness that Hooker's memory lies embalmed in our mausoleums of dead heroes, and that in lesser commands his career was patriotic and useful. The disaster at Fredericksburg in December, 1862, had left its mark upon the ever faithful Army of the Potomac.

It had lost its confidence in its chief, but not in itself. Burnsides retired in January, to the satisfaction of all, but carrying away their affectionate regard.

Hooker succeeded to the command. His soubriquet of "Fighting Joe" aptly but superficially characterizes him. Few men could handle a division—perhaps a corps—to better advantage under definite orders. None gloried in the act of war more than he. Lacking not conduct, yet the dramatic side of the art, military was dearest to him, and his ubiquity and handsome bearing made him better known to the army at large than many of his more efficient brothers in arms.

The troops accepted Hooker with the utmost heartiness. He had been identified with their history. He was bone of their bone. He seemed the very type and harbinger of success. Men and officers alike joined in the work of rehabilitation. Under well digested orders—for Hooker was a good organizer—the lamentable laxity of discipline soon disappeared; eagerness succeeded apathy, and the Army of the Potomac once again held high its head.

On April 30th, 1863, the morning report showed "for

duty equipped 131,491 officers and men, and nearly 400 guns (cannon) in the camp near Falmouth. Confronting this overwhelming body of men lay the weather-beaten army of Northern Virginia, numbering some 60,000 men and 170 guns" (cannon.) This force was posted from Banks' ford above to Skenker's neck below Fredericksburg, a distance of some fifteen miles.

Every inch of this line was strongly and intelligently fortified. The *morale* of the Confederate army could not have been finer. To numbers it opposed superior position and defenses, and its wonderful success had bred that contempt of danger and that hardihood which are the very essence of discipline.

Perhaps no infantry was ever in its own peculiar way more permeated with the instinct of pure fighting—ever felt the *gaudium certaminis*—than the Army of Northern Virginia at this time.

The Army of the Potomac could not well risk another front attack on Marye's Heights.

To turn Lee's right flank necessitated operations quite in evidence, and the crossing of a river 1,000 feet wide in the very teeth of the enemy.

Hooker matured his plans for a movement about Lee's left.

On April 12th the cavalry corps was ordered out upon a raid via Culpepper and Gordonsville, to the rear of Lee's army, in order to cut his communications and to demoralize his troops at the moment when the main attack should fall upon him.

"Let your watchword be fight! and let all your orders be fight!! fight!! fight!!!" was Hooker's aggressive order to Stoneman. The performance of the latter, however, was in inverse ratio to the promise of these instructions. The start was delayed two weeks by a rise in the river, and the movement was so weak from its inception that the cavalry raid degenerated into an utter failure, and the first step in the campaign thus miscarried. The operations of the calvary corps scarcely belong to the history of Chancellorsville. They in nowise affected the conduct or out-come of the campaign.

In order to conceal his real move by the right, Hooker made show of moving down the river, and a strong demonstration with the First, Third and Sixth corps on the left under command of Sedgwick, covered by Hunt's guns, on April 29th and 30th. Pontoons were thrown at Franklin's Crossing and Pollock's Mills; Troops were put over and bridgeheads were constructed and held by Brooks' and Wadsworth's divisions. Lee made no serious attempt to dispute this movement, but watched the disposition, uncertain how to gauge their value.

Meanwhile the Eleventh and Seventh corps, followed by the Fifth, with eight days' rations, marched up to Kelley's ford. Here all three corps crossed the Rappahannock on the night of Wednesday, the 29th, and on Thursday the two former crossed the Rapidan at Germania ford, and the latter at Ely's, and all three reached Chancellorsville Thursday afternoon. Here Slocum assumed command. Gibson's division of the Second corps had been left to guard the Falmouth camps and do provost duty, while French and Hancock, after United States ford had been unmasked, crossed at this point and joined the forces at Chancellorsville. The Third corps was likewise ordered from the left, by the same route, to the same point. Thus far, everything had been admirably conceived and executed. Small criticisms can be passed upon Hooker's logistics. They were uniformly good. Two of our corps had centered the enemy's attention upon his right flank, below Fredericksburg, while we had massed four corps upon his left flank, with a fifth close by, and had scarcely lost a man.

Hooker's vaunting order of this day is all but justified by the situation.

But one more immediate and vigorous push and the army of Northern Virginia would have been desperately compromised, practically defeated.

Lee had not been unaware of what the Federals had been doing, but had been largely misled by the feint below the town and had so little anticipated Hooker's movement by the right, that less than 3,000 of his cavalry were on hand to observe the crossing of the Rappahannock and Rapidan.

Stuart had not, until Thursday, fully gauged the importance of this movement and only on Thursday night had Lee ascertained the facts and been able to mature his plans for parrying Hooker's thrust. Anderson had received on Wednesday orders to check at Chancellorsville, as long as possible, our advance, supposed to be partial only, and then to slowly retire to the Mine Run road.

This he had done, and here Lee's engineers were speedily engaged in drawing up a line of entrenchments. Early was left at Hamilton's crossing. Barksdale remained in the town and Lee, with the bulk of his forces, hurried out to meet the Army of the Potomac. At an early hour on Friday morning Jackson arrived at the Mine Run line and took command.

Hooker's tardiness in advancing had already allowed the erection of a difficult barrier. The headquarters of the Army of the Potomac had remained at Falmouth till Hooker personally reached Chancellorsville. After the transfer hither, the chief of staff, for ease of communication between the wings, was kept at the old camp at Falmouth.

Hooker now announced his plan to advance Friday in force and uncover Banks' ford so as to be within quicker reach of Sedgwick. It had been a grave error not to make this advance on Thursday afternoon. On Friday morning, after reconnoitering the ground, he accordingly ordered an advance toward the open country to the east, while Sedgwick should threaten an attack in the neighborhood of Hamilton's crossing to draw Lee's attention.

In pursuance of these orders, Meade advanced to within grasp of Banks' ford quite unopposed. Sykes and Hancock on the turnpike, on leaving the forest, ran upon the entrenched divisions of Anderson and McLaws, whom they engaged. Slocum, with the Eleventh and Twelfth corps on the plank road, was arrested by the left of this same line. The opposition was nowhere serious. The troops were there to fight, Hooker should have carried out his programme in full by ordering up fresh troops and by driving back the largely overmatched forces of the enemy. Every reason demanded this. The Army of the Potomac had just emerged from the wilderness, in whose confines no superiority of force could be made available, as it could be on open ground toward Fredericksburg. It was essential that the two wings should be got within easier communication. The enemy had been surprised and should be followed up. The plan had succeeded well so far; to abandon it would create a loss of *morale* among the troops. Suddenly every one concerned was surprised by an order from Hooker to withdraw again into the wilderness.

Here may be said to have begun the certain loss of the campaign. The proceeding was absurd. Hooker had reached Chancellorsville Thursday noon with 40,000 men, fresh and abundantly able to advance toward and seize Banks' ford, his first objective point. To delay here until Friday noon was a grave mistake. Still had the advance on Friday been pushed home by a concerted movement by the left so as to seize Banks' and cover United States ford, it was by no means too late to gather the fruits of the vigor and secrecy exhibited thus far in this flank march. But the advance on Friday was checked by Hooker without personal examination of the situation, to the surprise of every one, and against the protest of many of his subordinates.

A more fatal error cannot be conceived. Here first appeared Hooker's lack of balance.

The troops retired and Jackson at once took advantage of the situation by advancing his left to Welford's.

The Army of the Potomac on Friday night lay huddled in the chapparal around Chancellorsville instead of occupying, as they might, a well defined position on the open ground in front of Banks' ford. Gradually during the night the several corps drifted weary and disheartened at this unexplained check in the midst of success without any idea of fighting there.

The line was thus a haphazzard one, on the worst conceivable ground, where cavalry was useless, artillery confined to the roads or to a few open spaces, and infantry hidden or paralyzed.

Reynolds was now ordered from the left wing to Chancellorsville. The line lay from left to right—Meade, Couch, Slocum, Sickles and Howard. Hooker determined to receive instead of delivering an attack. He knew how vastly he outnumbered Lee; he could gauge the advantage he had gained from his initiative; he could not be blind to the wretched terrain around Chancellorsville, and yet he sat down as if already worsted. Nothing but a sudden loss of moral force can explain such enigmatic conduct. Hooker had come to the end of his mental tether. The march had taxed his powers to their limit. He had no more stomach for the fight.

During this night, while the Army of Northern Virginia was moving into position in front of its gigantic, but apparently unnerved enemy, Lee and Jackson developed a plan for an attack upon our right, which, though posted on high ground, was really in the air. Lee may have originated the plan, but it bears a distinctly Jacksonian flavor; and surely without such a lieutenant to execute it, Lee would never have dreamed of such a risky move.

The plan gave Jackson about 24,000 men with which to undertake a march around our right flank to a position where he might cut us off from United States ford.

It was ultra-hazardous, for it separated a small army in the presence of a large one.

It was justifiable on the ground that Hooker evidently meant to retain the defensive; that the movement would be screened from his eye by the woods; that there seemed no more available plan; that some immediate action was demanded.

Had it failed it would have met the censure of every soldier. No maxim of tactics applies to it so well as the proverb, "Nothing venture, nothing have."

Although Jackson's corps had been on foot and partially engaged for some thirty hours, the men set out on his new march with cheerful alacrity. They could always follow "Old Jack" with their eyes shut. Stuart's cavalry masked the advance.

Jackson did not know that his column would have to pass some open ground in full view of our line at Dowdall's until too late to have it follow a better concealed route.

Early Saturday morning the movement was discovered by the Third corps and a reconnoisance was pushed out to embarrass its advance.

After some trouble and a slight and successful attack,

Birney ascertained and reported that Jackson was moving over to our right.

The conclusion which Hooker drew from this fact was, apparently, that Lee was retreating.

Jackson, meanwhile keeping Sickles busy with a small rear-guard, advanced along the Brock road until toward afternoon he was abreast and in the rear of our right flank. While he was thus massing his men to attack the army of the Potomac in reverse, Hooker continued to authorize Sickles to deplete the threatened wing by sending a large part of its available strength, (Barlow, Birney, Whipple and Geary in part—some 15,000 men), out into the woods in hopes of capturing the force which had long ago eluded his grasp and was ready to fall upon our rear.

Hooker's right flank of barely 10,000 men was completely issolated.

And yet though scouts, pickets. and an actual attack at 3:30 P. M. proved beyond a peradventure Jackson's presence at this point, Hooker allowed this flank to be held by an untried corps, composed of the most heterogenous and untrustworthy elements in the army of the Potomac. This march of Jackson's might at first blush have been construed by Hooker to be either a retreat or a strategic march by Lee to new grounds, or to be a threatened flank attack. Either would have been accompanied by the same tactical symptoms which now appeared.

If the former, Hooker had his option to attack at an early or late period, more or less vigorously, as might appear best to him. Hooker afterwards claimed that he believed in the flank attack. But the testimony of his dispatches at the time finds him riding both horses, and he acted on the retreat theory. At 9:30 A. M., he had notified Slocum and Howard to look out and prepare for a flank attack, and to post heavy reserves to meet one. He telegraphed Sedgwick at 4:10 P. M.: "We know that the enemy is flying; trying to save his trains."

In the meantime he had removed the heavy reserves in question and sent them out on Sickles' wild goose chase to the front. He made no inspections of the right except one early in the morning.

Howard, commanding on the right, misled by Hooker's orders and apathy, held to the retreat theory. He had, on the receipt of the 9:30 order, disposed Barlow's brigade and his reserve artillery so as to resist an attack along the pike road, but Barlow had been ordered by Hooker to join Sickles.

General Devens made several distinct attempts to impress on Howard the danger of an attack, but the latter took his color, as well as his orders, from the commander of the army. General Carl Schurz, under whom I served that day, also held strongly to the flank attack theory, and scores of men in the Eleventh corps, after the picket fight of 3:30, fully believed that another attack would be made in the same place. Common generosity to the memory of Hooker, who was a gallant and successful corps commander, leads us to think that at the time he believed that the enemy was retreating. His neglect of the right was otherwise criminal.

In him alone centered all the information of constantly occurring changes.

To him alone was reported each new circumstance. His subordinates knew but the partial truth. They relied on him for the initiative.

At 6 P. M., then, the situation was this: The left and center lay as before. Howard held the right—the "key of the position." 10,000 men, a half brigade of Devens' only astride the pike, the rest of Devens' and Schurz's facing south, and Steinwehr massed at Dowdall's. Howard's best brigades were gone, and there was not a man to support him between Dowdall's and Chancellorsville, for this portion of the line, under Sickles, had been advanced into the woods nearly two miles. On the right flank of this little force lay Jackson's corps of over 20,000 men, whose wide wings, like the arms of a gigantic cuttle-fish, were ready to clutch it in their fatal embrace.

To cover Jackson's march Lee, at intervals during the day, tapped at the lines in his front, principally where Hancock lay.

During all this afternoon, Hooker had a chance to handsomely redeem his Friday's error in retiring into the wilderness. Whatever the reason, the fact that he had divided his army remained clear.

Lee, with the right wing, had but 18,000 men. Hooker knew that he conld not have more than 25,000. He himself had 70,000 splendid troops.

He could have crushed Lee like an egg shell and then have turned on Jackson.

But, with a knowledge of Jackson's habit of mystery, of his wonderful speed and fighting capacity, and of his presence on our right, with all means of knowing that this same right flank was isolated by two miles of impregnable woods from any supporting force, he sat still, folded his hands, as it were, for sleep, and waited events.

The Eleventh corps was cooking or eating supper. Arms were stacked. Breastworks looking south were but fairly substantial. Facing east were none. Some carelessness was apparent, in that ambulances, ammunition wagons, pack mules and even a drove of beeves were close behind the line. Everyone was at ease, though a few were not wanting in anxiety.

Little Wilderness church, near by, endeavored to stamp a peaceful air upon the warlike scene. The general feeling seemed to be that it was too late to get up much of a fight today. Jackson, in three lines, rides in advance, Colston next and A. P. Hill still coming up, lay close by. He had caught Hooker's right *flagrante delicta.*

At 6 P. M. the order was given and twenty-two thousand of the best infantry in existence closed rapidly down on the flank of ten thousand of the least hardened of the troops of the Army of the Potomac. No division in the Army of the Potomac, not the old guards, not Frederick's automato, could have changed front under the staggering blow. The fight was short, sharp, deadly, but partial only.

But the force on the right was swept away like cobwebs by Jackson's mighty besom. Some of Schurz's regiment made a gallant show of resistance under the terrible ordeal of friends and foes breaking through their hastily formed lines; some melted away without burning a cartridge. Bushbeck's brigade threw itself into some breastworks, constructed across the road at Dowdall's, and made a desperate resistance.

It was here that Howard had asked leave to place his line, but had been refused. A ridge made the line well available for defense. The whole situation was confusion worse confounded. The attack had been so sudden that the stampede of the regiments on the extreme right swept away many of those which were endeavoring to form near the fork of the roads. The droves of beeves, the frightened teamsters and ambulance drivers, officers, servants and hundreds of camp followers, were rushing blindly to and fro seeking an escape from the murderous hail of lead.

The enemy came on with remorseless steadfastness. Never was an army more completely surprised, more absolutely overwhelmed.

Few, even among the old soldiers, preserved their calmness, but many did their duty.

The higher officers were in the thickest of the fray. An occasional stand would be made, only to be again broken. Everywhere appeared the evidence of unpreparedness. It is a small wonder that the corps made no resistance worthy the name.

Rather wonder that, under the circumstances I have detailed, the onset of Jackson was actually checked by this surprised and overmatched, this telescoped force, considerably more than an hour, at a loss of one-third its effective strength. Could more have been expected?

The worthlessness of Hooker's dispositions now became apparent.

Jackson's small rear guard had been playing with Sickles, while his main body had extinguished Howard. Nothing now lay between Jackson and the headquarters of the army except a difficult forest through which a mass of panic-stricken fugitives were rushing in dire confusion, out of range.

Happily, night was approaching, and Jackson's troops had to be halted and re-formed, his three lines having become inextricably mixed.

Anderson had made a serious attack on our center as soon as the guns of Jackson's corps were heard, so that Hooker had nothing at hand to throw into the gap but Berry's division of the old Third corps. Other troops were too far away. This division was now hurried into position across the pike. The artillery of the Third corps and many guns of the Eleventh corps were assembled on the Fairview crest. Sickles faced about the 15,000 men he had led into the woods, and disposed himself to attack Jackson in a more practical fashion. Between good use of several batteries and a gallant charge by a handful of cavalry, a division upon his flank was created, which, coupled with Berry's desperate resistance and the heavy artillery fire from Fairview, arrested Jackson's onset.

It was after this check, while reconnoitering in front of his troops, that this noted soldier received from his own lines the volley which inflicted on him a mortal wound.

A midnight attack was made by Sickles upon Jackson. Sickles' claims that he drove the enemy back to Dowdall's is scarcely substantiated.

The attack had no particular results. Sickles regained once more his old position at Haze Grove which he held until daylight Sunday morning, when he was ordered back to Chancellorsville by Hooker.

The latter seemed unaware how important this height might prove in his own—how dangerous in Lee's hands. For, as his lines here made a salient, it behooved him to strengthen it by just such a height or else to abandon this line of defence.

On Sunday morning at daylight, Stuart, who succeeded Jackson, ranged his twenty thousand men opposite the Fairview crest and supported them by batteries on this same Hazel Grove. Fairview was crowned by our artillery and defended by about an equal infantry force on the next ridge below, consisting of the entire Third corps and Williams of the Twelvth corps. Anderson and McLaws, with seventeen thousand men, still confronted Geary and Hancock with twelve thousand men. Reynolds had arrived during the night but was posted on the extreme right away from the scene of actual hostilities. No other troops were brought into action.

Thus the superior tactics of the enemy enabled him to outnumber us at every point of attack, while an equal number of available Union troops lay upon their arms close by, witnessing the unneeded slaughter of their comrades.

The attack of the Confederates began shortly after daylight with "Jackson" for a watchword, and was gallant in the extreme.

Anderson pushed in on our left center as Stuart did on the right center, both contending for the Chancellor House, which barred their possession of the turnpike. No praise is too high for the staunchness of the attack or the stubbornness of the defense; but after heavy fighting during the entire forenoon, the Army of the Potomac yielded to the Confederate pressure and retired to a new line already prepared by its engineers and which had its apex at the White House. Time does not allow the barest details of this struggle to be entered upon. Suffice it to say that the loss of the Third, Twelfth and Second corps of 4,000, 3,000 and 2,000 respectively, effectually gauges the bitterness of the contest.

The Confederate loss was, if anything, higher than ours during Sunday morning.

Lee was reforming for an assault upon our line when rumors from Fredericksburg diverted his attention. During this fight of Sunday morning, the general plan of the Confederates was to obtain possession of the direct road by which they could keep to themselves the communications with Fredericksburg. Hooker's plan, after failing to attack one or the other of Lee's divided wings, should have been to retain this road, the key to which was the Chancellorsville crest and plateau.

But he seemed to have no conception of using the forces at hand. The First, Fifth and Seventh corps were not in action at all, though of their 47,000 men 30,000 could easily have been spared from the positions they held.

Reynolds could have projected a strong column upon Stuart's left flank, and was eager to render this simple service. From our left several divisions could have made a diversion against McLaws' right. Our forces at Fairview could have been doubled at any time. But all Hooker seemed able to do was to call upon Sedgwick, a dozen miles away, to perform an impossible task in succor of his own overwhelming force.

To be sure, Hooker was disabled for some hours by the falling against him, about 10 A. M., of a column of the Chancellor house, which was dislodged by a shell.

During this period Couch acted as his mouthpiece. But this disablement cannot excuse the error which preceded it, and Hooker was beaten, morally and tactically, before this accident; for he had predetermined retreat by the erection of the new lines, and had taken none of the measures which ordinary military nous demanded while he was able-bodied. There is no palliation to be found in this accident. There is nothing approaching tactical combination to be seen on our side in this campaign after Friday's withdrawal in the wilderness. It has been surmised that Hooker, during this campaign, was incapacitated by a habit of which, at times, he had been the victim. There is rather evidence that he was prostrated by too much abstemiousness when a reasonable use of stimulants might have kept his nervous system at its normal tension. It was certainly not the use of alcohol during this time which lay at the foot of his indecision.

Let us now turn to Sedgwick, who properly formed the left wing of the Army of the Potomac, though, as the operations eventuated, his corps was rather a detached command.

Sedgwick had lain on the Falmouth side with one division across the river guarding the bridge-heads.

During the afternoon of Saturday Hooker ordered him to cross and pursue what he called the "flying enemy" by the Bowling Green road. Sedgwick did cross and began skirmishing with Early to force the latter from the road back into the woods. After the Eleventh corps had been crushed, the same evening Hooker ordered Sedgwick, at 9 P. M., to march to Chancellorsville "destroying any force he might fall in with on the road." This order was received by Sedgwick at 11 P. M., when he was intent on pursuit in the opposite direction. Sedgwick sent out his orders to change dispatch, but it was after midnight before he could get his command faced about and fairly headed in the new direction.

The Fredericksburg Heights were held by Generals Early and Barksdale with 8,500 men and plenty of artillery. In December a few brigades had here defeated the entire Army of the Potomac.

Hooker himself, with his battle-worn veterans, had then pronounced the task impossible.

It was after midnight, Sedgwick had fifteen miles to march after capturing this almost impregnable position, and all this to be done before daylight—that is, within three hours, if he was to carry out his orders.

So soon as his head of column reached the town, four regiments were sent against the rifle pits but were speedily repulsed, with considerable loss. Before Sedgwick had sufficiently altered the disposition of his troops to warrant an assault, day broke.

Brooks still held the left of the line, Howe the centre and Newton the right. Gibbon, who had been left in Falmouth, threw a bridge above Fredericksburg, crossed and filed in on Sedgwick's right.

Both Gibbon and Howe made demonstrations against the enemy's flanks but the nature of the ground precluded their success.

Two storming columns were formed, one from Howe's front and one from Newton's.

These dispositions were not completed until 11 A. M., after a delay perhaps not justifiable, in view of the stringency of the orders.

But their work was well done. Without firing a shot, these columns advanced, rushed upon and over the intrenchments and carried them at the point of the bayonet, with a loss of over one thousand men. This cut the Confederate force on the right in two and gave Sedgwick possession of the plank road, the direct way to Chancellorsville.

If Sedgwick had captured the heights before day-light, and, leaving a strong rear-guard to occupy Early's attention, had advanced straight toward Chancellorsville, he might have reached Hooker by 9 or 10 A. M., the hour when his chief was worst pressed. And some of Sedgwick's subordinates think this could readily have been done. But, while it is hard to-day to insist that this much might not have been accomplished, the probabilities certainly are that a night attack in force would have resulted either in defeat or in giving Early, who was entirely familiar with the ground, a chance to deal some fatal blows at Sedgwick's moving column, which would be more or less disorganizing by the night assault and march. Be this as it may, Sedgwick's movements were certainly more speedy than those of Sickles', and his work stands out handsomely when contrasted with any done on our side in this campaign. Another delay now occurred in giving Brooks the head of the column in advance toward Chancellorsville.

Though technically proper, Brooks not having been engaged, the nature of Sedgwick's orders certainly did not warrant this delay. Newton followed Brooks; Howe brought up the rear. By noon word reached Lee that

Sedgwick had captured the Fredericksburg heights. Wilcox, cut off from Early, alone separated Sedgwick from Lee's rear.

McLaw's and a part of Anderson's men were at once dispatched to sustain Wilcox.

These troopes arrived at Salem church by 2 P. M; Brooks and Newton shortly came upon the field and endeavored to capture the position they had taken, but, though 1,500 men were lost in the attempt, our troops finally recoiled. A pontoon bridge was now thrown across at Banks' ford, and nearer communications were opened with headquarters. Up to this time, be it noted, Hooker in no wise reflected on Sedgwick's tardiness, though aware, through Warren, who had been his representative with Sedgwick, of all the Sixth corps had done or failed to do. His dispatches to Sedgwick are plainly couched in terms of approval.

During Sunday night Lee concluded that he must permanently dispose of Sedgwick before he could again assault Hooker's lines. Early had recaptured the Fredricksburg heights and Gibbon had recrossed the river.

The balance of Anderson's force now joined McLaw's.

With Anderson, McLaws and Early, some 25,000 men, Lee thought he could fairly expect to dispose of the Sixth corps, which was now reduced to 5,000 less and felt it lack of success. After this he could turn again upon Hooker. Jackson's corps alone was left to watch Hooker. Here, then, we have the spectacle, happily rare in war, of a slender force of 20,000 men who had been continuously marching and fighting for four days, persuing in their defences an army of over sixty thousand (60,000) men, while its commander cries for aid to a lieutenant who is miles away and beset by a larger force than he himself commands. And this slack-sinewed commander is the very same who intimated the campaign with the watchword: "Fight! Fight!! Fight!!!" and with the motto: "Celerity, audacity and resolution are everything in war." Despite which lamentable fact, this same commander's after-wit sought to lay half the blame of his defeat upon this lieutenant's failure to come to his assistance. The other half fell upon Howard on equally invalid grounds. So soon as Sedgwick became aware of the presence of the bulk of Lee's forces in his front, he disposed his three divisions so as best to cover Banks' ford, both from south, east and west, and to hold a footing on the plank road substantially. Newton faced west, Banks south and Howe east. Lee, after some hour's preparation, made ready to press in Sedgwick's centre.

It is worth while, perhaps, to note the fact that Lee's delay in attacking Sedgwick was fully as great as Sedgwick's in forcing Mary's Heights. And yet his haste was quite as pressing, for at at any moment Hooker might decide to move toward his lieutenant.

Many dispatches passed between Hooker and Sedgwick at this time. Sedgwick must, of course, be judged by the time of their receipts. At 4 P. M. of this day, Monday, he received word to "look well to the safety of his corps," and to cross at Banks' ford to the north side, if desirable.

These dispatches he answered, but he could not be sure that the answers reached Hooker. Later Hooker ordered him to hold on to Banks' ford if possible. Then again, on receiving Sedgwick's report of insecurity of his position, Hooker ordered him to withdraw, and still later again to hold on. This last dispatch, however, was reseived by Sedgwick too late. For under the former authority to the same effect, he had determined to retire across the river as soon as night should fall. At 6 P. M.

Lee attacked. McLaws fell upon the corner held by Brooks; Early assaulted Howe. The latter's onset was very hardy. Our loss was over two thousand men, but no serious impression was made.

During the night Sedgwick withdrew and took up his pontoon bridge. The corps had lost over 5,000 men. Lee, having accomplished his task, sent Early back to Fredericksburg and himself returned to Hooker's front. While Lee was considering how he might best attack the Army of the Potomac, Hooker called his corps commanders together to ascertain their feelings relative to advance or retreat.

All except Sickles were in favor of a vigorous advance. Sickles thought that political reasons favored retreat, less the Army of the Potomac should suffer an overwhelming defeat, which, at this time, might discourage the war party of the north. Moreover the rations brought by the troops had been exhausted and the river was now rising and threatening the bridges.

Here, again, it may be noted, that unless retreat had been actually predetermined, the past three days should have been used to revictual the army for a possible advance. For Hooker was, as a rule, careful in these matters. Under all these circumstances, and after hearing all opinions, Hooker decided to retire.

A new line was accordingly made to protect United States ford, and during the night of May 5th the army recrossed the last troops about 8 A. M., of May 6th. Lee did not interfere with this movement.

He was glad to see an end put to his dangerous situation, for his army was absolutely exhausted. But had he known the precarious situation of our troops, huddled that night in the *cue-de-sac* at the bridge-heads, he might have inflicted terrible damage upon us. The total loss of the Army of the Potomac was 17,000; of the Army of Northern Virginia, 12,300.

On arriving at its old camps, the Union army received an order tendering it the congratulations of its chief on the achievements of the last seven days. Lee recommended the Southern troops to unite in ascribing to the Lord of Hosts the glory due his name.

Two years later Hooker, in his testimony before the committee on the conduct of the war, stated that in his opinion, there was nothing to regret in regard to the Chancellorsville campaign except that he did not accomplish all that he moved to do, and that he did not consider the campaign a defeat.

Up to thursday noon Hooker's manœuvre was a pronounced success. His subsequent defeat may be ascribed to the following tactical and logistic errors:

First—Failure to move his cavalry effectively. This is probably more Stoneman's fault than Hooker's.

Second—Failure to move the entire army out into the open country and to seize Bank's ford on Thursday afternoon.

Third—This having been neglected, failure to make a vigorous rush toward the same objective point on Friday morning.

Fourth—Weakness to fight a defensive battle after a successful offensive flank movement.

Fifth—Failure to order (after 9:30 A. M.) on Saturday, and personally to see, that suitable dispositions were made on the right flank to resist a threatened or possible attack at that point.

Sixth—Weakness in allowing a partial, slow and inaffective movement against such a wily tactician as Jackson to produce a gap in his line, which robbed his right flank of all support.

Seventh—Failure to fall in force upon one or the other

of Lee's separate wings Saturday afternoon or early Sunday morning.

Eighth—Not having done so, failure to hold Hazel Grove as head of salient on Sunday morning.

Ninth—Failure to sustain the gallant struggle at Fairview with some of his unused divisions, which themselves outnumbered the enemy, or to attack the enemy's flank in its support.

Tenth—Failure to attack whatever was in his front in support of Sedgwick's advance and fight at Salem church during Monday.

Eleventh—Failure to ration his army while his communications were open, so that he might again advance on Tuesday.

Twelfth—Failure to keep Sedgwick on the south side of the river so as to aid in a new joint advance.

The direct result of Chancellorsville was a second invasion of the Northern States by Lee, which culminated in a defeat of the Army of Northern Virginia two months later on the hills of Gettysburg.

Tried by the rule of brilliant success against vast odds, Lee's work in this campaign is scareely open to criticism.

The hero of the Chancellorsville campaign is Thomas J. Jackson, the most able lieutenant of our civil war, while historical accuracy obliges us to place the onus of this lost campaign upon Hooker, and, while his own bitter perverseness toward his lieutenants may lead some asperity to our criticism, it will not do to forget Hooker's excellent services to the country.

As a brigade, division and corps commander, previous to Chancellorsville, he had earned an enviable record in the Army of the Potomac.

Subsequently, in lieu of retiring in dudgeon, he went to Chattanooga with the Eleventh and Twelfth corps, and there did worthy service. Hooker's efficiency was always weakened by his peculiar desire to work for the public eye and by his characteristic shortcomings. But Hooker was a brave soldier, a true patriot, and, within his limitations, a reliable general officer. He did not, however, possess that rare combination of self-reliance, intellectual vigor and military common sense which enables a man to bear the strain laid upon him by the command of an army opposed to such a captain as General Robert E. Lee.

Here, for the hundredth time, American manhood engraved with steel its name upon the brazen shield of *fame*. The Army of Northern Virginia, led as its valor deserved to be led, showed that resolution which can accomplish the all but impossible.

The Army of the Potomac, held in the leash by blunders which bowed its head in shame, but which it could not repair, illustrated that fidelity which always shone forth from disaster with a refulgence which even a victory scarce could lend it. Every virtue which crowns the brow of the soldier was typified in the ranks of either army. The ability of the conqueror to-day elicits our admiration; the errors of the conquered leader have long since been forgiven.

We hold the laurel wreath above the heads of those who fought here and still live; we lay it tenderly upon the graves of those from whose devotion to either cause has sprung that brotherly respect and love which best insures the perpetuity of the union.

Rest to their ashes! Peace to that nobler part which dieth not.

CHAPTER VIII.

The Gettysburg Campaign.

We remained in our old camps a few days and moved out about half a mile to a new camp in a pleasant oak grove, where we had nothing to do but drill and a little picket and guard duty, until about the first of June.

Here in this camp our regimental chaplains held divine service day and night. Our beloved General Gordon was often among the worshipers. He had become almost an idol in the brigade with officers and men, often leading in the prayer and exhortation service. A great many professed religion, joined the church and were baptized.

The last of May we drew plenty of clothing and shoes. Every gun was examined and if they were not all right we had to get one that was. Our cartridge boxes were filled, and we knew *something was up.*

General Lee had been reinforced until his army was eighty thousand strong.

On the first day of June we were ordered to cook two days rations, which we did. We left our camp about dark for the Gettysburg campaign. The first little branch that we came to every man was trying to walk the foot-logs, when General Gordon jumped off his horse and waded the branch back and forth, to show the boys how to wade.

We marched all night and camped just before day in very thick woods. We were not permitted to have any fire.

Ewell did this to keep Hooker's balloon spies from seeing us moving. Generals Ewell and Hill were both promoted to corps commanders, and Jackson's old corps was divided between them. Early's division was assigned to Ewell's corps.

We remained in camps all day quietly, and started again just at dark: we marched all night again and got out of sight of the balloon spies. At Culpepper Court House we rested two or three hours. There was a brisk cavalry battle going on near Brandy Station, a few miles from Culpepper. The Union cavalry fell back across the Rappahannock. After this we marched only in day time and got along finely.

General Ewell had us to march two miles and then rest ten minutes. By doing this we could march all day, and all the boys who were well could keep up.

We had but few straglers. The wagon trains kept up and we drew rations regularly. We made excellent time. We crossed the Blue Ridge mountains through the gap into the great Shenandoah valley at Front Royal, situated right at the foot of the mountains on the Shenandoah river.

We arrived at Front Royal about five o'clock P. M. and camped for the night.

The next morning Early's division took one road and Rhode's and Johnson's divisions took another. They all left about two hours before day. The Sixty-first Georgia Regiment was left to guard Early's wagon train on the march. It was said that there was a regiment of Union cavalry somewhere in the valley, so we had to protect our division wagon train.

Colonel Lamar was commanding our regiment. He deployed us along side of the wagon train, with orders to all rally in case of an attack, or to partially rally according to the number of the enemy, but we saw no enemy.

We marched alongside of the wagon train all day and

arrived at Kernstown about 5 o'clock. Ewell was at Winchester trying to capture Milroy, who had about five thousand soldiers stationed there.

We heard heavy cannonading and then the small arms. Finally we heard the rebel yell. It was Gordon's brigade and other troops charging the fort and Milroy's works.

Generals Rhodes and Johnson had Milroy cut off from the Martinsburg road and the fords on the Potomac river at Williamsport and Shepherdstown. The firing and yelling soon ceased, and Milroy's little army was nearly all captured and made prisoners of war. We captured about five thousand men, thirty-four cannons and some army stores. General Milroy and a few of his cavalry escaped. This was on June 13. Gordon's brigade lost about one hundred and fifty men, killed and wounded. Among the killed was the brave and daring Captain Hawkins, who fell at the head of his company. General Gordon also captured Milroy's fine horse, which he rode during the Gettysburg campaign.

Ewell left next morning very early with his corps and made all possible haste to Martinsburg, W. Va., which is thirty-four miles from Winchester, on the Baltimore and Ohio railroad. He captured it before night, with all the commissary stores. We again guarded the wagon train.

In Martinsburg we had to load the wagons with fresh supplies and guard them to the Potomac river. We then rejoined the brigade.

Ewell pushed his corps to the Potomac, at Shepherdstown and Williamsport, held the fords and waited till the wagon train could arrive.

Early's division crossed the river at Shepherdstown while Rhodes' and Johnson's divisions crossed at Williamsport. I do not think a man wanted to put his foot in the river, because they had gotten tired of Maryland the year before, and we expected to have trouble in the enemy's country.

We soon got over into Maryland, near the old Sharpsburg battlefield of the year before. We marched through Sharpsburg and crossed Antietam creek, on through Hagarstown into Pennsylvania. We seemed to have no opposition, for we had never had more quiet marching.

Our regiment was the first infantry to march into the town of Chambersburg, Pa. I saw a little girl, probably about eight years of age, standing on the stoop in front of her house, and heard her say, "Mamma, are those men rebels?" "Yes, my daughter." "Why, mamma, they haven't got horns; they are just like our people."

We marched on without opposition. Our quartermaster and commissary departments took every cow, sheep, horse, mule and wagon that they could lay their hands on, besides bacon and flour. Foraging was strictly prohibited among the men in line.

The cavalry and commissary department did this work. We boys, with guns, had more strict orders here than we ever had in our own country; we just had to stay in line, and sometimes we almost suffered for water.

Early's division, consisting of Gordon's Georgia Brigade, Hays' Louisiana Brigade, Pegram's Virginia Brigade, hurriedly marched in the direction of Harrisburg, the capital of Pennsylvania, by the way of Shippensburg to Carlisle and on to near Mechanicsburg, and would have taken Harrisburg if it had not been on the north side of the Susquehanna river.

We then turned down the river to York, Penn. Here we had a little combat with the Pennsylvania militia: captured and paroled about 5,000 of them, and ran the rest through Waynesboro and across the Susquehanna river at Columbia. They burned the bridge behind them.

Gordon's brigade carried the Confederate flag further north than any other troops.

We returned to York, where we were ordered to prepare two days rations. We did so and hurried off on the York and Gettysburg road. It seemed that Ewell, Lee, Hill and Longstreet, as well as all the Yankee army were pulling for Gettysburg on different roads.

The head column of Meade's army, commanded by General Reynolds, seemed to get there first, and Heath's division of Hill's corps, of General Lee's command, came up. He and General Reynolds opened the terrible battle of Gettysburg. This was July 1st.

Judging from the firing the conflict between Reynolds' and Hill's men was very severe at times. Our brigade (Gordon's) and the rest of Early's division formed in line of battle and advanced. We met the enemy at Rock creek. We attacked them immediately, but we had a hard time in moving them. We advanced with our accustomed yell, but they stood firm until we got near them. They then began to retreat in fine order, shooting at us as they retreated. They were harder to drive than we had ever known them before. Men were being mown down in great numbers on both sides.

We drove them across a fence, where they stopped and fought us for awhile. We advanced and drove them into and out of a deep road cut and on to the almshouse, where the Yankees stopped and made a desperate stand. Their officers were cheering their men and behaving like heroes and commanders of the "first water."

Here the gallant General Barlow, the enemy's commander, fell into our hands, severely wounded. He was treated kindly. We drove them on through Gettysburg and had them greatly confused. General Rhodes, of

Ewell's corps, seemed to drive in the enemy about the same time, badly torn up. We pursued and when the enemy got into Gettysburg they became one confused mass.

Their officers seemed to lose control of them and we captured some five thousand prisoners and drove the enemy through and out of the town, and we occupied the town.

Early's division seemed to be partly in the town and on the left. Johnson's division was on our left and extended to Rock Creek. Rhode's division of Ewell's corps was on our right and extended to Hill's corps.

Thus ended the first day's fighting on our part of the line.

Some of Hill's corps had a desperate fight on our right and drove the Yankees to Cemetery Ridge.

The second day everything seemed comparatively quiet, with some skirmishing and cannonading, until about three or four o'clock in the afternoon. Longstreet and some of Hill's corps had some severe fighting on our right. About six o'clock Hays' Louisiana brigade and Hooks' North Carolina brigade of our division, (Early's) charged and took some of the enemy's works but could not hold them. Late in the evening Johnson's division of Ewells's corps took some of the enemys's works on the left, but could not hold them. We (Gordon's brigade) were not generally engaged that day except heavy skirmishing and terrible shelling.

The principal part of the fighting by our lines on the third and last day, was done by Hill's and Longstreet's corps. One of the most desperate and fruitless charges of the whole war was made on the evening of the third day by General Pickett and his division of Virginians and Thomas', Wrights' and Wilcox's brigades of Georgians.

They broke the Union line under General Webb and captured their breastwork but could not hold it. There were about five hundred pieces of artillery playing at one time by the two armies and that many shells exploding. We could seldom distinguish one gun from another and the ground trembled under our feet.

No one that fought in this terrible battle or heard the thunder of the artillery and the explosion of the shells can ever forget it.

I heard a responsible man of Thomas' Georgia brigade, who was wounded and captured in this battle, and is now an eminent minister of the gospel, say that the ground around the enemy's battery was nearly covered in fragments of shells, and that it was the worst sight he had ever seen.

Men and horses were lying dead in piles. A wounded Confederate said to one of the officers, "It looks like you have a lot of men killed here." The officer replied, "H—ll, yes; how could we help it, when the ground is covered three inches in shells?" He further said, "You have given us h—ll and we have given you h—ll, too." An Irish prisoner then replied, "An' shure it's h—ll all around."

Our brigade's losses in the battle was very severe, though not so bad as it had been in the Second Battle of Manassas or Sharpsburg. Here Major Peter Brannon, of the Sixty-first Georgia, was killed. Company D, of the Sixty-first Georgia Regiment, had three men killed which were as follows: Sergeant John Everett, Privates John Anderson and Harrison Rushing. Lieut. James Mincy was severely wounded. For the rest of the killed and wounded of the Sixty-first Georgia I refer the reader to the muster roll and casualties in the back of this book. Lieutenant-Colonel McLoud, of the Thirty-eighth Georgia Regiment, was killed while gallantly leading his regiment. The Thirty-eighth Georgia Regiment carried about four hundred men into the battle, and reports say they had twenty-eight killed and seventy-six wounded. Among the killed were Lieutenants Goodwin and Oglesby. Major Matthews was severely wounded. Col. C. A. Evans, of the Thirty-first, was severely wounded in side and hip. Sergeant-Major Philip Alexander, Thirty-eighth Georgia, was also severely wounded. He got so close to a Union officer until he killed him with his sword. He in turn was shot through the hips by a Union soldier.

I would gladly report more about the casualties of the different regiments of the brigade if I had their reports like I have the Thirty-eighth Georgia, but I have not been able to obtain them.

On the 4th of July both armies lay quiet. It seemed like both of them were exhausted, and neither cared to make any advances. General Lee made preparations to retreat. Details were sent from each company to cook three days' rations.

Lee's wagon trains, which consisted of more than one thousand wagons, started to move back to the Potomac, and were under good way before night. It traveled all night. About day a squad of cavalry cut down about one hundred on the road among the mountains. They were run off by some of our soldiers who were guarding the wagon trains.

When the trains arrived at the Potomac, it was so swollen on account of the recent heavy rains that they could not cross it. They had to wait till pontoon bridges could be put down.

The sick and wounded crossed over in a large ferryboat that could carry about one hundred men at a time.

Lee's army started to fall back on thenight of the 4th of July. It fell back about twelve miles that night.

We leisurely marched out of Gettysburg and hardly left a wagon, ambulance or a piece of artillery.

We fell back to near the river and formed a line of battle near Williamsport, Md., until the wagon trains could cross, and General Lee could get all his "booty" over that he had taken in Pennsylvania and Maryland, which was immense.

The enemy came up and threw a few shells at us, but we stayed there three or four days—till all was over the river and the pontoon bridge taken up. The river had fallen till the army could ford it.

Company D thought Lieutenant James Mincy was left with some of the rest of our wounded at Gettysburg, but he was rescued by Rube, his faithful negro servant.

When Rube found that his master was going to be left, he stole a horse and wagon and got his master in the wagon and followed in the rear of our wagon train. We were proud to see Lieutenant Mincy back and we were proud of Rube, who could have remained in Pennsylvania and have been free, but I believe that he hated the Yankees worse than we did.

After the battle of Gettysburg I was sick and came out on our medical wagon to the Potomac and was sent on up the valley to Jordan Springs, of pure sulphur water, where there were a great many of our sick and wounded. There were so many wounded and so few doctors and experienced nurses and so little accommodation, that I offered my services as nurse, as I had served as nurse in Richmond during the winter of 1862.

The doctors all seemed worn out—some were very nearly sick. I told them that I would help them if they wished me to do so, as I had helped to perform several amputations and had considerable experience. One of the surgeons requested me to help him. He asked me what I could do. I told him that I could do anything he wished me to do. He was almost sick himself then.

Our first job was on a North Carolina lieutenant who had a ball shot through his foot and ankle. We put him on the surgeon's table and the doctor examined his foot, and told the lieutenant that he would have to take it off. The surgeon put him under the influence of chloroform and corded his leg so that it could not bleed. He then showed me where he wanted it taken off and put me to work while he held the chloroform.

I did the whole job except sawing the bone, and the surgeon pronounced it a "first-class job." I assisted them till they got through with the amputations and helped them to render the poor wounded fellows all the assistance in my power.

The doctors sent the wounded that were able to be moved on towards Stauton, Va, After remaining here about a week, resting and drinking the pure sulphur water, the most of the sick were about able for duty again.

We heard that Early's division was on the march and that they would soon pass near where we were, so I and about one hundred of our regiment and brigade went out to the road where they would pass. After waiting awhile Gordon's brigade came along and I soon recognized the Sixty-first Georgia Regiment, and you may be sure that I was glad to see them again on our own soil; and they all appeared to be proud to know that I had gotten out safe.

We marched leisurely along and had plenty to eat. We went on up the valley by Winchester, Newtown, Strasburg, Woodstock, Mt. Jackson to Newmarket.

On this march between Strasburg and Mt. Jackson the brigade was marching along about eleven o'clock, it being very warm and dusty and a great many wanting water. Everyone was tugging along in the hot sun with seldom ever a word being spoken.

A real fine looking man rode up along side of the Sixty-first Georgia Regiment. He had on a fine looking high crowned, broad brimmed, gray hat, the brim turned up on one side and a large silver looking star on it. He had on heavy calvary boots with a large pair of brass spurs, and a large white linen duster that reached very nearly to his feet, and was riding one of the poorest horses, almost, I ever saw any one riding. The poor old horse was so weak that his back was badly swayed. I suppose he had ridden side of our regiment for more than a half mile. I saw several of the boys eying him and was expecting some of them to poke some fun at him. Finally one of them hollowed out: "Come down out of that gown mister; I know you are there for I can see your legs hanging out." The poor fellow took exceptions at it and apparently got very mad and used language that is not in the *Bible.* He turned and rode up near us and wanted to know who in the h—l it was that insulted him and used some bad language. We all marched along, no one apparently paying the least attention to him. He finally turned to ride off and one of the boys said, "Y-a-e-a-h!" It was a signal, for I suppose more than fifty of the regiment began "y-a-e-a-h!" "y-a-e-a-h!" and raised a big yell at him. We everyone had to laugh at him. I have never seen a poor fellow sold worse than he was. The boys asked him whose coat he had stolen, and what would that poor preacher do who he had stolen it from, and where he had gotten it, in Pennsylvania, Maryland or Virginia. Some one asked him if he was a feeling man and a friend to the poor. Others would advise him to get down and tote the poor old horse. They carried him so high until he would not say a word.

About that time the bugle was blown for a stop to rest ten minutes. He then rode up to Colonel Lamar and wanted him to punish the regiment for their insults. The colonel told him to go on and not notice the boys, for they were always going at every fool they met, and for him to pay no attention to them. He left very mad but some wiser than he was, for he had found out what the boys thought of him.

Near Mt. Jackson in the big "Horseshoe-bend," of about two or three thousand acres of land, in the Shenandoah river bottom, we saw some of the cattle and sheep that we had taken in Pennsylvania and Maryland. The bend was about full. They were on both sides of the road for about two miles, and all were feeding about at will on the clover.

When we got through the herd I asked one of the men who was guarding them how many there were, he replied, "About twenty-six thousand head of cattle and twenty-two thousand head of sheep." I think we could see that many cattle, but I do not think we could see half that many sheep. Most of them were brought from the great Cumberland Valley of Pennsylvania.

We rested one day at the foot of the mountain and started across the Blue Ridge early in the morning, at what I think they called Swift Run Gap or Brown's Gap. It was really no gap, for it was right over a high mountain. The road was a winding road with a heavy upgrade. We found many of the coolest, purest and best springs of water I ever saw. While we were going up the mountain we could look down and see seven different roads and wagon trains and soldiers, apparently marching in different directions, while all were going across the mountain on the same road.

We got to the top about noon. It was about fifteen miles up a heavy grade. We rested awhile, and I suppose every one felt well paid for his march, for it was a very high mountain, from the top of which we could view some of the grandest scenery I ever saw. We could stand in one place and see eleven beautiful little Virginia towns with the natural eye, some on one side of the mountain and some on the other.

We ate dinner and started down the mountain. We were rejoicing, for we thought we would have easy marching in the afternoon, because it was down grade. We marched for two or three miles very well. Our knees began to get weak, and our toe-nails felt like they were slipping off our toes. Before we reached the foot we could hardly keep our feet under us. We reached the foot just before dark, and it looked like everybody was mad.

We were marched out into a large clover field, halted and ordered to stack arms and camp for the night. We sat down, pulled off our shoes and tried to rest. Our feet were blistered and our toe-nails were bloodshot. Seme were so mad till they gave vent to their feelings by cursing. Oh! such horrible oaths! It looked like some could curse "by note." They cursed out the Union, the Yankees, "Abe" Lincoln, Jeff Davis, the Confederacy, and the whole negro race.

It seemed like chickens began to squall, owls to hooting, hogs to squealing, cows to lowing, sheep to bleating, horses to neighing, mules to braying, dogs to barking and cats to fighting. I had never heard just such a noise or things better mimicked. It finally wound up with a rebel yell, and the bands began to play. We soon lay down and went quietly to sleep. A great many did not have anything to cover with. Next morning we marched about three miles and found a nice grove. Our officers marched us out and camped for the rest of the day. They finished getting the wagons and artillery across the mountain and let the teams rest as well as the men.

The next day we resumed our march. We went on down to the south side of the Rapidan river, about four miles from Clark's mountain, and camped for about two months in a pleasant oak grove.

CHAPTER IX.

The Battles of Bristow Station and Mine Run

While we were in camp we drew more clothing and shoes. We also drew plenty of our Pennsylvania beef; rested several days withont anything to do.

We privates could not hear anything about the Yankees. It seemed for a long time likĕ we had either killed them all or had left them on the north side of the Potomac. We afterwards found out that this was not the case.

Our regimental chaplains began to preach day and night, assisted by Jackson Wright, a private soldier of Company E. He had been on the entire Gettysburg campaign, and was one of the most devoted Christians and preachers we had. He has long ago crossed over the *river* to the great *beyond* and received his reward. He would often march hard all day and hold public prayer meeting before he would retire.

In this camp a great many of the boys professed conversion, joined the church and were baptized. Brother Wright often baptized from ten to fifteen in a day for two or three weeks.

A great many of the sick and wounded that had been left before we started to Gettysburg, returned to the army. We recruited up till it seemed that we were about as strong as we were before we started to Gettysburg.

While we were in camp my dear mother went to see me and stayed about ten days. When she left it was indeed a sad parting to us; but I felt like the the great *God* promised me, after I bade her good-by, and before she was out of sight, that I should live to see her again. She died in 1869.

About the 10th of September, 1863, we heard cannonading in the direction of Culpepper C. H. We then packed up and went down to the Rapidan river and camped at the foot of Clark's Mountain. The Union cavalry came in sight, threw a few shells at us and drew off.

We stayed here about three weeks and while we were here we had Dr. A. Broadhurst, of Kentucky, and another minister by the name of T. H. Prichard, from Maryland, with us.

They had been put into our lines by the Union authorities because they were true Southerners and advocated Southern rights. They went to General Lee and he appointed them army evangelists.

They preached for our brigade about a week, and I don't think I ever heard better preaching. A great many more joined the church; among them was W. H. Bland, of Company D.

Dear reader, with your permission, I will relate a little of Dr. A. Broadhurst's experience as he related it to us in one of his sermons. It was so striking and showed the power of the great God of heaven so plainly until I am sure I can never forget it.

I do not think it will hurt any one to read it, besides it corresponds with my own experience in the month of May before, or at least his troubles and mine were so near alike. Not that I was raised by a rich widowed mother as he was, or that I had ever cursed, gambled, drank whisky or horse-raced like he said he had done, yet I think my heart-troubles had been like his.

He said he was raised by a Christian, widowed mother, that he had always been petted and spoiled until he was about eighteen years of age. He said that he was very wicked and profane, would get drunk, gamble and horse-race, and was very wild, and, in fact, was as bad a boy as could be found. He said it was nearly killing his dear old mother and sister and his crippled aunt, and that they had begged him to quit it and reform, and how little he cared for what they said to him. He said one day a fearful dread of death and judgment, and the horrors of the infernal regions came over him, and that he tried to pray, but got no relief, and that he became one of the most miserable beings on earth, and felt to be the worst sinner on the earth, and felt that God could not be just and save such a wretched sinner.

He said that he went to his mother, sister and aunt and asked them to pray for him. He said that he could see no way of escape for days and weeks; he was afraid to go to sleep for fear of awaking in torment. One evening just as the sun was going down he said he felt worse than ever and felt as though he would not live to see it rise again, and he told his mother and sister that he could not live, and that eternal destruction was his just doom.

He said he went to his room and, I think, said he had retired and had given up all hope, when all at once his room seemed lit up, he raised up on his feet and his burden of sin left him. He slapped his hands and said: "God has pardoned my sins." He said that he could then see that Jesus was his Saviour, and that God could be just and save sinners through the meritorious sacrifice Jesus had made for sinners.

He said he went to sleep and slept well, and when he

got up next morning he was in a glow of rejoicing, and told his mother and sister that God had pardoned his sins. He said he looked down the lane and saw his good old crippled aunt coming in the rain, hobbling along with her stick. He told his mother and sister to not tell aunt about it, and he said he "had no thought of telling her himself," but when she came in and looked at him he felt so happy till he got up and met her and said: "Aunt, God has pardoned my sins." She almost shouted, and they all shed tears, thanked God and rejoiced with joy unspeakable. Please excuse me for digressing and I will return to the history.

One day we saw there was something up from the stir among the couriers, who were carrying orders.

In the afternoon Captain Kennedy and I went up to the top of the little mountain, which was about 500 feet high, where General Gordon was with his field-glasses. Here he could have an excellent view of the enemy's maneuvers. Captain Kennedy saluted him and asked him the news. He said: "The enemy is moving to the right," but we could not see them. Captain Kennedy asked the general for his glasses. He took them, looked and said: "Yes, they are going down the river." He looked at them for several minutes, then I asked Captain Kennedy to let me see. He handed the glasses to me. I looked and could see the men marching, could see their guns and could see the brass buckles on their cartridge boxes and bayonet

General Gordon told us that it was fifteen miles to the road they were marching on. The Yankees went into camps and seemed very quiet. We remained here a few days longer and Ewell's corps was ordered on a long circuit, flank movement to near Madison C. H. and Warrenton.

We struck the rear of the retreating Yankees at Bristow Station, nine miles from the old Manassas battle field. Company D was on skirmish. We advanced, struck the enemy's skirmish line and moved it without any trouble. We saw that they had big, heavy knap-sacks and we wanted them, so we took after them in a run and got so near them till we ordered them to surrender. A great many did surrender and the rest threw their knap-sacks, haver-sacks and guns down and ran for dear life. The writer and Anderson Woods got some distance ahead and got two or three knap-sacks and haver-sacks apiece and several prisoners.

We plundered their knap-sacks till the rest of the company came up. I got two tent flies, two fine flannel over-shirts, a good oilcloth, some stationery and one of the best blankets I ever saw. As it was getting late in the fall (Oct. 17th, 1863), we greatly needed them.

We pursued them till we were halted. The men whom we had been running were some raw troops that President Lincoln had recently called out and had not been accustomed to service, or we would not have had such an easy time with them. Some of them refused to throw down their guns after they surrendered, for fear they would have to pay for them, but we made them give them up.

We camped for the night, and next morning everything was quiet. We were furnished with tools and went to tearing up the railroad that the Yankees had been getting their supplies over. The way General Lee had it done was to draw the spikes, pile up the ties and fire them, then lay the railroad irons on till they got hot enough for the ends to touch the ground; we would then take the ends, go to a tree and twist it around and leave it. We tore it up in this way back to the Rappahannock river, which I suppose was about fifty miles.

We crossed over the river about three or four miles,

camped and began to build winter quarters. We had to do picket duty across the river, a brigade at a time from Early's division.

One evening while Hay's Louisiana Brigade was on picket, the Yankees surprised them and captured about half of them. The balance swam the river and made good their escape. We ran to assist them but were not in time. Everything now in camp was in a stir for a few days. We could hear the whistles blow on the rail road that we had torn up, for the Yankees were building it back again.

General Lee fell back to the south side of the Rapidan river, where we fixed up some temporary winter quarters and rested quietly for some time. Late in the fall our Pennsylvania cattle were too poor to be eaten, and the officers and men refused to take it for rations. After this we drew nice bacon.

General Meade made a flank move on Lee. He crossed the Rapidan river below us and we met him at Mine Run. We built good breast works and desired for him to advance on us, but he did not come as we expected. One morning the enemy ran into our skirmish line. It fell back to the line of battle and we waited awhile for the enemy to advance but they did not.

Our officers sent out a new skirmish line, with instructions to drive in their skirmishes. Company D volunteered to go; so we advanced to the old picket line without seeing a Yankee. They were back in their old skirmish line, about 250 yards from ours. We would shoot every one we saw.

Late in the afternoon they started to advance on us, and we had a real hard skirmish battle. There were nearly enough trees where we were for every man to get behind one. Madison Warren and I had to stand behind one tree, which was about ten inches in diameter, or one of us be exposed.

The battle continued till nearly dark, during which time the tree was struck by eight balls, from knee high up to as high as our heads. We had about exhausted all of our ammunition. The Yankees recrossed the Rapidan that night. None of our company were hurt. This ended the skirmish fighting at Mine Run.

We now returned to our camps and after remaining a few days we moved into the wilderness and fixed up permanent winter quarters. We fared very well all winter. General Lee gave one man from each company a twenty-four days furlough to go home. W. H. Bland, William Holloway, William Alderman and Dock Waters all received furloughs and returned.

As I have finished the campaign of 1863, I will continue this chapter with a joke that some of the boys got on a lieutenant in one of the Georgia brigades, as it was told to me by a responsible man of Hill's corps. He said that it was certainly truth, or I would not tell it.

He said they had a regular rear guard commanded by a bigoted lieutenant (we will call him D—). He would take everything he could from the boys who had been out foraging. He kept this up for some time till all of the boys got to hating him. So three of the boys that were acquainted with him before the war determined to get ahead of him. They went out, caught and killed a real fat dog, dressed him nicely, cut off one of his hind quarters, cut off the foot, wrapped it up and came up in the rear of the guard in a real suspicious way, apparently trying to conceal it.

The ever vigilant lieutenant saw that they had something and asked them what it was. The fellow stepped back a few steps and the lieutenant cursed him and went to see. The man apparently gave it to him very reluctantly, and said it was a piece of lamb. The lieutenant took it and gave it to his negro cook and told him to cook it for his supper. The boys went on to their camps well pleased.

The negro cooked some and the lieutenant sat down to eat it. He cursed the negro and told him that he had poisoned it, for he had never eated as *strong* mutton as that was. The lieutenant then cooked some himself, but it was no better. The next day he asked the man whom he had taken it from what it was. He said in a low, drawling way, "Why, Lieutenant, it was a piece of a *dog*." Such a laugh as that raised!

It was such a good joke it was all over the camps in a few hours. Men would hollow out, "Who eat the dog?" and you would hear answered from all over the camps, "Lieutenant D." My friend told me they run that so far till "D." ran away and quit the army.

CHAPTER X.

From January 1st, 1864 to May 1st, 1864.—Skirmish Battle at Morton's Ford.

January, 1864, came in fair and warm for Virginia. On the morning of January 4th we heard firing at the picket post at Morton' Ford about five miles from our camps. We hurriedly fell in line and double-quicked (ran) most of the way. Gordon's Brigade was the first troops to get there, but Gordon himself was not present. He was said to have been at Orange C. H., and General Lee was in Richmond.

Colonel Evans, of the Thirty-first Georgia Regiment, was in command of Gordon's brigade and formed the line of battle. We found that the Yankees had crossed the river in some force and had driven off our pickets. The Yankees fired at us as we came up, at long range (about 600 yards). There were some works about half a mile from the ford and we were ordered into them.

Colonel Evans ordered out a heavy skirmish line and companies D and F, of our regiment, were put on skirmish, with about the same number of men from each regiment of the brigade. Captain Kennedy was in command of the skirmish line from the Sixty-first Georgia. We were ordered to advance, which we did, with the Yankee sharp-shooters shooting at us all the while.

There was a deep ravine about 100 yards from the Yankee skirmish line, and we went into it and remained nearly all day. The Yankees were well posted in and around Dr. Morton's house and negro houses. There were about six of the negro houses and they were built of brick, and were about twelve feet wide and twenty feet long, with spaces of about four feet between each house.

When the sun was about half an hour high, our batteries threw about a dozen well-directed shells at the Yankee line, and we were ordered to charge them away from the houses, which was directly in companies D and F's front. We advanced with a yell, and they fired one volley at us but did not hurt any one; they then left the houses in a run.

Dr. Morton's house was on a high elevation from which we could see all over the enemy's lines and ours.

We had our "sights" up, so we went right on past the houses. An order came down the line to halt and occupy the houses, but Captain Kennedy wanted to go right on. He said; "We could run the whole d—d fixings into the river." (This was the only profane word I ever heard him speak in the whole war). We reluctantly returned to the houses and the fun began.

The Yankees wanted this position back, for it overlooked their line and ours and was not over 250 yards from the river. We went to shooting at them with a vim. Everybody seemed cool, yet determined to do them all the harm they could. They tried to charge us twice with their skirmish line and did get near us, but their officers could not get them any nearer than about fifteen or twenty yards, for they could not stand the firing and would fall back, leaving the ground strewn with their killed and wounded, while some would come on and surrender.

They then tried a solid line of battle which advanced to within about one hundred yards of us when the men refused to advance any nearer. It appeared that some of their officers did everything in their power to advance their men but they would not advance. We loaded and shot them just as fast as we could. They retreated, rallied and tried it again. Three Yankees came to me and surrendered and gave me their guns. I sent them to the rear. A great many of the boys captured as many or more than I did. All of them were sent to the rear.

One large Yankee who seemed well in whisky, walked up to Sergeant William Alderman with his gun loaded, cocked and capped, with his bayonet on and ordered him to surrender. Alderman also had his gun loaded and ordered the Yankee to surrender or he would shoot him. They faced each other for about a minute, each telling the other to surrender or he would shoot. They were about six feet apart and the Yankee advanced to put his bayonet into Alderman. Alderman leveled his gun and fired and it seemed to me that the fire went through the Yankee for I saw it pass him. He fell dead and did not even groan. I think Alderman centered his heart.

I shot thirty-four rounds in this little fray. I had an excellent rifle, one that shot very close, and I never took better aim at a bird or squirrel in my life than I took at those Yankee soldiers. And I never enjoyed a party in my young days any better.

The Yankees did not charge any more on our part of the line. In this battle the Yankees were never farther away than 250 yards, and were sometimes as near as fifteen or twenty yards. Just as it was getting dark, a Yankee officer, or at least his uniform indicated that he was one, rode along our picket line about half a mile. When asked who was there he would say, "General Hayes." There was a Confederate General Hays in our division, and all who saw him thought it was our Hays. This was all that saved his life.

By some means our skirmish line gave way on our right, although there was no hard fighting on any part of the line except that part occupied by Companies D and F. It seemed that the Yankees slipped around us on our right, where our line had given way, or had not advanced when we did ; for about dark I heard them talking behind us, and could see their caps.

I could tell by their caps and their Dutch brogue that they were not Southerners. I could see our men slipping out on our left. The Yankees were stirring about slowly, and seemed confused. About this time a gun fired, and the Yankees began to cry, "Washington! Washington!" which, I suppose, was their countersign.

I gathered up my own gun and the three Yankee guns and slipped towards our left. I went about thirty yards and stumbled and fell headlong. Dr. Morton's garden palings had been torn down by the Yankees, and I had run against the bottom lath to which the slats had been nailed. When I fell with my turn of guns it made a fearful noise, and I expected the Yankees to shoot at me, but they did not. I got up with a first-class pair of bruised and skinned shins I gathered up all of my guns and went on around them, near enough that I could hear them talk and call for certain ones among them as "Shim, Shon and Sho." I found some of our boys near a house, about eighty yards in the rear of where we had been fighting, and they were partially formed in line. I met Captain Kennedy. By this time it was very nearly dark, and he said: "Is that you, George?" I said, "Yes." He said: "Stand right here and watch till I see whether the line is formed or not." He walked on and left me standing by the house just referred to. I heard some one move in the house, and when he came back I told him about it. About this time Sergeant Hogan, of Company F, came along the line from the other direction. He, too, was examining the line to see if it was all right. Captain Kennedy informed him that it was, and asked him if he would go with me into the house to see if it was a Yankee. He replied, "Shure, and I will." (He was an Irishman.) Captain Kennedy called out, "Who is in this house?" No reply. "If you don't speak I'll fire the house." We all heard some one move and speak out: "It is nobody, boss, but poor old Luce." He said, "Strike a light, for we must see." She lit a candle, and Sergeant Hogan and I went in, but we found no one but an old colored woman with her head nearly as white as snow, scared nearly to death. We told her not to be scared, for we would not hurt her. We took the candle and went up stairs, but we found no Yankee.

When we came out of the house we found that Colonel Evans had sent in other troops and we were relieved. We returned to the line and were complimented by all the boys in the brigade. We found we had sent 150 prisoners to the rear, and there were 117 dead on the field. The Yankee general told W. H. Bland (our prisoner) that he lost 500 killed, wounded and captured. We only lost four, all told. We only had two small companies, (D and F, of Sixty-first Georgia,) not exceeding twenty-five men each, engaged in this skirmish battle. Our casualties were as follows: One of company F killed (Patrick Ryan). One of company D wounded (A. M. Rimes), and one captured, (W. H. Bland). One was killed about 600 yards in the rear by a stray ball. The enemy carried off their wounded and were all across the river before morning.

In this little skirmish battle the brave Captain Robt. T. Cochran, of company F, Sixty-first Georgia Regiment, captured a Union officer and eight men. He took the officer's sword, which was a very fine one and was as bright as silver. Captain Cochran has it yet and praises it very highly, and keeps it bright. Captain Cochran was one of the bravest men in the Confederate services. He is now living in Rockmart, Ga.

Our Yankee prisoners were guarded at our line. Next morning General Lee came riding along the line with General Gordon. We cheered them. The Yankee prisoners all seemed anxious to see General Lee, and they seemed to admire him greatly. Some of them said: "Look! he is the most graceful rider I have ever seen." Others would say: "What a *soldier* he must be," and still others: "He is the *grandest* General that ever lived," and I heard one say: "I wish that we had such a commander."

We returned to camp and rested quietly during the remainder of the winter; had a tolerable plenty to eat, with nothing to do but guard and picket duty. Our picket post was at the fords on the Rapidan river near Clark's Mountain, six or eight miles above our camp. A regiment would have to go at a time and stay two days.

One time when our regiment had to go the weather was very cold; the river was frozen over at least eight inches thick. We heard a terrible racket up the river and could not understand what it could be. The noise approached us rapidly and we soon saw the cause; it was the river rising and breaking the ice. The rising water would break the ice and keep it piled up ahead on the solid ice three or four feet high. Large pieces which would have weighed one hundred or more pounds would be sliding along ahead of the breaking ice. Broken ice floated along all that day.

That night I had to stand picket guard one hour. I came near freezing to death. When relief came I was so cold till I could hardly get back to the fire.

Elder A. B. Woodfin came to us and was appointed Chaplain of the Sixty-first Georgia Regiment. He was one of those noble Virginians and one of as good chaplains as there was in the brigade, and seemed to take as much interest in the meetings of the brigade as any of the chaplains from our own state. He was as pleasant a man as I ever met. He was a young man and an excellent preacher, and always seemed to get enthused when he was telling us about the *blood* of the *Blessed Jesus* so freely spilt for sinners on the crop and *its* being the only way from this sinful world to the *Glorious Paridise above.* (He is now living in Hampton, Va.)

In these winter quarters we built a brigade chapel, daubed the cracks with clay and made a large fire-place in it and had preaching almost every day and night, with but few in attendance at first. One night one of the regimental chaplains said he wanted every Christian in the house to make the worst man in his company a special object of prayer for two weeks. He said he felt that we would have a revival and would have the house filled when we had divine worship. (This was probably our Chaplain A. B. Woodfin.) It struck me with great force, and I studied who is the worst man in Company D? I could not decide. There were two who could hardly speak without a horrible oath, and it did not seem that they cared for themselves or anyone else, yet they were excellent soldiers. I could not decide which was the more wicked of the two. Something presented or suggested that I take them both; so I went off to a secret place in the snow and prayed for them, and it seemed that I became burdened for them. Next day I went to their tent and to my surprise and joy they were not playing cards no using profanity. The next night both entered the chapel and took the seat nearest the door. The stayed till preaching was *over*, and I think it was the *first* time I had ever seen either of them at preaching.

I went to their tent the next day and to my joy, both were reading the blessed word of God. They took a seat the next time near the center of the chapel and seemed greatly affected as they listened to the preaching. They asked the preachers to pray for them. Their condition filled me with rejoicing and prayer for the dear boys. In about four weeks both of them joined the church, told bright experiences and dated their convictions to the very night I offered the first special prayer for them. They were received and baptized.

In one week after that good servant of God made the request that the Christians pray for the worst men in their companies, our chapel was full unless the weather was too very cold. We had a great revival and could seldom hear a profane word spoken.

We had plenty of fun and exercise in camps—snow-balling each other and having snow battles.

In the latter part of April every gun, gun-lock and

tube was examined and all that were not all right were sent off and good ones put in their places. We also drew clothing and shoes.

History tells us that the Union general, E. M. Law, said of the Confederate Army: "A new pair of shoes or an overcoat was a luxury and full rations would have astonished the stomachs of Lee's ragged Confederates. I have often heard expressions of surprise that these ragged, barefooted, half starved men would fight at all; but the very fact that they remained with their colors through such privations and hardships was sufficient to prove that they would be dangerous foes to encounter upon the line of battle." This he found to be true before the campaign ended.

Everything was put in readiness and every man sent to us that could be. Our wagon and artillery teams were made good by exchanging those that were broken down for good ones. We felt sure that the campaign would soon open.

CHAPTER XI.

Battle of the Wilderness.

On May 3rd we noticed that couriers were riding around, sometimes in quite a hurry. We felt sure that something was on the verge of happening. On the 4th we had to prepare two day's rations, and could hear cannonading down the river about Germania ford.

We broke camp and marched down to Locust Grove. The courier and staff officers were in a stir; we knew something was up and we dreaded it, for we heard that General Grant was in command of the Army of the Potomac, and that he was a terrible "bull-dog," and that he never turned loose. We heard that he had massed 200,000 men in our front, and we knew that General Lee did not have over 60,000 to meet him with, and we knew we were going to have a terrible struggle.

Next morning, May 5th, we were ordered up early and put on the march at quick step. We soon heard heavy musketry and some cannonading. We met troops (Doles' Brigade) coming out badly confused, with General Lee in the rear right by himself. He seemed burdened. I think his mind was taxed to its utmost capacity.

Our company (D) was at the head of our regiment; our regiment at the head of Gordon's brigade and Gordon's brigade at the head of Early's division.

The first words General Lee said was: "General Gordon, there are Yankees in front and lots of them, and they must be moved or the day is lost. They have our position and if they are not moved we will be forced to retreat, and we are not prepared for it. Can you move them?" The gallant Gordon replied: "We will try, general." General Gordon turned to us witn a deep determined look—to move them or die. The regimental officers and men looked the same way.

General Gordon addressed us in about these words: "Boys, there are Yankees in front and lots of them, and they must be moved or the days is lost, and *we* must move them. Now all who are faint hearted, fall out, you shall not be hurt for it; for we do not want any to go but *heroes—we waut brave Georgians.*" We cheered him and General Lee. General Lee said: "General, right and left your men into line and forward *at once.*"

We filed to the right, and loaded our guns as we marched along. We were informed that General Gordon addressed all the regiments with about the same words that he addressed ours with. The next regiment to ours filed left. All the regiments filed right and left till the brigade was formed across the road. If I mistake not, the Thirty-eighth Georgia was the last one to form.

The brigade forwarded in thick woods in the wilderness. Every man seemed anxious to go ahead, and it seemed that every one had an iron will—determined to move those Yankees from General Lee's chosen position or die in the attempt.

It has been thirty-four years since this memorable campaign opened, on this awful 5th day of May, 1864, but it seems almost as fresh in my mind now as it did then.

Just as we were ordered forward, Irvin Spivy, of the Twenty-sixth Georgia Regiment, hallooed. He could halloo the queerest that I ever heard any one. It was a kind of a scream or low, like a terrible bull, with a kind of a neigh mixed along with it, and it was nearly as loud as a steam whistle. We called him "The Twenty-sixth Georgia's Bull," and the Yankees called him "Gordon's Bull." He would always halloo this way when we charged the enemy, and we were informed that the Yankees understood it as a signal for them to move back. We have heard that Spivy is yet living in Coffee county, Georgia.

We forwarded and soon struck the Yankees. They began to fire at us and we at them. I never heard such a yell as we raised. We could scarcely hear a gun fire, and could hardly tell when our own guns fired, only by the jar it gave us.

We soon routed the first Yankee line. We all pushed right on and on with the yell, until we had driven the first line into the reserve line. The two lines did not stand but one or two volleys before both began to waver and retreat in confusion. We soon had them into the third line, and on into the fourth, and on until we seemed to have five or six lines in one confused mass, with many of them lying down and surrendering, or coming back with their hands up to show that they were surrendered. We would send them to the rear. Our officers could hardly get a man to go to the rear with them.

We killed a great many of them, and drove them off of Lee's position and on for nearly two miles.

Our regiment's position was on the extreme right, and we kept getting further to the right until Company D was not more than a skirmish line. We found that the enemy had retreated so far from our front till they were all out of our sight. We came to an open field, or open place in the woods, and found that they had divided and some had retreated to the right and some to the left of this open field. So Major J. D. VanValkenburg, of our regiment, was left with our company and a part of his old company (Company I, if I am not mistaken in the company) to watch that side and prevent a flank move by the enemy.

General Gordon had driven the enemy from Lee's position and General Lee sent Gordon orders to fall back. Colonel Lamar sent Lieutenant Eugene Jeffers with orders to Major Van to fall back to the line. We had just gotten started when we saw a regiment of Yankees between us and our line. I felt bad, for we did not have over forty men and there were about five hundred Yankees.

They appeared badly confused to see Confederate soldiers coming up in their rear, when they were not expecting any. We stopped and Major Van advanced, for his quick military eye took in the position that we were placed in. He walked up with a quick step and with drawn sword and ordered their commander to surrender. He refused and ordered Major Van to surrender. He refused and hallowed back to tell General Gordon to send up a brigade, for we had an obstinate regiment cut off and they refused to surrender. Captain Kennedy and the rest of us, in a low voice, began to command forward. Major LeGrand B. Speece, the commander of the Yankee regiment, ordered his regiment to stack or ground arms. He expected a volley from a brigade. We hurried up and Major Van commanded: "Officers to the front." All the officers came to the head of the regiment and Major Van led off and ordered the enemy to follow him.

Captain Kennedy took their flag and carried it out, and we, forty men, formed a thin guard around them and marched them out. I tell this truthfully. for I was an eye-witness.

The enemy told us after we got past our lines that they had been sent in to re-inforce their line and that they came up through that open field referred to above, and that they never saw any of their retreating men and that when they saw us and Major Van's actions, they thought that Gordon's Brigade had them cut off. They said we had captured every man in the regiment but one, who was sent back to inform their commander that they could not find any men only their dead on the battlefield.

When we got them out and they found that they had been captured by Major Van's strategem they were the worst set of mortified officers and men I have ever seen. Major Van turned them over to the provost guard and took a receipt for about forty regimental and company officers and four hundred and seventy-four non-commissioned officers and privates. If I am not mistaken it was the Seventh Pennsylvania Regiment of reserves that we captured.

GEN. CLEMENT A. EVANS.

On General Gordon's return (so we were informed) Gen. Lee met him with a big smile, jerked off his glove and gave him a hearty hand shake, calling him *Major General Gordon.*

So you see General Gordon was promoted from brigade to major general on his return from one of the most successful charges of the war, where Gordon's Brigade of six Georgia regiments of not much, if any, over two thousand men, had captured about twenty-five hundred prisoners, had killed and wounded about as many more and had routed five or six times our own number.

That noble Christian, Colonel Clement A. Evans, of the Thirty-first Georgia Regiment, who was almost an idol in the brigade, was promoted to the rank of Brigadier General and assigned to the command of Gordon's old brigade. Lieutenant Colonel J. H. Lowe was promoted to the full rank of Colonel over the Thirty-first Georgia Regiment.

I believe from General Lee's actions that he wanted to promote the whole brigade; for he told Gordon to take his men to the rear and rest them, for they had done enough for one day. Our mouths were all black with powder and our faces were nearly black with smoke. We were all hoarse from halloaing the Rebel yell so long, and *we* were willing to go to the rear. We had been put on the march about 4 o'clock A. M. had marched about eight miles and had done some excellent work. It was then about 8 or 9 o'clock and we had had no breakfast. Nearly every man had picked up one or two well-filled haver-sacks with coffee, sugar, condensed cream, bacon, hardtacks, etc. We began to make and drink our coffee; were all full of life, for we had not lost a man out of Company D. though several were killed and wounded in the regiment and brigade.

The noble captain, John T. Erwin, of Company G, was

severely wounded and carried off the field by that noble member of the litter corps, George Hopkins. He never recovered sufficiently to return to the company.

While we were eating breakfast one of the regiments was called for and put in line by the famous Louisiana Brigade, to fill up a gap in the line, of the balance of Early's division that had been formed and fortified in General Lee's well chosen position that we had driven the Yankees from. The Thirty-first Georgia was the one that answered the call.

We soon heard our sharp-shooters or skirmish line begin to shoot. They were soon driven in by the enemy. We heard three tremendous huzzars! and the Yankees came up in a most excellent line to meet a terrible slaughter and defeat. They charged and recharged our line several times before noon in our front, but did not break any part of it. Our brave Virginians, North Carolinians and Louisianians were there to stay. When the enemy would "huzza," they would raise the "Rebel yell."

Our brigade did not have the pleasure of being in this part of the battle, but I am sure that four-fifths of the brigade would have volunteered to go to the line and fight the Yankees. Some of our regiment asked permission of the officers to go.

Hill's corps was on the right of Ewell's corps and did most of the fighting in the afternoon. The battle raged there for hours, and judging by the amount of cannonading, musketry, huzzaing and yelling it must have been fearful.

Some of Longstreet's corps came from Gordonsville and took position on Hill's right and were engaged in battle before it ceased. Hill was pressed severely.

It ceased late in the afternoon and everything was comparatively quiet along the whole line. Our boys passed word down the line asking Longstreet's and Hill's men how they got along with the "Yankees." In a few minutes we received the answer: "We have whipped everything in our front." We talked back and forth for some time and it was better than a telephone line, for the whole army could hear and it seemed to buoy up the whole line, for the whole line raised the Rebel yell. It was surprising how quickly a dispatch could go several miles and return.

We had a good night's rest and next morning we got up, cooked and eat a hearty breakfast of our Yankee bacon, crackers and coffee. There was no fighting on our part of the line till late in the afternoon. Our brigade was marched around on a circuit-flank movement on the extreme right of the Yankees.

We found them massed five or six lines deep, all resting, cooking and eating; with their guns stacked, their blankets spread down and some of their little tents stretched.

We came up in thick woods in the wilderness and were in about 100 yards of them before their guards saw us. A few of them fired at us and killed Giles Chapman, of Company I, in our regiment. We fired one volley at them, raised a yell and charged them. They fled at once, leaving their guns, blankets, knapsacks, haversacks, tents, canteens, some hats and, in fact, everything they had.

We could not give them but two volleys. It seemed like scaring up a bunch of partridges or crows, for the Yankees left us almost as quickly as partridges could. It was like shooting birds "on the wing." They left stampeded and panic stricken. I am sure there were enough guns to have armed our brigade three or four times, and several car-loads of blankets, tents, clothing, etc. The Yankees never tried to retake this position and I never heard of but one man getting hurt in the brigade. That was the one above referred to.

We took some prisoners, and among them there were two generals. One of them, General Seymour, was a very tall man. I suppose he was six and one-half feet high and would have weighed 150 pounds. The other, General Shaler, was a regular cut-short Dutchman about five feet high, and would have weighed about 250 pounds. There was quite a contrast in them as they were marched out.

Next day the enemy had left our front and I feel sure thot General Grant decided that he had struck a "snag," and that if he ever got to Richmond he would have to try a different road.

We tramped over the field of battle, where we fought the first day. It was thick woods in front of our line with much small growth. We could not find a bush without the sign of a ball on it. The bushes were literrlly shot to pieces. It looked surprising that any one could live in the midst of such carnage. The enemy's losses were severe, while ours was very light.

CHAPTER XII.

Battle of Spotsylvania Court House.

On the 8th of May Ewell's corps was ordered from the extreme left to the extreme right of Lee's army, and on down to near Spotsylvania C. H. A part arrived on the evening of May 9th. General Grant was trying to swing his immense army around Lee's right flank. We ran a few cavalry back and reconnoitered. We saw the enemy coming in full force, and we had a little battle on the evening of the 9th, and stopped the enemy. We captured a Union staff officer, and if I am not mistaken, he said that he belonged to General Hancock's staff. He was a fine looking man and was very intelligent He rode a very fine black horse.

The next day the rest of Ewell's corps came up and we began to fortify. Hill's corps, which was commanded by General Early on account of Hill's sickness, also arrived on the 10th and took position. Longstreet's corps arrived later in the day, and General Lee formed his line of battle in the shape of a horse-shoe, with the wings extending from the heel in right and left angles. Ewell's corps occupied the shoe. Gordon's division (Early's old division) was in a well fortified line about two hundred yards from the toe of the shoe and extended from one side to the other. General Evans' brigade was on the reserve line near the left side of the shoe.

We spent the 11th in fortifying. General Grant moved up his army and reconnoitered and found how Lee's lines weref ormed. On the night of the 11th every one knew Grant would make a desperate effort to break Lee's lines. We could hear them arranging their artillery and getting it in position. We could hear them moving all night.

About 3 o'clock on the morning of the 12th we could hear them getting up as close to Johnson's line in the toe as they could. Gordon and Evans had their lines up and in perfect readiness. One of the heaviest fogs I ever saw had risen. It was so dense we could not see a man thirty feet from us, even after the sun had risen.

About 4 o'clock we heard Hancock's men start to advance, and we expected to hear the battle open and did hear some of Johnson's pickets fire ; but I suppose they fell back to their line of battle, and found very nearly all of the men asleep, for Hancock's men ran up and found them in that condition. A few guns were fired. We heard the Union men cheer with their huzzas, and we knew Johnson's men were prisoners. Hancock captured General Johnson and two thousand and eight hundred of his men.

Hancock captured Johnson's men from a little to the left of the toe of the shoe, and down to the right of our line to some distance past where we were connected with the shoe line, which was the front line. This gave some of Johnson's and Gordon's men a stampede. This placed Evans' brigade and the rest of Gordon's division in a bad condition. We were ordered out of our works, and Lee's line, on our left, moved from left to right and filled our places. We cut off the victorious Yankees and formed our line.

Here General Lee came to us and took position in front of the Thirteenth Georgia Regiment to lead us. General Gordon told General Lee that his men had never failed to do their duty, and they would not fail now, and entreated General Lee to go to the rear—to his place, for he was worth 10,000 of us. He said: "Here are my brave Georgians, and there are my brave Virginians, (pointing to General Pegram's Virginia brigade) who have never failed and they will not fail now." The men in the line began to cry "General Lee to the rear!" "General Lee to the rear!" Others would say: "General Lee, if you will go to the rear, we will move the enemy out of our captured line." Here some of the men in that noble Thirteenth Georgia Regiment rushed to General Lee, seized his horse by the bridle, and led him back through our line. General Lee turned up our line towards our left, and Evans' and Pegram's brigades raised a yell and made a most gallant charge in a dense fog. While our dear boys were being mown down at every step, and after a desperate struggle, we succeeded in recapturing our line on the right of where the reserve line connected with the captured line, and had everything safe so far as a solid line was concerned.

Our regiment (Sixty-first Georgia) was on the extreme left of Evans' brigade. We charged the enemy where we did not have any support on our left, and our color bearer, Francis Marion McDow, planted our battle-flag on the works and we had a hand to hand battle with club-guns. Our line being very thin and the enemy's fully three times as strong as ours, we were overpowered and a great many of our regiment had to surrender. Here the enemy captured sixty-five of our regiment, McDow and our old tattered and torn battle-flag.

I must stop and say a few words about Sergeant Francis Marion McDow. He was an Alabamian by birth and as brave as the great hero General Francis Marion, after whom he was named. He was like the brave Sergeant Jasper, unlettered. He was about 23 years of age and had received a severe wound at Sharpsburg, Md., while carrying the flag so bravely. He was complimented by the noble and brave Colonel Douglas just before Colonel D. was killed. The flag was nearly shot to pieces by shot and shell. It was nothing but a tattered and torn rag, for it had been in every battle the regiment had ever been engaged in, and the regiment loved it and its noble bearer. We mourned the loss of McDow and the dear old flag. Sergeant McDow died in the Fort Delaware prison. He was a good member of the church.

Evans' brigade was cut to pieces, for we had lost severely. When I saw such officers as Captains J. J. Henderson of Company A, Daniel McDonald of Company C, Adjutant J. J. Mobley, Lieutenant J. D. DeLoach, Lieutenant F. N. Graves, Sergeant Hilary Wright, and our good preacher, Jackson J. Wright, Private M. J. Green, and many others, whose names I do not recollect, begin to surrender, I turned and ran back for dear life. I just abhorred the idea of being a *prisoner*. It seemed that I almost preferred *death*, and would take my chances in getting away, with several others. There were not many shots fired at us, for the fog was so dense that the Yankees could not see us more than 30 feet away. We ran back to the reserve line, which was about 75 yards in the rear, and found it full of our men, who were in readiness. This helped my feelings, for I was afraid that the Yankees would get the best of us. (This charge was made just at daylight in a dense fog.)

The reason why our regiment lost so many prisoners was because we ought to have stopped and occupied the reserve line when we drove the Yankees past it. Our orders were to do that, but we did not understand them. Generals Gordon, Evans and Pegram succeeded in establishing Ewell's line on the reserve line and on down the line to the right angle, while General Hancock held the most of the toe of the shoe the rest of the day.

When we got to the reserve line and knew that our regiment was so badly hurt in killed, wounded and captured, we asked the men where the rest of Evan's brigade was, for the fog was so dense we could not see. They said they did not know. We could not see where to go for the fog. About one hundred of our regiment and brigade turned up on the line towards the left angle. We were badly confused and mortified. About 150 yards from the angle we again found General Lee sitting on his horse trying to look and listen to find out what the enemy was doing.

I went to him and asked him where we could find Evan's brigade. He said it was on the right. He asked us, (for there were about one hundred of us with two officers) if we belonged to that brigade; we told him that we did. He then told us to fall in line and occupy a piece of the line near him that was not occupied. We fell in and just filled up the gap and made the line solid. General Lee told us to hold it at all hazards, and we promised him to do our best, and we *did* hold it, though we had a hard struggle. After driving the Yankees back our brigade occupied the line that they had recaptured the rest of the day.

I will leave the brigade and tell what our squad of one hundred saw and did the remainder of the day.

General Lee's line from the left, on the angle, was like a worm fence, and in every jam a piece of artillery was planted, about twenty-five feet apart, behind very strong earthworks. As well as I recollect he had about twenty pieces there and all the space between filled with men with small arms, and boxes of ammunition set all along the line, so the supply would not run short.

On the part of the line where our squad was stationed a four-gun battery was planted behind very strong earthworks in the line of the shoe. General Grant soon began to throw shot and shells at the batteries from a great many of his cannons, (probably one hundred).

It seemed to rain shot and shells for nearly an hour. Our batteries replied for a few minutes and nearly ceased firing. I could understand the reason why they ceased. It was because the enemy did not have their range and they threw very nearly all their solid shot too high and cut their shell fuse too long. There was a thick pine grove in our rear and they cut down about five or six acres of it, seldom ever hurting a man or injuring one of our cannons.

By this time the fog had risen and we could see a line of battle coming over the top of the hill about 500 yards from us. It advanced in excellent order and our batteries opened on them with shell. The lines kept rising and coming over the hill till we could see five lines coming in excellent order. They cheered with their "huzzas" and our line answered them with the Rebel yell.

The enemy advanced in a run towards our line and every piece of our artillery and small arms opened on them in earnest. When our massed batteries would pour in their double charges of grape and canister shot, it would mow them down like grass before the scythe. They advanced to within about 125 yards of us and stopped. Some of their officers acted extremely brave, for they would put spurs to their horses and rush to their battle-flag, take it and raise it aloof on their horses, cheering and leading their men on, when probably the next volley horse, man and flag would all go down.

I never saw officers act more bravely or with more courage than some of those Union officers acted. While I was their enemy and was doing everything in my power to kill them, I could admire them for their bravery and true courage. They finally advanced to within about sixty yards of us and then began to reel and waver and retreat in confusion, when, if possible, our cannoneers and infantry loaded and shot faster and with more accuracy than ever. Our line raised a yell in earnest and would have scaled their own works and pursued them if our officers would have permitted us to do so.

When their line began to retreat, some of them threw down their guns and threw up their hands and came in prisoners of war.

Here I must tell the readers of this little history the heroic deed of one of General Lee's spies as it was told to me by a friend of mine whose veracity cannot be doubted. He told me that he saw the spy when he came in. General Lee wanted to know where Grant's extreme right rested, which was of great importance to General

Lee, so he could know how to meet an attack from that quarter.

The spy put on full Yankee uniform and went around on Grant's line and found out precisely.

He had no way of getting back in time only to come with the enemy on this charge, and, when they retreated, to come on to our line. When the Federal soldiers began to retreat, he rushed ahead, pulled out a white handkerchief, held it before him, and when he arrived at our works, unhurt, he jumped over them, elated, and said, "Where is your colonel?" "On the right," was the reply. He said, "Well, I *must* see him." He went to the colonel and in two minutes he was on a good horse, going, at very nearly full speed, to General Lee.

Here they charged and recharged in the same place eight or ten times during the day, but they never had any better success or succeeded in getting any nearer than they did on the first charge.

After one of their charges and retreats, and the enemy had gone out of our sight, one of their men, who was lying near us, and who seemed to be a mere boy, got up, and from his actions he was severely wounded. He had a stick or officer's sword, and went back walking very slowly, using it for a walking cane. He was limping badly and was bareheaded. Our men did not molest him. I am sure there was no one in our line who wanted to harm him.

This battle was the worst slaughter I ever saw. It seems that I can yet see and hear it as I write (May 10th, 1898). Such groans! such cries! and such pitiful calls for water and other assistance; but none could go to them, for the enemy would not let us go and we would not let them go. I am sure hundreds died because they lacked attention. They bled to death and perished near where there were so many Southerners who would have willingly gone to their assistance, and would have taken care of them. But the Yankees would have shot us if we had given their own wounded, bleeding and dying any assistance. But *such is war.*

We had a complete cross-fire on the Union soldiers, and if Grant could have broken Lee's lines here where he tried so hard and sacrificed thousands of lives, he could have ruined Lee's army, for Ewell's corps would have been surrounded and the rest of the army cut in twain. It was nearly an all-day's fight. Grant shelled us all day.

Our part of the line fired about one hundred and sixty rounds, and was exposed to Grant's shells all day, but only two of our squad were hurt. Grant drew off from our part of the line in the evening and made a desperate charge on the right angle, but with no better success than he had on the left.

In this battle at Spotsylvania, Evans' brigade had one of the hardest struggles it ever had, and was placed at a sad disadvantage, for it had to fight the enemy after they had been flushed with victory. We had to drive them out of our own fortifications that they had previously captured from General Johnson.

They killed and wounded a great many of the brigade, though our losses in killed and wounded were not as great as it was at Manassas, Sharpsburg, Fredericksburg or even Gettysburg; but more were captured in this battle than in all of the other battles.

Among the killed was the brave and noble Lieutenant-Colonel C. W. McArthur, of the Sixty-first Georgia Regiment, and Lieutenant D. L. Gray, of Company K, in the same regiment. Lieutenant Frazier, of Company G, was severely wounded and captured. He died in the northern prison. Lieutenant F. N. Graves, of Company F, was also captured. Sixty-five valuable officers and men were captured in the regiment. Company D lost two killed, who were, Corporal William Lee, a fine young man and one who was ever willing to do his duty, and Private Henry Oliff, one of as brave and fearless young men as I ever saw. He had been on every march, had been in every battle and skirmish the brigade had ever been engaged in. He had worn out one gun and I never saw him the least excited or nervous in the worst battles. Colonel Devant, of the Thirty-eighth Georgia Regiment, was captured; also Lieutenants Maddox, Vaughn and Law were captured. The gallant captain, L. W. Farmer, and Lieutenant Sid Farmer, of Company G, were killed, also Lieutenant-Colonel Jones, of the Thirteenth Georgia Regiment. I suppose Evan's brigade suffered worse in this battle than any part of Ewell's corps, except the brigades of Johnson's division that were captured. This was caused by the brigade making the first charge at day break to arrest the Federals who had broken Johnson's line.

About three or four days after the battle the Yankees all seemed to have left our front. Our brigade went to reconnoiter. We marched over the ground on which they had charged and re-charged our batteries so many times on the 12th. In places, the dead Union soldiers were lying almost in piles. They were as thick as corn hills. I saw an officer's horse lying on five men and two or three men were lying against the horse.

Here in this death angle there were several acres of ground the worst strewn with dead men I saw during the war. I saw an oak tree, probably eighteen or twenty inches in diameter, that was very nearly cut down with canister shot and minnie balls, and the ground around it was covered with dead men, it being on the lowest ground the enemy had to advance over and where our batteries and small arms had a full sweep on them. Those who were not very badly mutilated were swollen as long as they could swell. Their faces were nearly black and their mouths, nose, eyes, hair and the mutilated parts were full of maggots!

This is a horrible picture, but I know it is not overdrawn. What an awful scent! It just makes me feel bad to-day as I write about it. I know that hundreds, and probably thousands, died for the want of attention. There were many mothers deprived of kind, loving husbands; their children were made fatherless; their darling sons, whom they had nursed and dandled on their knees while babes, and watched carefully over them while children, and gave them good advice, praying to the great God to spare them to return to them in peace, lying on the cold ground in this horrible condition.

Oh! how I long to see the time come when the prophecy in Isaiah will come to pass, second chapter and fourth verse: "And *He* shall judge among the nations, and shall rebuke many people: and they shall beat their swords into plowshares, and their spears into pruning hooks. Nation shall not lift up sword against nation, neither shall they learn war any more."

After the battle was over and the wounded very well cared for and night had closed around us, one of our bands began to play "The Dead March" just in the rear of the "death angle." You could hardly ever hear a man speak, and it seemed that we all wanted to shed tears of real sorrow; some that had lost relatives or dear friends did have to wipe their eyes. When our band ceased playing, one of the Union bands played "Nearer, My God, to Thee;" then our band began to play "The Bonny Blue Flag," after which the Union band played "The Star Spangled Banner;" then our band played "Dixie Land," and the Union band finally struck up "Home, Sweet Home;" this probably brought tears rolling down many powder-blackened cheeks in both armies.

When the Union band played "Star Spangled Banner" we could hear their soldiers huzza, and when our band struck up "Dixie" it looked like it cheered every man, and we raised a yell; but oh! how different when "Home, Sweet Home," was played. It brought to our mind two of the sweetest, dearest words in the English language —*Home* and *Mother*.

Can any one, either Union or Confederate, ever forget these historic times?

We found the rear of the Yankee column about four miles from the field of battle, and they were moving towards Lee's right. It was nearly dark. A heavy column of them turned and came meeting us. We moved out about 100 yards from the road and lay down in ambush. We kept very quiet and it was too dark for them to see us, but they halted when they got to the part of the road nearest where we were lying. Many of them were cursing, and some shot towards us. We, privates, expected to have to fire a volley into them and charge them, but we did not. They soon all went back and we returned to our command.

We rested two or three days and both armies seemed quiet. Yankee prisoners afterwards told us that Grant was waiting reinforcements and received forty-seven thousand men. I suppose he had lost that many in the battles of the Wilderness and Spotsylvania.

CHAPTER XIII.

THE BATTLES OF NORTH ANNA AND COLD HARBOR.—SKIRMISH BATTLE AT LYNCHBURG.—A VISIT TO THE NATURAL BRIDGE AND STONEWALL JACKSON'S GRAVE.

After resting a few days General Grant started on a flank movement, but we cut him off at North Anna river and Hanover Junction and fortified. Grant did not try to move us, but he tested the strength of some parts ot Lee's lines. A heavy skirmish battle was in our front. Grant moved on to our right not far from South Anna river and we had to cut him off again at a place called "Turkey Ridge," near South Anna river. Here while we were coming up and forming in line the Yankee sharpshooters killed Sergeant J. A. J. Cruce, a splendid man and excellent soldier. He had joined the church just before the campaign opened. William Kicklighter was also killed on the sharpshooter's line of our brigade. "Billy" was an excellent soldier; also John Self, of Company C, was killed.

The Thirty-eighth was sent out to run off the enemy's sharpshooters and skirmish line. They did so and held their position.

Grant made another flank movement and we had to move a few miles further. We cut him off at Cold Harbor. Here our brigade was reinforced by the Twelfth Georgia Battalion of seven companies. It was something over one thousand strong. They were excellent soldiers and commanded by Lieutenant Colonel Henry D. Capers.

We built excellent earthworks and formed our lines. About the last of May or the first of June Companies D and H were put on skirmish with the Twelfth Georgia Battalion and ordered to advance. We had a very heavy skirmish line, for we were placed about two and one-half spaces apart. We were afraid that the battalion would not do its duty, for we saw that some of the companies were about 160 strong, with a great many boys in them, and they had a fine silk flag with the words "Fort Sumpter" on one side and "Battery Wagner" on the other. They were also fixed up in better garb than wc were, and some of our boys said that some of their officers looked too proud and dudeish for soldiers, and they were afraid they would give way and the enemy would flank us.

The skirmish line was commanded by their colonel, Henry D. Capers, He was ordered to drive in the Yankee skirmish line and find out the strength of their battle line. We advanced and soon saw that the battalion boys kept in excellent line, and I have never seen better behavior in officers or men. We soon found that they "had no flies on them," and we had to do our best to do as well as they did.

We advanced and soon found a very heavy skirmish line, composed entirely of New York zouaves, who wore red shirts, pants and caps, and blue coats trimmed in red. They all seemed to be very large men and were very hard to drive at first; but we kept advancing on them till we got within about thirty yards of them. They turned and fought us all the way back to their line of battle; but they were poor marksmen, for they seldom ever hurt one of our boys. We killed a good many of them. We drove them through and out of a piece of woods, through an open field, across a creek or branch and up a hill.

I was a little in advance of the line, and went a little

way up the hill. I saw a very strong line of works and a battery of several pieces of artillery. The skirmish line was getting over their works. While one was standing on their works in a daring way, I fired at him, but I do not know that I hurt him; but I do know that he fell from the works.

I could see thousands of heads and guns and the cannoneers in readiness, though no one shot at me. They were probably holding the fire till more could come in view. I was about one hundred and fifty yards from their works. I went back down the hill and told Captain Kennedy what I saw, and begged him not to go further up the hill, but he would go in spite of my entreaties.

They saw him, and I am sure more than one thousand guns fired at him. A peachtree that he was standing under was shot to pieces and Captain Kennedy covered up in the limbs. He came back looking very pale. I went and asked him if he was hurt. He said, "No."

The Twelfth Georgia Battalion was on our left, and did not have as good a hill for protection from the enemy's works as we had, and they advanced to a more exposed place, though not as near the enemy's line as we were. Colonel Capers was in advance and leading his men like a noble hero and commander. He was severely wounded and carried off the field. This seemed to us to be a calamity to the battalion and to the army to lose such a commander. He was never able for service again, and is now living at West Union, S. C., and is one of the leading lawyers of the State. We never had any doubts about the fighting qualities of the officers and men of the Twelfth Georgia Battalion again. They won the respect of the brigade at once. We had accomplished what we were ordered to do—to find out if the enemy had left our front—so we fell back some distance. We had nearly exhausted our ammunition. We were soon relieved and returned to the line.

In about two or three days our regiment was again put on skirmish duty. The night was very dark, and I was put on vidette duty. I had to advance about two hundred yards in front of our skirmish line to find out whether the enemy was moving or not. I heard a Yankee crawling in the leaves. I was by a large oak tree, and remained very quiet. He came in a few feet of me, but I could not see him and did not shoot at him. He turned and crawled back.

The next day the skirmish line was in the thick woods and not more than one hundred yards in advance of our line of battle. We had good rifle pits about twenty-five yards apart, with about five men placed in every pit. We had a good line of works and plenty of artillery, though our troops were so scarce till General Gordon's division only had a half line in the works. The boys in the pits had to keep firing to keep the enemy from advancing near us. The pit that I and four others were placed in was in an old road, which was an avenue to the battery which we had driven the Zouaves in a few days before.

We thought it was about one thousand yards to it, and the avenue was about twenty feet wide, and there was one limb projecting out a little further in the road than the rest. We decided that if we would shoot about as high as that limb we could pitch our balls just about to the enemy's battery. Our orders were for every man to shoot once in every five minutes, so, instead of shooting in the woods as we were ordered, we pitched our balls at the battery. The enemy pretty soon opened fire on us with their artillery and we got a terrible shelling. Our batteries, right in our rear, replied, and we had to lie very low. They cut a limb from a tree and it fell on

Ziba Collins, of Company K, and hurt him, so he had to go to the rear.

We pitched our balls at them several times during the day and they would shell us every time. Our officers found out what we were doing and stopped us. On June 2nd there was heavy skirmishing on our right. The next morning just at day Grant threw his force on Lee's Army at Cold Harbor where Lee and McClellan had fought two years before. The battle raged severely for about thirty minutes, then all ceased except picket fighting. This was all on our right and mostly in General A. P. Hill's corps, though some of our division were engaged. Our brigade expected it, for the enemy drove in our skirmish line. Histories tell us that Grant lost 14,000 men in about thirty minutes. The Federal General, McMahone, says General Grant lost 10,000 men in eight minutes in this charge on the morning of June 3rd, 1864, at Cold Harbor, while Lee's losses were but little, if any, over one thousand.

On the 3rd there was heavy skirmishing in our front. The 4th, 5th and 6th of June all was quiet.

Grant had lost about sixty-five thousand men in this overland campaign or battle march of one month's time, which was as many as Lee started with at the battle of the Wilderness.

On the 10th of June a part of Ewell's corps (Gordon's and Rhodes' divisions) was ordered to the rear of Lee's army, where they went into quiet camps. The next day we rested and washed our clothing. On the 12th we cooked three day's rations and about 2 or 3 o'clock on the morning of the 13th we started on the march with General Early in command.

We marched hard all day, but we privates did not know where we were going. We marched through the battlefield where the Confederate and Union cavalry had fought at Travillion Station, about the 10th or 11th. It looked to have been the hardest contested cavalry battle I ever saw, from the amount of dead horses. We had to march terribly hard for three days and arrived at Charlottesville, Virginia, on the 16th. Gordon's division was in the front; there were six trains of cars that came for us. We boarded them and started for Lynchburg as fast as steam could carry us, leaving everything but our guns and cartridge boxes, which were well filled, and our other equipments.

We arrived at Lynchburg about sundown and marched out at once. Many citizens met and told us that we were just in time. Our officers hurriedly marched us through and out of the town, about one-half mile, and formed us in line of battle, and we fortified it. We stopped the Union general, Hunter, from coming into Lynchburg. We could see his camp fires. The cars left as soon as we got off and went after Rhodes' division and had them there the next morning by 8 o'clock.

We had brisk skirmishing during the day. On the night of the 17th General Hunter began to retreat. The next morning we took after him with a vim, though we were not prepared to give him a good race, for our forage and commissary trains, pot wagons, ambulances and the officers' horses were all left behind, except the general's staff officers' and couriers'. The colonels, majors and doctors were all tramping like we privates, and they soon had sore and skinned feet—yes, some of them straggled. We privates were glad to see some of them in that condition, especially those that had been tainted with the "big head," and could curse out some poor, sick, bare-footed, broken-down private if he could not keep in his place on the line of march.

We ran Hunter to the North or Alleghany mountains. Our cavalry captured some of his wagons and artillery and cut down a great many. Hunter spiked the rest of his cannons and left them, and made good his escape towards Charlestown, W. Va.

On the march after Hunter we found a Union soldier who had been mixed up with a bee hive, and it appeared that the bees had gotten the better of him. His face was swollen till his eyes were completely closed and the poor fellow appeared to be very sick. Some of our boys cursed him for a thief, for they thought he had stolen the hive; but no one hurt him.

After getting Hunter across the mountains of West Virginia, and his cannons captured or spiked, we returned to the valley turnpike road and rested for a few hours, till our wagon trains could arrive. We drew and cooked rations and took the valley turnpike for Staunton, Va. It was very warm weather, but we got along finely. We would march two miles and rest ten minutes. We would always start very early in the morning and rest a long while at noon. We all felt better than we did when we had to face Grant's army almost every day, and sleep at night with gun in hand.

One day we found General Gordon stopped at a fork in the road. He told us that the right hand road crossed over the great natural bridge, one of the wonders of the world, and all that wished to see the bridge could go that way, that it was but three miles out of the way and that we would not have to march very far that day, and we would have time to go by and rest one hour at the bridge. He said that he was going by it. Nearly all of our regiment went to see the bridge.

The bridge is where a prong of the James river runs through a high hill, and the road is situated on the top of the hill, with a good slope each way. You could cross over the bridge and not know that the waters of a bold little river was dashing over the rocks 200 feet below.

I went to the edge and looked down, but I drew back quickly. It made me right nervous. We went around and down to the water and under the bridge, and took a good view of it. The walls are about seventy-five feet apart and are smooth lime rock with no veins in them. The walls and arch overhead all seem to be one piece of solid rock. The arch is about 100 feet wide and about forty or fifty feet thick, and is covered with soil on which grows grass, trees and bushes.

I had read about how George Washington and other great men had climbed these walls and cut their names in the rock; but I think it must be fiction, for I could not find them. No brick or stone mason could build such a bridge as this. We all felt well paid for our trip.

On the march we had to pass Lexington, Va. Here the Virginia Military Institute had been located, and it looked like it had been a very fine place; but Hunter had burned it out. I have never seen a finer parade and drill ground.

Lexington had been the home of Stonewall Jackson, and in the Lexington cemetery was where he was buried. We marched by our much-beloved old commander's grave, which was covered with beautiful flowers that had been put there by the fair ladies of Lexington. I saw strong men and officers, who did not flinch in the fiercest battles, shedding tears. We marched by the grave with heads uncovered at reverse, trail arms, every one making a bow at the grave.

Lexington is one of the prettiest towns in Virginia, and is a place noted for good women and pretty girls. I never saw more kindness shown poor, dirty, footsore soldiers. They had large tubs of buttermilk, bread, pies, cakes, and all kinds of baked meats, there in abundance, perfectly free for the soldiers, on tables in the street by the sidewalks. It seemed that they wished to show their appreciation of their friend and fellow-citizen's (Stonewall Jackson's) old command. I never saw prettier girls. How I did want a nice suit of clean clothes and permission to stop with them a week or two. Well, to tell the truth, I love them yet. They could hand us so many nice things to eat as we marched along! I hope God has blessed them. They were dressed like queens and they treated us like kings and princes. They did not want any more Yankees in their town, especially those that loved the torch, like General Hunter. Their tender hearts were full of old Virginia patriotism.

We went on to Staunton and rested a part of one day, drew clothing and shoes, and everything was put in readiness.

CHAPTER XIV.

Battles of Maryland Heights, Monocacy, March to Washington and Skirmish Battles—Return to the Valley of Virginia.

On the morning of the 28th of June, 1864, we started down the valley by the way of Harrisburg, Va., New Market, Mount Jackson, Woodstock, Fisher's Hill, Strasburg, Middletown and arrived at Winchester on the 2nd of July. At Middletown the Yankees had burned a great many houses that were owned by the best Southerners, among them the city ministers. At Winchester the great Shenandoah valley widens out, and General Early divided his corps and marched on different roads. Early went to Harper's Ferry with part of his men, and captured it, with a great deal of army stores. The gallant General Gordon was in command of the rest of the corps, and went directly to Martinsburg, W. Va.

Martinsburg is a beautiful town situated on the Baltimore and Ohio railroad, and was one of the strongest Union towns I ever saw, while Winchester was one of the strongest Confederate towns in the South, and the two towns are only twenty-two miles apart. We arrived at Martinsburg before night, and ran General Sigel off and captured the town, with a considerable quantity of army stores. Sigel retreated across the Potomac at Shepherdstown to his strongholds on the Maryland Heights.

We burned the railroad bridge across the Opequon river and destroyed some of the Baltimore and Ohio railroad. We then went to Duffie's Depot, where we rested a few hours. Five companies of the Thirty-eighth Georgia Regiment were left at Martinsburg to guard the army stores we had captured.

On July 5th we crossed the Potomac at Shepherdstown into Maryland. We crossed Antietam creek, and on the 6th Gordon's division drove the enemy into their works on the Maryland Heights. Here we drew plenty of good shoes, of which we were in great need.

The Yankees shelled us severely from the Heights, killing and wounding some in the brigade. None of Company D got seriously hurt. I got my leg considerably bruised with a piece of shell, which partially crippled me. But I kept my place on the march.

On the morning of the 8th we marched through South Mountain, at Fox Gap, to Frederick City, Md. Here we found a large force of Yankees commanded by General Lew Wallace, who retreated across Monocacy river and took a position in a road leading towards Washington. McCausland's brigade of cavalry crossed the river in pursuit and raised a row with them.

Evans' brigade crossed the river, formed in line and advanced on their position about three-quarters of a mile through an open field. Wallace's men were well posted in a road that was washed out and graded till it was as fine breast works as I ever saw. Here our brigade suffered as bad as it ever did in battle for the amount of men and the length of time engaged, especially the Sixty-first Georgia Regiment and the Twelfth Georgia Battalion. General Evans was shot off his horse in the charge, the ball passing through his body.

We advanced to within thirty yards of the line of Yankees, but we would have had to fall back, for our men were killed and wounded until we did not have but a mere skirmish line. If it had not been that Hay's Louisiana Brigade crossed over the river and formed a line on our left and flanked the Yankees out of their position, we would have suffered worse than we did. It made our hearts ache to look over the battle-field and see so many of our dear friends, comrades and beloved officers, killed and wounded. Our loss was terrible, while the Yankees lost but few. I only saw three dead Union soldiers and I did not see one that was wounded, though I did not go over the field. We could not see a Yankee on our part of the line during the whole advance. All that we could shoot at was the smoke of their guns, they were so well posted. It was called our victory, but it was a costly one, for it cost Evans' Brigade over five hundred men, in wounded and killed. It was said that it was raw troops that we were fighting, but I never saw old soldiers shoot better. The Sixty-first Georgia Regiment went into the battle with nearly one hundred and fifty men, and after the battle was over we could not stack but fifty-two guns by actual count.

Our beloved Colonel J. H. Lamar and Lieutenant Colonel J. D. Van Valkinburg (the hero of the wilderness) were both killed on the field. We truly mourned the loss of these good men and noble Christian commanders.

Colonel Lamar was quite a young man and a military graduate, and was very profane when the war begun, but thank *God!* I hope and believe that he died a Christian. He had joined the church and often led in the prayer service at divine worship. His life seemèd to be the life of the humble followers of Christ.

It looked like half of the Twelfth Georgia Battalion were killed or wounded. Company D had the sad misfortune of getting Lieutenant James Mincy severely wounded. He was carrying our battle flag. He had picked it up after the fifth man had been shot down while carrying it in this battle and he was likewise shot down at once. He had already been wounded at Manassas and *severely* wounded at Gettysburg. Here he was shot through the left lung, the ball just missing his back bone. Bloody froth from his lungs would come out of his mouth and nose, and in the front and back where the ball passed through. He has since told me that the Yankee doctors drew a silk handkerchief through him and treated him *very* kindly.

He had a strong constitution as well as an iron will. He was a very fine man and was as brave as could be and we *all* loved him and mourned his loss. We had but little hope of ever seeing him again. He was an orphan boy.

James J. Hendrix, of Company D, was also severely wounded, and many others of the regiment, that you can find in our causalities in the back of this book.

Here I saw one of Company A of our regiment, Thomas Nichols, (though no relative of mine) with his brains shot out. When I saw him he was sitting up and wiping his brains from his temple with his hand. I went to try to render him some assistance and did so by giving him some water. He seemed to have some mind, for he said he wanted to go back to Virginia and get a horse and try to get home and never to cross the Potomac again. He lived twelve hours before death came to his relief.

In this battle the noble Colonel J. H. Baker, of the Thirteenth Georgia Regiment, was also wounded.

Captain W. H. Harrison, Company E, Thirty-first Georgia Regiment, was severely wounded while leading his company so bravely. He was left at Frederick City a prisoner.

The Thirty-eighth Georgia Regiment only had five companies, the rest being left at Martinsburg, W. Va. It lost five killed and thirty wounded. I suppose it, our regiment and the Twelfth Georgia Battalion was a fair average of the casualties of the brigade. I heard a member of the Twenty-sixth Georgia Regiment say that a Yankee shot at them from behind a shock of wheat, and that several of his regiment shot at the shock of wheat and they hit the Yankee with eighteen balls.

We camped on the battle-field, drew and cooked rations and left early the next morning (July 10th). We took the road leading directly to Washington City, with McCausland's cavalry in front. It was extremely hot, dry, dusty weather. We camped near Rockville, and were started by daylight next morning. It was one of the hottest days I ever felt. It had not rained for several weeks and we could not get but little water on the road. We were enveloped in clouds of dust and a great many of our dear boys fell by the roadside from exhaustion and we had several sun-strokes, but we pulled on the best we could.

When we got in sight of Washington City they began to shell us from Fort Stephens and other forts. We formed in line, deployed skirmishers and advanced till we got near the fortifications. Some of our skirmish line had a fight with the enemy in Montgomery Blair's yard. We privates wanted to charge and take the city, and we wanted to capture "Uncle Abe." I suppose it is a good thing that we did not capture the city, for I feel sure that we would have burnt it, for we had marched, fought and seen so much hardship at the enemy's hands, and so much depredation—in burning houses, barns, etc., in our own country, till I fear we would have burnt it in retaliation. We could see church steeples and the dome of the capitol building, and could hear the city clocks strike.

We could see clouds of dust rising and it was said to be troops coming up from Grant's army to reinforce the troops at Washington. We lay around all day (the 12th) and skirmished, and pretended like we would charge the enemy's works till night, when we left, unmolested, on our way back to Virginia. We returned by the way of Rockville. Here two of our boys were out trying to get some water—it was William Alderman and Sam Turner. The Union cavalry rode up in a run and captured Turner. I must say a few words about him. I was never acquainted with what you could call a better man. He was our company's commissary up to this time. He was brave, honest and truthful, and almost as kind and tender hearted as a lady, and an excellent cook.

I never heard him speak a profane or vulgar word. War is the place to try men's souls, principles and honesty. But Sam had all of these essential qualifications, and was a perfect gentleman. Alderman ran out with the Yankees halting and shooting at him.

From Rockville we went by Poolsville and crossed the Potomac river at White's ford, on the east side of the Blue Ridge mountains, into Virginia, on the morning of the 14th, bringing all the prisoners we had captured, and everything else in perfect safety. Our cavalry had captured a great many cattle and horses. The Union cavalry followed in close pursuit, and the Confederate and Union cavalries had a brisk battle before we crossed the river. In the evening our batteries and the Yankee batteries had a battery duel across the Potomac river.

We were all glad to get back to Dixie land, for we never loved to cross the Potomac, going north.

We rested all day, in good shades, on the 15th, and it was the second day we had rested all day since we had left winter quarters, on the 4th of May. Our officers aid we had averaged marching twenty-seven miles per day since we left General Lee and started on the valley campaign. We would often have nothing to eat but green corn roasted in the ashes. We left General Lee near Richmond on June 13th. On the march we had gone by the way of Charlottsville, Lynchburg, Salem, Natural Bridge, Lexington, Staunton, Harrisburg, New-market, Mt. Jackson, Woodstock, Fisher's Hill, Stras-burg, Middletown, Kernstown, Winchester, Bunker Hill Springs, Dartsville, Martinsburg, Duffie's Depot and Shepherdstown, in Virginia, and Sharpsburg, Frederick City and Rockville to Washington City, and back by Rockville and Poolsville, in Maryland. We had marched all of this route in one month and one day's time. We had fought four battles and marched 850 miles.

On the morning of the 16th we retreated back into the valley through Snicker's Gap, in the Blue Ridge Mountains. The Yankees were in pursuit and captured some of our wagons, but were driven off by another division of our troops.

We crossed the Shenandoah river July the 18th. The Yankees had crossed the Blue Ridge at Snicker's Gap behind us, and crossed the Shenandoah river below us. They advanced up the river on us with a heavy force. Gordon's division fronted them and held them in check, while Rhode's division flanked them. We advanced on them and drove them back in great confusion, killing and wounding many of them and capturing a great many prisoners. Our loss was slight.

On the 17th we skirmished with them all day across the river with but little loss to us. On the night of the 19th we started to fall back. It was reported that there was a flanking party of Yankees sent out from Martinsburg, which was true. We fell back to New Town. Ramsuer's division had a hard fight with the enemy at Stephenson's Depot.

Our sick and wounded were sent to Strasburg.

Early's entire command reached Strasburg on the 22nd. We rested the next day and washed our clothes the best we could in Cedar Creek, and had to put them on wet, for we had no more.

On the 24th we started back to Winchester and found the enemy posted for us in full force at Kernstown. Here General Breckinridge flanked the enemy on our right and stampeded their left wing. We advanced and the rout became general. We pursued them through Winchester to Stephenson's Depot and camped after dark.

On the morning of the 25th we moved out early to Bunker Hill Springs, twelve miles from Winchester, and rested the remainder of the day. The enemy retreated in great confusion with our cavalry after them. They never stopped till they reached Maryland Heights. The road was strewn with caisson boxes, wagons, ambulances and old broken-down horses that were killed and left in the road. The wagons were cut down and some of them were burnt.

We went to Martinsburg on the 26th and tore up the railroad the remainder of that day and the next, and burnt the new bridge across the Opequon river. General Early went with the rest of his corps to Williamsport on the Potomac. He sent Rhode's division across the Potomac river with General McCausland's brigade of calvary and sent the cavalry to burn Chambersburg, Penn., which he did in retaliation of Hunter's and Crook's depredations in the valley of Virginia, in burning houses, barns and parts of towns. It seemed to me that this should have been beneath the dignity of either side. It did not seem right for a great Christian, civilized nation to stoop so low down in heathenism as to burn non-combatant's houses and their contents and turn innocent women and children out with nothing to eat, no bed but the cold ground and no shelter but the skies of heaven. I can't think that a great big Christian heart, full of the love of God, would do or command such a thing, yet this was Hunter's and Crook's tactics and Early's retaliation.

On the 31st we marched back to Bunker Hill Springs, where we rested the 1st, 2nd and 3rd of August, with a large detail out threshing wheat and having it ground.

This is such a beautiful spring, and it made such a lasting impression on my mind, I wish to describe its beauty to the readers of this little history. They boil up from four to six inches high in a little sink or pond which covers about two acres of ground. The bottom of the sink is covered with lime rocks and the water boils up through holes in the rocks from two to six inches in diameter. There seems to be several hundred places through which the water boils.

The spring is surrounded by a few little hills, and the water was so cold till it made our teeth ache to drink it. The spring is the head of a bold little stream, on which there was a fine mill about five hundred yards below the spring. The building was made of stone, and was about one hundred feet square, three stories high and had fourteen sets of runners on the first floor.

General Early kept these mills busy grinding the wheat he had threshed, and I think the flour was the best I have ever seen. The mill was situated in the lower valley of Virginia, and was in the finest wheat country I ever saw.

On the 4th we marched back to the Potomac and crossed the river at Shepherdstown on the 5th and took position at Sharpsburg, near the Maryland Heights. We recrossed the Potomac August 6th and marched back to Bunker Hill Springs on the 7th, and rested on the 8th and 9th.

On the 10th we moved to the southeast of Winchester to guard the Berryville road. The Union cavalry advanced on us at New Town on the 11th, and we had a very heavy skirmish battle. We fell back to Hupp's Hill, between Strasburg and Cedar Creek, on the 12th and began to fortify. In the afternoon we fell back to Fisher's Hill and again began to fortify.

Grant had given General Sheridan the command of the Union army in the valley, and he reconnoitered our position for several days, during which time we had three or four heavy skirmish battles without much loss to either side. In one of these battles Dr. Price, assistant surgeon of the Thirty-eighth Georgia Regiment, was killed while riding up and down our skirmish line. He had no business there and was doing us no good, and he made an excellent target for the enemy to shoot at. I heard brave officers and men say that he acted more like a fool than a brave man.

Near Fisher's Hill are two mountains—the Three Tops mountain and Little North mountain—and a bold creek runs from the foot of Little North mountain across the valley and makes its way into the Shenandoah river at the foot of Three Tops mountain.

Fisher's Hill is situated on the south side of a creek,

and is a very strong natural position, and we had it well fortified. The Three Tops mountain rises almost abruptly from the Shenandoah river and forms a high peak which overlooked the Shenandoah valley, Luray valley and Sheridan's and Early's positions. Early had a signal station on this peak, and Sheridan sent a force of men up there who drove our signal corps off. Then General Gordon sent Captain Keller's company of sharp-shooters up there and recaptured it. This company was a picked volunteer company, and was composed of some of the best "stuff" in our brigade.

Corporal Eli Martin and Private Alfred Kicklighter, two extra fine soldiers of Company D, had joined it, and in the fight above mentioned Martin was severely wounded in thc leg, and had to retire from service. Our company often volunteered to go with that company on a skirmish fight.

The Yankees fell back on the night of the 16th, and we followed them on the 17th, and had a fight with their cavalry near Winchester. We drove them back across the Opequon river.

On the 19th, we again moved to Bunker Hill Springs.

On the 20th, we had a general move. Gordon's division went on a flank move and struck the Yankees in heavy force near Charlestown, W. Va. We had very heavy skirmishing, which continued till night. The next morning the enemy had all left our front. We followed them the next day and drove their cavalry through Charlestown to a very strong position near Maryland Heights and Harper's Ferry, where they were under protection of their heavy guns.

On the morning of the 25th of August, General Early left some of his troops fronting Sheridan, and moved with the rest of his command to near Shepherdstown, on the Potomac, passing through the villages of Leetown and Kearneysville. We met a large force of Sheridan's cavalry and a supply train of several days' rations. They had started on an expedition in our rear. We had a sharp engagement with heavy losses to the enemy, while our losses were not so heavy.

Our beloved General Gordon was wounded in the forehead, over his right eye, by a piece of shell or ball from a loaded shell. He was in front of our skirmish line when he received the wound. The general turned his horse and rode back slowly, and his wound seemed to be bleeding very freely.

I ran to him and asked him if he was badly hurt and if he needed any assistance. He said that he did not think he was hurt very much and that he could get along very well. He went to the rear, had it dressed, and was back in about thirty minutes.

We succeeded in cutting off their retreat at Shepherdstown. They went below and crossed the Potomac into Maryland.

On the 26th we moved back to Leetown, and to Bunker Hill Springs the next day, leaving our cavalry at Shepherdstown and Leetown. On the 29th the enemy's cavalry crossed the Opequon river and drove in our cavalry. We advanced and drove them *back* across the river. We had a sharp artillery duel across the river. Everything was quiet on the 30th and 31st.

On the 2nd of September we moved back across the Opequon river and again had to fight the cavalry. Rhodes' division had a battle between Martinsburg and Bunker Hill Springs. The next day Early went with the most of his corps to Whitepost and Berryville. He had a severe battle down there, but our division was not engaged, for we had been left at Stephenson's Depot to cover the roads to Winchester and Berryville.

On the 6th the enemy's cavalry made heavy demonstrations at us on the Martinsburg road and Opequon river. We whipped them out and ran them off.

On the 10th of September we again had to fight the Union cavalry at Bunker Hill Springs and Darksville. We succeeded in driving them back.

On the 11th we returned to Stephenson's Depot and rested the next day.

On the 13th a large force of cavalry, supported by artillery and infantry, advanced on us from Summit Point. We met them at Smithville, and after having a severe little battle, drove them off again. Here William Jackson of Company I was killed.

The 14th, 15th and 16th all were quiet. Gordon's division went to Martinsburg and ran off some cavalry and again burned the railroad bridge across the Opequon river. While in Martinsburg we heard from citizens and newspapers that Grant had sent up large reinforcements from Richmond and Petersburg to Sheridan. It was also reported that Grant himself had come up and was with Sheridan at Charlestown. This made us, private soldiers, feel very bad, for we knew if it were true, we would soon have trouble.

On the 18th we fell back a few miles and camped in a nice piece of woods. We had a heavy rain in the afternoon. We had to get water out of an old staunch Union citizen's well, and he was very much opposed to our getting the water. General Evans rode up and asked the old man if he could have his headquarters at his house. General Evans had just returned from the hospital, where his severe wound had been treated, and was not yet recovered, and the ground was wet.

The old gentleman replied: "I have no shelter for no d—d Rebel."

The noble general replied: "All right, I suppose I can make out."

Yet he wanted to protect the old man, and he said: "Old man, you had better let me station a guard at your house to protect you and your property."

"I can protect my own property," said the old citizen.

"Yes, but my men might kill your sheep." (The old gentleman had a fine bunch in his pasture, near the house.)

"The d—d Rebels are welcome to all the sheep they can catch. I will guard my own place."

General Evans said: "Well, if my men kill all of your sheep, I will not punish them for it."

(Some of Company D heard this conversation.) There were only three sheep left in his pasture the next morning. I admire brave men, but I never could admire this old man's judgment.

CHAPTER XV.

Battles of Winchester and Fisher's Hill. Sheridan's "Burn Out" in The Valley.

On the morning of the 19th of Septtember, 1864, we started very early to fall back to Stephenson's Depot, where the rest of General Early's command was. We marched several miles with quick-step and began to see that something was wrong, for we would march a short piece and stop. The couriers and staff officers were in a stir, riding at rapid gaits carrying orders. Our wagons and artillery were being moved as fast and cautiously as possible. We would march a short piece and have to wait for the wagons to move on.

Evans' brigade was marched out about a quarter of a mile on the left of the road and we privates knew that trouble was up. We had to march through open fields, woods, etc., along with the wagon trains, which had to keep the road. We marched here in order to protect them. Four other men and I were sent about one hundred yards to the left of Evans' lines and had to march along for sometime to look for the Yankees.

We could hear heavy cannonading on our left front. We five walked up on a line of Yankees lying down in thick high clover. We were in ten paces of them before we saw them. They raised up and captured us and made a dash on our brigade. They fired a volley into and charged it, and threw our men into considerable confusion. It was the first time that our brigade had ever retreated without orders.

The front Yankee line followed Evans' retreating men.

The Yankees paid but little attention to us—only told us to go to the rear and we would be taken care of.

Along came the second or reserve line and we had not thrown down our guns, so a little Dutch officer of one of the Maine regiments ran up to me and said: "You dosh throw town your cun." He jerked it away from me. It was a very fine one and I had had it nearly two years, and had shot about eight hundred rounds at the Yankees with it. The officer saw that it was a fine gun and said: "Here, Yokup—here dosh be one d—d fine cun, an you dosh trow town your old von, and take the good von." He then told us to go to the rear, but sent no guards with us. He asked us what brigade we belonged to. I told him Gordon's old brigade. He halloed out to his men: "Gordon's brigade is retreating; let us press it." They all went ahead and left us prisoners standing there.

The other men went on to the rear and I stood looking at our retreating men, with the Yankees following them with two lines of battle. I felt like I had about as soon die as to go to prison. I was in a terrible strait, for I knew it was only Evans' brigade retreating. I was satisfied that our boys would rally when they got in proper shape to do so. I knew that the rest of our division was not more than 500 yards away, marching by the side of our wagon trains. So I decided to risk consequences and take chances, and follow on behind the reserve line of Yankees. I was satisfied that our men would send the Yankees back faster than they were advancing, yet they all seemed very resolute and determined to go ahead. I have never seen prettier lines than they had or advancing in better order.

I followed about fifty yards in their rear. There were a few of our men killed and wounded all along. There was a good sized hill between the Yankees and the road where our men were traveling. By this time our men had all gone over the hill and the Yankees were following, rising and going over the hill, and the battle soon opened in earnest. General Battle's Alabama Brigade and the first line of Yankees seemed to make it very interesting, having a terrible battle.

Some of our artillery had gotten into position and were throwing grape and canister shot into the Yankee line at a rapid rate. By this time the reserve line of the enemy had gotten to near the top of the hill. Their officers commanded them to lie down, which they did, and it paid them to do so, for our grape and canister shot were flying like hail just over their heads.

I saw that none of them were paying any attention to me, so I walked up and lay down, about twenty yards in their rear, like I was dead.

By this time the front line of Yankees had a decent whipping put on them and they were retreating in a run, badly confused, and the fighting seemed to cease.

I heard one of the Yankee officers say, "the Rebs are flanking us on the left." I turned my head and looked up the valley about 600 yards away and could see our men swinging around them in excellent order at right shoulder, shift arms; their guns shining in the morning sun like silver.

I felt then that if I could act dead I would soon be back with the Confederates, and I suppose I did it very well.

I could hear our men coming over the hill, the officers commanding—forward—forward—forward. And along came the front line of Yankees into the reserve line. The Union officer in command of the reserve line commanded them to fall back.

They jumped up and ran right over me. I had my legs, hands, head and arms all arranged to make them believe that I was dead, and they all had enough respect to not trample on the dead, as they supposed.

I could hear our men just over the little sharp hill, coming. When I knew that all of the Yankees had passed over me I was so elated till I raised up and thanked *God* for my success, The two lines of Yankees were all mixed up and running for dear life. Just then there was no shooting on this part of the line, but I knew there would be soon, so I laid down again.

The Yankees jumped over a ditch of pure spring water and were rising the next hill.

I heard our men very close by, and heard a few guns fire. All at once our men got to the top of the hill and in full view of the retreating Yankees. And I have never seen such a deadly volley fired as those noble Alabamians fired at the retreating enemy. It was so terrible that it really looked sickening. It seemed that the first volley cut down half of their line. Our men went on with a yell, and some of the Yankees acted bravely, for they stopped and shot back at the Confederates. Among the bravest was their color-bearer. He stopped, drew his pistol and emptied it at the advancing Confederates, and he did this walking backwards.

This was a very hilly place, and I was between two fires, the balls passing me from each way, but none touched me. Our men went on after the retreating Yankees and I went to the line of dead and wounded Yankees. Oh! such lamentations and cries for water. Many of them were in a few feet of nice spring water, but were not able to get it. They called me and said, "Johnny Reb, for God's sake give me some water," or, "Do, Johnny, give me some water." I had the pleasure of devoting about thirty minutes to giving those wounded Yankees water. I would fill their canteens with water and give it to them. Several died while I was there. Our litter corps came to their assistance.

I got one of their guns and found a silver fork in a haver-sack that had been thrown down, with the name Herbert engraved in the handle.

I went to hunt the brigade, and found it and Company D in about fifteen minutes, all resting quietly in line of battle ready for another fray. When I walked up the boys gathered around me and seemed so proud that I had gotten away. I told them the story of my escape, and I well remember a remark that Sergeant Lum Bass, of Company A of our regiment, made. He said: "Boys, I'll be d—d if Nichols is not the smartest general on the field, for he has out-generaled the Yankees, and I'll be d—d if General Early has done it."

Some of our regiment were killed and wounded. Our color-bearer was shot down, and that noble Christian, Sergeant Henry Hatcher, of Company F, from Quitman county, Georgia, picked up our flag and carried it only a few steps when he was likewise shot dead. We all loved Sergeant Hatcher, for he was such a noble Christian man, and could pray so fervently. He crossed over the river into the great beyond, and I feel sure that he met a happy reception and received a crown of life where there are no more wars.

Our noble lieutenant, S. L. Williams, picked up the flag and carried it through. Lieutenant Simon never backed down from duty.

I hate to have to write any more about the balance of this day's work, but I must do it, and will tell the truth as I saw it.

Our wagons and artillery got back to a safe position. We soon fell back to a new line nearer Winchester and made connections with the balance of Early's command. Here the fighting began on our right, south of Winchester. It was a desperate battle and soon became general all along the line. Late in the evening we found that the Yankees were driving Rhodes' division, which was on our right, and the cavalry made a heavy charge on one of our brigades on the Martinsburg road on our left, and surrounded it about three to one. It formed a hollow-square and fought its way out with some loss.

Evans' brigade and the balance of Gordon's division held their ground all right, though we were soon ordered to fall back, which we did in perfect order, Generals Gordon and Evans riding along the line, keeping everything in perfect order. We fought as we fell back about one or two miles, till we got in sight of Winchester. We were rising a hill with the Yankees advancing on us about 150 yards in the rear.

A ball struck me on the back of the thigh, which made me fall to my knees, but I got up again. Captain Kennedy ran to me and asked if I was hurt. I told him that I was. He looked and said that the ball had not gone in. I suppose it had struck the ground, bounced and had struck me sideways. I could not bear any weight on my foot, so Captain Kennedy helped me along for some distance. He helped me to the line and told me to get out if I could. I used my gun for a crutch and got along somehow on my gun-crutch and one foot in a storm of balls.

Jack Collins, of Company K, received a severe wound in his foot and he too, was using his gun for a crutch.

While we were rising the hill a ball cut a strip out of my hat, which was on my head. It cut my hair and addled me so much I fell to my knees again, but soon got up, with the balls flying thick and fast around me. I was in a confused, addled condition, and went on. By this time our line was near me and took position in some old breastworks on top of the hill, near Winchester, and remained there. It was then after sundown, and Collins and I went on to Winchester.

Our wagons and artillery were tangled up in the retreat at Winchester, but soon began to move out in a run.

Just before dark an ambulance came in, in a hurry. It stopped and the driver told the captain of the rear guard that General Rhodes was killed, and that he was in that ambulance. I have since found out that the captain of the rear guard was my friend, Captain John L. Johnson, one of the firm of John Flannery & Co., of Savannah, Ga. He was doing all he could to get the wounded on, telling us to go right on towards Strasburg.

I went on, passed the town about one mile, and sat down. All the fighting had ceased on the lines. The Yankees began to camp and make fires. I sat down and rubbed my thigh, which had partly come to its feeling, and I could walk on it some.

We had lost some of our best officers, and a great many of our good men were killed, wounded or captured.

We had also lost some of our wagons and a lot of artillery. It was said that Sheridan had 35,000 infantry and 10,000 cavalry. Early did not have over 8,000 or 10,000 infantry and 2,000 cavalry.

The death of General Rhodes was a terrible blow, for he was like Gordon and Evans—a most excellent general and commander—and was greatly beloved by the entire army.

About an hour after dark our shattered and confused army began to come marching leisurely along. When Evans' brigade came along I fell in line. We marched to New Town, about ten miles away, that night and struck camps after midnight.

On the morning of the 20th we fell back across Cedar creek, and began to fortify on Hupps' Hill, between Cedar creek and Strasburg; but in the afternoon we fell back to Fisher's Hill—a very strong and well fortified position. Sheridan advanced to Hupps' Hill and fortified it and made heavy demonstrations in our front. We had a severe skirmish battle, getting some men killed and wounded.

On the evening of the 22nd Sheridan sent out a flanking column around Little North mountain, and broke our line where we had a few dismounted cavalry, and made a dash on our rear. We did not know what it meant at first, for we saw our men leaving our works on our left and begin to fall back in a run. We were ordered to leave our works and fall back.

Sheridan advanced his whole line and the rout became general. All of our men left the works badly confused, though all of them got their guns and other equipments. To make it worse, the Yankees gave three huzzas and began to shoot at us with a vim. The shooting did but little harm, only to add to the confusion. I was never fleet footed and could hardly keep up. Some tired down and stopped and surrendered.

We ran about two miles, and got out past the flanking party. We readily stopped and formed in line; but it looked like we were ruined. Our artillery was nearly all captured and a great many of our wagons, and many prisoners had been taken. Captain DeLoach, of Company H, was captured. He had been severely wounded in the knee at Gettysburg and it had never gotten well enough for him to run fast, and he had to surrender. He remained in prison till June, 1865. He is now living at Beard's Creek, Liberty county, Ga.

As soon as it began to grow dark the enemy quit pressing us and camped. If night had not put an end to the contest I suppose we would have been ruined worse than we were. We fell back twelve miles that night and camped near Woodstock. All of the army was nearly exhausted. I was so fatigued till I spit blood. The wound that I received at Winchester on the 19th was paining me and was swollen badly, but I did all I could to keep out of prison.

The next morning we fell back to Mt. Jackson, where we formed a line of battle and remained till our sick and wounded could be moved back towards Staunton. In the afternoon we had to fight the enemy's cavalry, which we drove back. We then fell back to Rudes Hill, between New Market and Mt. Jackson, and camped.

On the 24th of September we had to fall back again with Sheridan's whole force pursuing us. The valley here is almost entirely open and cleared up. There are some high hills. We could see thousands of Yankee infantry in our rear and cavalry on our flanks, but we retreated in good order.

General Early formed his whole command in line of battle across the valley turnpike road and fell back in line of battle. We often had to fight as we marched along. We would sometimes come in sight of our wagon trains, which could not move fast on account of our having poor, broken-down teams and heavy loads. Our army was very small. I heard a Yankee prisoner say afterwards that they thought it was only our rear guard,

They would run cavalry batteries up on top of the hills and shell us severely. We kept in excellent line, but we nearly perished for water. We were all nearly exhausted and I tried to get some of the boys that were better off than I was to take some canteens and go and try to get some water, but they would not, so I told them if they would carry my gun along that I would go. John Yeomans took my gun and I took nearly every canteen in the company, which was only seven or eight, and hurried on ahead about 400 yards and found a well and filled the canteens in a few minutes. While I was getting water I heard the Yankee batteries open fire and could see the dust rising where the shot and shells struck, right where I left the boys about fifteen minutes before.

About the time I had filled my canteens I saw them begin to get up and fall back. When I got near them with the water, I saw that all of them looked very solemn. They said: "George, John Yeomans is killed. He was shot nearly in two, and your gun and his are both broken." I gave the boys their canteens of water and Captain Kennedy told me to go ahead, overtake our ordnance wagon and get a gun from Sergeant Mimms. I did so. We all loved John Yeomans, for he had been our company's commissary ever since Sam Turner had been captured at Rockville, Maryland. He was a brave, honest, Christian gentleman. He left a good wife and several children at home in Emanuel County, Georgia, to mourn the loss of a kind, loving husband and father.

I got another gun and sat down and rested nearly an hour, waiting for the company to come up. Just as the command got near me they made a stand and fired a few volleys at the enemy. All the firing ceased and the Yankeés camped and began to build fires. We fell back a few miles and camped for the night.

Next morning we started early, marched a few miles and left the valley turnpike road then, went to Port Republic and took a very strong position in the Blue Ridge Mountains. This is where our brigade first joined the famous "Stonewall" Jackson, in June, 1862. Our army was now reduced to only five or six thousand men and seemed badly discouraged and looked like they thought it was useless to fight any longer. We had an elevated position and could see Yankees out in the valley driving off all the horses, cattle, sheep and killing the hogs and burning all the barns and shocks of corn and wheat in the fields, and destroying everything that could feed or shelter man or beast.

They burnt nearly all the dwelling houses in the valley. The valley was soon filled with smoke. We remained at Port Republic two days, and very cautiously moved along some mountain roads to Waynesboro, near the great tunnel through the mountain, and through which the Richmond and Staunton railroad passes. We ran a few Yankee cavalry from Waynesboro and occupied it.

After Sheridan had burnt out the upper valley, he fell back to Strasburg and we followed him to Woodstock, and then returned to New Market. We found that he had burnt every barn and nearly every dwelling house from Staunton to Strasburg. Most of the dwelling houses in the towns were spared.

The distance, I believe, from Staunton to Strasburg is seventy miles, and we heard that Sheridan reported to Lincoln and Grant that "a crow would perish in the valley." And it was one of the finest and richest places I ever saw before this merciless "burn out."

The commanders, who were the real perpetrators of such horrible deeds as this, are all dead, and I have been made to wonder if they met the great Judge up yonder in peace.

CHAPTER XVI.

Battle of Cedar Creek and the Closing of the Valley Campaign.

About the 5th of October Early was reinforced by General Kershaw's division, from Richmond, consisting of about 3,000 infantry and a brigade of cavalry. This made our command about as strong as it was before the disasters at Winchester and Fisher's Hill.

On the 12th of October we advanced to Fisher's Hill, and on the 13th we moved out in line to Hupps' Hill, and had a small engagement with some of the Yankees' cavalry and drove them across Cedar creek, and found that their infantry was well posted in a good fortified position, and we returned to Fisher's Hill and went into camps near our works. We stayed here and rested until the evening of the 18th. About 3 or 4 o'clock all of our regimental and company officers were called for. They assembled at Generals Gordon's and Evans' headquarters. Here the plans of a great battle were made known to them and they made it known to us.

We were commanded to cook two days' rations and be ready to leave at dark, which we did. We were not allowed to carry anything that would make a noise, so we had to leave our canteens and the officers had to leave their swords. We marched and crossed the Shenandoah river and went around the Yankees through a trail in the Three Tops mountains. We got within 300 yards of their pickets, and got around to another ford in the Shenandoah river, which was almost in the rear of the enemy.

Our division (Gordon's) had gotten there and was massed by 3 o'clock in the morning and all ready to cross the river at the proper time. We had not made enough noise to cause the enemy's pickets to notice us, and it was reported to us private soldiers that General Gordon managed to capture one of the Yankee pickets, and that he gave General Gordon the countersign correctly, and that Gordon had all of their pickets relieved near the ford and had Confederates put in their places, and had all of the Yankee pickets captured. I do not yet know whether this report was true or not.

[Since writing the above I have learned, through Major J. L. Crider, who was raised and lived six miles from Winchester, and who was one of Stonewall Jackson's scouts, that a private soldier by the name of Billings, of the Twelfth Virginia Regiment of cavalry, captured the Yankee picket that gave General Gordon the countersign.]

Just at the break of day we marched across the river in four lines. Evans' brigade started up the road at double quick step ahead of all the rest, but the rest were following immediately in the rear. There was a big frost on the ground, and as we had to wade the river and were wet up to our waists, the run up the hill did us good, for it warmed us up.

We advanced up the road at double quick to a certain place and stopped. We faced the Yankees' camp and advanced through the woods in fine order. The enemy was not aware of our being anywhere near them till a few of their camp guards began to shoot at us. It was then light enough for us to see their camps.

We advanced in a run and raised the Rebel yell. At

this signal Kershaw advanced from a different place and raised a terrible yell. The Yankees fired a few cannon shot at Kershaw's men and then fled. We were soon in their camp. The most of them were still in bed when we raised the yell and began firing at them. They jumped up running, and did not take time to put on their clothing, but fled in their night clothes, without their guns, hats or shoes.

We were shooting them as fast as we could, and yelling as loud as we could to see them run. It was the worst stampede I ever saw. We captured about twenty stands of colors (battle flags); and some of Sheridan's men told me, in Savannah, Ga., the next June, that some of the Yankees ran to Winchester, which is fifteen miles away, in their night clothes, without shoes or hats. We took many prisoners and captured nearly all of their wagons, artillery, ambulances, horses, mules and a great deal of clothing, shoes, blankets, tents, etc. I saw one Union soldier who had been killed with only one shoe on. We ran in pursuit of them till we had gotten about two miles from their camp, and then everything was halted. A great many of us went back to their camp after blankets, shoes, clothing, etc., and to my surprise, General Early had his own wagons and artillery brought over Cedar creek.

It seemed that there were no Yankees in our front. Everything was as quiet as death. Some of our boys went to sleep while the others were plundering the camps. I got two nice new tent flies, two fine blankets, a fine rubber cloth, two new overshirts and two pair of new shoes. In fact, we could get anything we wanted except Yankee money.

It was reported to us privates that General Gordon planned and executed this move on the Yankees. If Early had moved all we had captured back to Fisher's

Hill it would have been one of the grandest successes of the war; but he did not, and it proved to be one of the greatest disasters.

Again, dear reader, I hate to have to write any more about this memorable 19th of October, 1864, but, as painful as it is, I must write it as I saw and heard it.

About noon Gordon had all his division to get to their places in the line. Late in the afternoon we heard the pickets or cavalry begin to fight on our right. Evans had his brigade well in hand and all well composed. The firing was about 800 yards from us, and it soon got faster and nearer and we saw the Yankees advancing.

General Sheridan was not present when the battle and stampede opened in the morning, but was at Winchester, and General Wright was in command of the Union forces in the valley. History tells us that when Sheridan heard the cannonading he put spurs to his fine black horse and met his flying men between New Town and Winchester and told them "We are going back, and all good men must rally and go back with me." All of them cheered him and rallied. He also had one of his corps camped at Winchester, and he had it hurried up and formed in line, and had full and ample preparations made to advance late in the afternoon. We private soldiers thought that General Phil Sheridan was one of the best commanders, or really the *best* commander we had ever had to fight, and never really found but one fault of him, and that was his merciless burn-out in the valley—the "Eden of America."

As just stated, we could see the Yankees advancing and our men falling back on our right. At first it was in order, though it seemed to be a poor, thin line. They began to retreat faster and finally began to run. General Evans then ordered us to fall back, which we did in perfect order for nearly a mile, but were finally ordered to double quick, as the other men were so far ahead of us and their officers had lost all control of them. Sheridan's cavalry was making a bold charge on them, shooting with their repeating rifles and making a lot of them prisoners.

We finally got into a perfect run, with the cavalry getting nearer all the time, and some of our men surrendering. To tell the truth, it all turned into a panic. The gallant generals, Gordon and Evans, were showing all personal bravery mortal men could do. Nearly every man would stop, face the enemy and shoot at them, while the rest of the line was running as fast as a herd of wild, stampeded cattle. We just had to get out or be captured, and we saw it, our officers losing all control over us.

Generals Gordon nor Evans nor any of the brigade were responsible for this panic.

We arrived at Cedar creek just before dark and I was completely exhausted. I was so worried till I could hardly keep my feet under me, but I was no worse off than a great many others were, and not as bad as some, for they tired down and gave up and were taken prisoners. When I arrived at the creek I left the command —or the command left me, rather, and I turned down the creek towards the Three Tops Mountains. I had to do this or be captured. I went down the creek about two hundred yards, stopped, got some water and sat down and rested. When the brigade got up the hill, the generals rallied the brigade and stopped the Yankees, covered the retreat and saved the army from complete destruction.

After resting a few minutes I started down the creek, which is very crooked. By this time it was very dark, and I knew that if I could go along down the creek I would be tolerably safe, so I went, I thought, three or four miles, and crossed a big turnpike road, and went up the hill about 100 yards from the road in a thick place of bushes. I spread down my blankets and lay down. In a few minutes eight other men and one lieutenant came near me and made a little fire out of some leaves. I saw it was Confederate soldiers, so I contented myself on my success in getting out safe.

Men and horses began to cross the creek at the road and go up the hill, and went into camps. I could hear the men talk, hear their horses neigh and eating corn. I felt sure that it was our men, but I was badly mistaken, for it was Yankees. I was about thirty feet from the men who had come up there near me, but I never made my presence known. All of us soon went to sleep, for we were very badly worried, as none of us slept any the night before.

I awoke about 2 o'clock the next morning; the other men were up and had made a little fire out of some leaves and sticks. I looked around, for the moon was shining very brightly, and was about four hours high. I expected we were about the foot of Three Tops mountain, and I was looking for the high peak of the mountain, which I knew was due east from our old position at Fisher's Hill. I could see it at a distance of about six miles south of where we were.

I went to the men near me and went to outing their fire, for let me tell you, I was scared. I knew we were in the rear of Sheridan's army. I told the lieutenant that we were all prisoners, or would be if we stayed there till daylight. He said: "Oh, no, we are not." I told him I *knew we were!* I then asked him to what regiment, brigade and division he belonged. He told me that they all belonged to a Mississippi regiment of Kershaw's division and that they had just come up from Richmond a few days before to reinforce Early.

I told him I was well acquainted in the valley and knew that if we did not get out of there we would be prisoners at daylight. I then explained about the high peak of the Three Tops Mountain and its being due east from our old position at Fisher's Hill. He recollected this very well. I then showed him the peak of the mountain at a distance. He then saw the perilous position we were all in, and all of them were as scared as I was. He asked me what we should do. I told him that we must get out of there before day. I told him that all of us had become turned round the night before and had gone in the wrong direction.

We decided to go to Cedar creek and go down the run of the creek to the Shenandoah river; cross the river and go up on the east side of the river by the foot of Three Tops mountain and re-cross the river where we crossed the night before. We packed and started at once.

When we got to the road at the ford of the creek, leading from Strasburg to Winchester, we found that it was the ford where we had left the army the night before. Lieutenant Baskett (for that was his name) asked me to lead the way, as I was well acquainted with the country. We went down the creek right by the run, often wading it, for it was very shallow and had a rock bottom and had no low bushes in it. We could often get along much faster wading than any other way.

When daylight came we were near the Shenandoah river, and I wanted to know if there were any Confederates or Yankees about, so I left the lieutenant and his men and went up the hill among the bushes a few steps and looked out in an open field (I being concealed) and saw a skirmish line of Yankee cavalry sitting on their horses, about one hundred yards in my front, with their backs turned to me and facing Fisher's Hill.

I could see the end of the skirmish line not over two

hundred yards to our left. I went back and got Lieutenant Baskett to look at them. He did so and we were sure we could get out for we could see how to get along. We hurried on down the creek about one hundred yards aud left the creek to our right, went through some thick woods which entirely concealed us from the enemy. We soon got to the river and crossed over where we could again see the line of Yankees. All of them were quiet. We were about three-fourths of a mile from them.

We hurried up the river and recrossed it again about a mile and a half from where we were and hurried on to Fisher's Hill, where we expected to find Early's command. When we got to the main valley turnpike road at Fisher's Hill, three of our cavalry were there sitting on their horses and the Yankee cavalry were advancing. Our cavalry told us that General Early left Fisher's Hill at 2 o'clock and was to be at Woodstock at daylight.

We started up the valley towards Woodstock as fast as we could, but had not gone over one mile when we heard our cavalry shoot and they went by us at almost full speed. They told us to get off that road and to the Three Tops Mountain or we would be captured. We left the road on a run and soon crossed the Shenandoah river. Here we saw an old citizen who showed us a trail that would take us across Three Tops Mountain into Fort Valley and to a road up Passing creek, between Massanutten and Three Tops Mountain, and he told us that when we got out we could get directions.

In Fort Valley we found very clever people and about 1,000 of Early's command. Old citizens told us that a Yankee had never been in that valley. It looked like there was a high mountain all around us.

When we got to the head of Passing creek we were out of the mountains. Here we found one of General Gordon's couriers who told us how to go and where General Gordon was stationed. We found our command at New Market four days after the battle and stampede at Cedar creek, all resting quietly in camps.

In the battle of Cedar creek our losses in killed and wounded were small. Our greatest loss was in prisoners. Jake Smallwood, of Company I, was killed and the noble Sergeant J. C. Jolly, of Company F, was severely wounded, (shot through the breast) and our beloved orderly' Sergeant William Alderman, was missing. We did not know what had become of him. He did not come home till the fall of 1865. He got cut off and went across North mountain to the south prong of the Potomac and worked with a citizen in West Virginia till the war was over, and till he came home. A braver and better soldier never shouldered the musket than Alderman was.

General Early lost nearly all of his artillery and his wagons and ambulances, and a great many of his officers and men were captured.

We could not help but blame General Early for all the disasters at Cedar creek. But I must say that General Early had always been an excellent officer and commander up to this time, but he never had the confidence of his men after the disasters at Cedar creek.

We private soldiers thought that he should have moved everything that we had captured in the morning back to the rear of Fisher's Hill, and he should have fallen back there when everything was quiet.

We rested quietly in the camps at New Market for some time, and had but very little to do.

On the 26th of October, the enemy's cavalry advanced to Mount Jackson, and we had to go out and meet them, but we had no engagement. They retired, and we returned to camps and rested till the 10th of November.

One day while in this camp, four other men and I were

sent out on provost guard duty with a lieutenant in command. We were looking around over the country taking up all the men we could find who were out of camps without passes. We took sacks along, and an old gentleman gave us as many apples as we could carry. I sold my turn for sixty dollars in Confederate money.

On the 14th of November we advanced to Cedar Creek and felt for the Yankees. We found them in a good fortified position at Newtown. We returned to New Market without any engagement except some light skirmishing. We remained in the valley with but little to do till we received orders to pack up and march out of camps on December 11th, 1864. This closed the ever memorable Valley campaign of 1864.

As I have some official reports before me from Generals Early, Sheridan, Hunter and Crooke, I will give them to the readers of this history.

Our little command of never over twelve thousand men had marched about two thousand and five hundred miles; had killed, wounded and captured about twenty-two thousand Union soldiers in the valley campaign, besides what we had killed, wounded and captured at the Wilderness, Spotsylvania C. H., North Anna, Turkey Ridge and Cold Harbor before we were sent to the valley. We had invaded Pennsylvania and Maryland; had been to the very walls of Washington; had been in thirty-five hard battles and skirmishes, and had lost about five thonsand men, killed, wounded and captured.

I do not think there was ever a little army which had done more real hard service, or could have gone through with more hardships, privations, and sometimes almost starvation, than we had; nor do I believe that we could have done much more than we had done. We were the worst set of broken down men I ever saw. I have never gotten over it. I was a mere boy, and was broken down before I matured into manhood, and I was too old to grow out of it.

We left our camps hurriedly about 11 o'clock on the morning of December 11th, and marched about twenty-six miles without resting, and stopped to camp just at dark.

We had held on to the blankets, clothing, shoes, oil-cloths, tent flies, etc., which we captured from the Yankees at Cedar creek. They were very useful, for it was now cold weather ; but they made a very heavy turn to carry. When we camped we were all badly worried. Our feet were blistered nearly all over. When I pulled off my shoes my feet were in a jerk like fresh-skinned beef. Ive Summerlin shook clotted blood out of his socks and wrung blood out of them.

We had to cook two days' rations. I was to get the wood, Ive Summerlin was to get the water and Madison Warren was to do the cooking for us three. I told them I did not feel like getting the wood, and Summerlin says: "George, if I were as well off as you are, I would be a mile from here, piling wood." The boys all laughed at Ive's foolish expression.

I managed to get the wood, Ive the water, and Madison did the cooking.

We left very early the next morning and soon got to Waynesboro, where we took the cars for Richmond. We went by way of Charlottsville and Lynchburg to Richmond, and arrived at Petersburg on December 14th. We were sent twelve miles south of Petersburg, where we began to build winter quarters.

LIEUT. COL. STEPHEN H. KENNEDY.

CHAPTER XVII.

Battles of Hatcher's Run and Deep Run and Capture of Fort Stephens—Closing Events of the War.

General Gordon was now promoted to the command of a corps, and General Evans to the command of General Gordon's division.

We camped twelve miles south of Petersburg. We had to build better winter quarters than we had ever built. We were building chimneys on Christmas day. We had about completed our winter quarters and finished cleaning up our camps by New Year's day, 1865.

About the 5th of January, 1865, some of our regiment were sent on picket on Deep Run creek, several miles from camps. In the afternoon a thunder cloud came up from the southwest, and we had a very heavy rain. After the rain ceased, a gale of wind began to blow from the northwest; every flaw seemed to get colder, and the ground was freezing before dark.

I had to go on vidette about 10 o'clock that night and stay one hour on top of a high hill. I was well wrapped in two good blankets, but there was not a tree or bush to protect me from this cold wind. I had orders to stand and watch, and that if I should see the enemy advancing, to shoot a signal gun and run back to the line of pickets. I did not stand, for if I had I am sure I would have been frozen in less than thirty minutes. I ran on the frozen ground until I was nearly tired down, and was very nearly frozen when relief came. It was about all I could do to get back across Deep Run and get to a fire. I told the officers in command that men could not stand to stay in that wind one hour. He saw how nearly frozen I was and changed the orders and had the videttes relieved every half hour.

This wound up picket and vidette duty with me, for General Lee sent out orders to give one man from every company a furlough for twenty-four days, provided there was a man in every company who had never been home since he enlisted, and had always been a faithful and obedient soldier and his home was not inside the enemy's line. I was the only one in Company D, so our good officers fixed up one for me and sent it off for approval.

I packed up and had everything in readiness. On the night of the 14th of January it came back approved. I was one proud boy, and was so glad I had not received one the winter before. Neal Browning, of Company C, Tom Bridges, of Company E, and Berry Birch, of Company K, all received furloughs at the same time.

Captain E. F. Sharp, of Company K, who had commanded the regiment since Colonels Lamar and Van Valkinburg were killed at Monocacy, Maryland, July 9th, 1864, received our furloughs. He sent for us to go up to his quarters where he told us to be ready at daylight next morning.

We were ready by time the next morning and received our furloughs. We had to go to Petersburg to get our transportations and four days' rations. There had been a terrible freshet which had washed up the railroads in several places between Petersburg, Virginia, and Bellfield, North Carolina, so we had to walk that distance, which was seventy-two miles. We started on a plain, pnblic road and made twelve miles of the distance on the 15th of January. We camped in a real good, comfortable unoccupied house that night.

We got up a plenty of wood, made a good fire, ate our

supper and soon went to sleep. Browning had married near Charlottsville, Va., the winter before. He left us at Petersburg and went to see his young wife instead of coming to Georgia.

We three were all happy, for we expected to soon see our loved ones at home. We got up early next morning and started for Bellfield, N. C, which was sixty miles away. The ground was frozen as hard as a brick and the ice on the streams was thick enough for us to cross on it. We met a great many wagons and cavalry who told us that trains going south left every morning at 8 o'clock.

We put in to be there at 8 o'clock the next morning, and marched fifty-two miles that day before dark and found a nice camp in thick woods where some one had camped the night before.

The fire had not gone out and there was plenty of wood already there and leaves on which we could sleep.

We ate supper and were soon asleep, for we were very tired. We were up and started early the next morning. The road was plain and the moon was shining bright. We crossed the Roanoke river where the railroad had been washed up, and arrived at Bellfield just as the sun was rising. We went to the station and asked what time the train left going to Raleigh, N. C. The agent told us it was due there at 1 and to leave at 2 o'clock.

We went to the waiting room, broiled some of our bacon and ate breakfast. The seven hours, during which we had to wait for the train, seemed to be very long ones.

We lay around and slept some, and just at one o'clock the train came puffing in, and so did Captain E. F. Sharpe, our regimental commander. He had sent off a furlough and it came back approved. He told us he got it and started the day before just at 1 o'clock, and had walked every step of the way from camps to Bellfied in one day, which was sixty-three miles.

We were all proud to see him, for he was a kind commander, always at his post and would not punish any one if he could help it.

The train started just at 2 o'clock with a great many furloughed soldiers on it. It had not gone its length before the front wheels ran off the track. We all jumped off and went and volunteered our services to help get it back on the track. The engineer looked at it and had us all move away, and he backed the train and, luckily, rolled it back on the track. He had the defective switch repaired and next time passed it all right. We got along finely, except a few misconnections.

When we arrived at Waynesboro, Burke county, Ga., we struck Sherman's track, where he had marched through Georgia, and we saw that there were other Federal commanders who were like Hunter, Crooke and Sheridan—loved the "torch," for only standing chimneys, coals and heaps of ashes were left to mark the places where happy homes once were.

I arrived at home, in Bulloch county, Ga., January 24th, 1865. When I met my dear mother she and I could thank God for preserving my life through so many hard contested battles and such bloody carnage. As I have said in a previous chapter, when she left me near Clarke's mountain, in Virginia, in August, 1863, on her way to Orange Court-house to board the cars to come home, I felt that the God of all Grace gave me the blessed assurance that I should live to see her again in peace. She told me that she received the same blessed assurance when she was not more than half a mile from me and saw me last wiping the tears from my eyes. She said she could see me through her tears and felt that God revived her with that blessed assurance, and she felt that *He* was my protector and would spare me to return to her again in peace. Dear reader, it is good to feel that we

GENERAL ROBERT E. LEE.

are just as safe in God's hands in one place as another.

I found all well and that the loved ones at home had a house to live in. My father had never owned a slave and his house was spared, but Sherman took every horse he had and a great many other things. This closed the war with me, for Sherman had me cut off from my command before my furlough expired, or I would have promptly returned to the army. But it did not take a prophet to tell me what the end would soon be.

As I was not with the army after the 14th of January, 1865, I will have to write the remainder of this little history from reports, given me by Lieutenant Colonel Kennedy, privates Remer, Franklin and Madison Warren, of Company D, and Captain F. L. Hudgins of Company K, Thirty-eighth Georgia Regiment, and knowing these men as I do I can assure the reader that it is the truth. I have written the campaigns of 1863 and 1864 as an eye-witness, except the march to York and Susquehanna river in Pennsylvania and the battle of Gettysburg, I being sick there and in our medical wagon.

I took down notes almost every day in all the campaigns of 1864, and also had other notes, or I could never have told how we raced with Sheridan's cavalry, or rather mounted infantry, for one of his men told me that the most of his cavalry were men taken from the infantry and mounted for gallantry. We had rather have fought his infantry at any time than his cavalry.

On the 18th of January, 1865, the Sixtieth and Sixty-first Georgia Regiments were consolidated into one regiment with only one stand of colors. Major W. B. Jones (Old Red) of the Sixtieth Georgia, was promoted to the rank of colonel, Captain S. H. Kennedy, of Company D, Sixty-first Georgia, was promoted to the rank of lieutenant colonel, and Captain Bedenfield, of the Sixtieth Georgia Regiment, was promoted to the rank of major of this consolidated regiment.

Companies B, C, D and H, of the Sixty-first Georgia, were all consolidated into one company commended by Lieutenant S. L. Williams, of Company D. The other six companies were consolidated into two companies, one of which was commanded by Lieutenant J. Rufus James, of Company I. The other company's officer is not known. About the 1st of February, Lieutenant S. L. Williams received a furlough and came home and was like I was, cut off from the army, and was never with the company again.

Everything went on quietly till the 5th of February, 1865. Evans' brigade of Gordon's division was commanded by Colonel J. H. Baker, of the Thirteenth Georgia Regiment; Evans was in command of Gordon's division, and Gordon in command of a corps. They engaged the Yankees near Burges' mill, on Hatcher's Run, and drove them back to their works after a very stubborn battle of one hour and a half. In the battle Major B. F. Grace, of the Twenty-sixth Georgia Regiment, was killed. Sergeant W. H. Williams, of Company D, was severely wounded. On the 6th the Yankees flanked around on the extreme right, and was met by Ewell's corps.

Our brigade was, as usual, first to get into the battle. It charged their works, but failed to rout them on the first assault. It had to fall back across a little boggy branch about 100 yards in the rear. Colonel Baker was wounded. Here General Gordon met and rallied it and made the second charge, and routed the Yankees badly in its front. This was a very stubborn battle, and the consolidated regiment had the sad misfortune of getting its gallant Lieutenant-Colonel S. H. Kennedy severely wounded while leading the regiment. He had to be carried from the field. This was on Deep Run.

A great many of the brigade were killed and wounded in this battle. The Sixty-first Georgia Regiment lost every one of its commissioned officers, either killed or wounded, and from this time till near the close it was commanded by sergeants.

The Sixtieth Georgia Regiment went into this battle with thirteen commissioned officers and had eleven of them killed or wounded, Colonel W. B. Jones and Lieutenant Rice being the only ones escaping unhurt.

Captain T. M. McRae, of Company E, came to the Sixty-first Georgia Regiment a few days before the evacuation of Petersburg, and was killed in one of the battles on the retreat, which left the regiment without a commissioned officer at the surrender.

In this battle Remer Franklin, of Company D, got eight holes shot through his clothing.

The Thirty-eighth Georgia Regiment lost fourteen killed, thirty-two wounded. The noble captain, R. H. Fletcher, of Company K, was killed, he being its tenth commander that had been shot dead.

After the battle the brigade and division relieved other troops in the ditches in front of Petersburg. Here it was almost a regular fight till the evacuation of Petersburg.

On the 25th of March the brigade was engaged in the battle of Fort Steadman on Hares' Hill, in front of Petersburg, and had a desperate battle and captured Fort Steadman.

Here Major John Y. Beddingfield was killed and Adjutant R. S. McFarlin was severely wounded, both of the Sixtieth Georgia Regiment. We had the sad misfortune to get our beloved brigade commander, Col. John H. Baker, of the Thirteenth Georgia Regiment, severely wounded. The brigade lost many valuable officers and men in this battle. Here while we were in the ditches in front of Petersburg, the Sixtieth and Sixty-first Georgia Regiments captured one of Grant's forts by surprise without losing a man, but lost some when they had to give it up. Here Remer Franklin was wounded by a piece of shell, but reported for duty in three days' time. In the battle of Hare's Hill and Fort Steadman Privates Moxley, of Company C, Smith, Company G, and Wiggins, of Company K, of the Thirty-eighth Georgia Regiment, carried out one of Grant's Morton guns.

M. O. Wiggins threw a Morton shell with a burning fuse out of our line and over our works before it exploded, and probably saved the lives of more than a dozen men.

By the 1st of April the severe wound that Colonel Kennedy received on the 6th of February had healed sufficiently, and he received a furlough and started home. He traveled by railroad by the way of Danville, Va., Greensboro and Charlotte, N. C. When the train got to where Sherman tore up the railroad, between Charlotte and Columbia, S. C., he had to walk through the country forty-one miles on his crutches, and he made the trip in a little over one day, to Abbeville, S. C. Adjt. J. J. Mobley, of the Sixty-first Georgia, and Captain McDonald, of Florida, were paroled from northern prisons, and were with him. They hired two old broken down horses and a wagon from an old citizen, with a negro driver, to carry them to Washington, Wilkes county, Georgia, a distance of forty-five miles, for which they paid him $700 in Confederate money. They had not gone more than two miles before the horses stumbled and fell, and when they were trying to get up they tumbled into a ditch. After a great deal of hard work they helped the old horses out with whole bones and made the trip after a long time without another fall. He then went on the train to Waynesboro and got private conveyance through the country to his home in Bulloch county.

On the 26th of March Lee's right wing was broken at the battle of Five Forks, and a great many of Ewell's corps were killed and wounded and 1,700 were taken prisoners.

On the 2nd day of April Grant massed his forces and made a heavy charge on our line of works, which was about thirty-five miles long, and Lee did not have but about 30,000 men with which to hold this long line. Grant broke it near Petersburg. General Lee was too weak to establish it, and had to evacuate Richmond and Petersburg. Then the final struggle began. General Lee had to march, stop and fight day and night, losing a great many of his men every day till April the 9th, General Grant succeeded in planting a solid line in Lee's front, rear and flanks and he had to surrender. General Lee and General Grant made honorable terms of capitulation. In these terms of capitulation General Grant showed himself to be a great and wise commander. And now the once great and powerful Confederate Army of Virginia were prisoners of war, and were honorably paroled.

General Grant refused to take Lee's sword, but allowed Lee to keep it, and the officers and men were allowed to keep their own private property—horses and side arms.

The Confederate and Union soldiers met and talked very friendly—once foes, but now friends. And the war of Secession was virtually ended.

The surrender was very humiliating to our officers and men. Most all of them shed tears freely. It was indeed a very sad parting with General Lee and his faithful and tried officers and men. Tears of true sorrow rolled down many a sunburnt cheek when tears were seen rolling down the cheeks of those beloved generals—Lee, Gordon, Evans and Colonel J. T. Lowe, our brigade commander.

General Grant allowed them to keep some wagons and teams for the men to haul rations for use on the marches home.

Our brigade went to Virginia in June, 1862, about seven thousand strong, and seven hundred and forty-seven surrendered at Appomattox C. H., commanded by Colonel J. H. Lowe, of the Thirty-first Georgia Regiment.

The war of Secession was four years of terrible war, and I know that if the Northern and Southern people could have known what the consequences would be, there would have been no war. Neither side could have been induced to have entered into such a struggle—such a sacrifice of human life and such a cost of treasures.

Slavery had once been in the North as well as in the South. The North had sold its slaves to the South and had received pay for them. The South bought them in good faith.

The negroes are all free and the whole nation is satisfied that such is the case. I, nor my parents never owned a slave and have never mistreated one.

They are now free, yet a great many are not faring as well as they did while in bondage. Yet they are better satisfied.

It is about like an old time darkey said to me a few years ago: "I do not fare near as well for something to eat as I did with old boss, but freedom is good for a dog; bind one down and he will holler." We know this is true and we old soldiers know that we had rather have our freedom and live on half rations, like we often had to do during the war, than to be in prison and have the best that the world could afford, (not that our prisoners fared well) and our sympathies are always great for people in bondage.

My dear surviving comrades, I love every one of you. Ah! yes, it's not half told, for I love the dust of all the dear ones who fell in the battle or otherwise. You are dear to my heart, and I would love to meet you all in a happy re-union, and I pray God, if in accordance with His will that we may all meet with Him in peace on the shores of sweet deliverance, where Jesus will be the captain of our salvation.

GENERALS LEE AND GORDON'S FAREWELL ADDRESS IN FULL.

General Lee's Last Order to the Army of Northern Virginia.

Headquarters, Army Northern Vinginia,
Appomattox C. H., April 10th, 1865.

General Order No. 9.

After four years of arduous service, marked by unsurpassed courage and fortitude, the Army of Northern Virginia has been compelled to surrender by overwhelming numbers and resources. I need not tell the survivors of so many hard fought battles, who have remained steadfast to the last, that I have consented to this result from no distrust of them, but feeling that valor and devotion could accomplish nothing that would compensate for the loss that must have attended a continuance of the contest, I have determined to avoid the useless sacrifice of those whose past service have endeared them to their countrymen.

By the terms of agreement, officers and men can return to their homes and remain there until exchanged.

You will take with you the satisfaction that proceeds from the consciousness of duty faithfully performed, and I earnestly pray that a merciful *God* will extend to you his blessings and protection.

With an unceasing admission of your constancy and devotion to your country and a grateful remembrance of your kind and generous consideration for myself, I bid you an affectionate farewell. R. E. LEE.

The soldiers were profoundly moved at the reading of this noble farewell address, and crowded around the beloved chieftain to shake his hand.

Responsive to their emotion he touchingly said: "Men, we have fought through the war together, I have done my best for you; my heart is too full to say more." And grandly indeed, had the simple utterances been attested.

It was a magnificent pageant from the Chichahominy to the final act at Appomattox Court House; sublime in its realization of valor, endurance and patriotism.

Freedom records no sacrifice surpassing it in magnitude.

And the grand hero, Lee, reilluminating the lustrous diadem of his mother, Virginia, is jointly enshrined in the reverential hearts of her sons with her Washington.

Crushingly overwhelmed, the starving Army of Northern Virginia laid down its arms, but its pitiful fate invested with mournful incense only its heroism and sacrifices.

Its achievements will increasingly command the admiration of the world during all time.

LIEUTENANT-GENERAL JOHN B. GORDON'S FAREWELL ADDRESS TO THE SECOND ARMY CORPS.

My Countrymen and Fellow-Soldiers :

Already has our great commander, General Robert E. Lee, spoken an affectionate farewell to the Army of Northern Virginia, No pen or words can add to his touching and patriotic address. I beg, however, as your late corps commander, the privilege of a few words in this sad hour of parting. Let me assure you that my heart goes out to each and every one of this gallant corps in this dark hour of disaster.

Do not doubt, my fellow-soldiers, that the future historians will give to you the full measure of your martial glory. Your battle-flags, now furled, tell of your heroic achievements. Thousands of your comrades, on almost every plain in old Virginia, sleep the sleep of death, yet the sleep of glory. But few survive the fierce conflict of civil war, and only a remnant is before me to-day to tell the story of the battles and privations of the Second army corps--the old corps of Stonewall Jackson. This corps and this Army of Northern Virginia will be remembered as long as the names of Stonewall Jackson and Robert E. Lee will be treasured by a grateful people. Overwhelmed by superior numbers and almost inexhaustible resources, together with the untiring energy and dauntless courage which has ever marked the military movements of the great leader of the Federal army, General Ulysses S. Grant, the Army of Northern Virginia—an army of heroes decemated by battle, disease and privation, through four years of almost continuous warfare—will now disband, never perhaps to meet again.

With our last parting, let me impress upon you one or two thoughts which, I trust, will go with you to your homes and firesides.

Remember that in God's providence we have surrendered, not to a foreign foe, but to our own countrymen. In the exhibition of your fortitude in the face of disaster, ever be as great and as good citizens as you have boen great and heroic soldiers.

Ever be the model citizens as you have been model soldiers. Obey the civil law, no matter how odious it may be temporarily. Discharge every duty as a citizen to your respective States and to the general government. Sustain the poor, help the feeble and succor the unfortunate in your midst, and by so doing you will command, not only the admiration and respect of the world, but win friendship and confidence of those who are now your political enemies.

Fellow soldiers, with my love and my benediction resting upon each and every one within the sound of my voice, I now bid you farewell.

May God, in his infinite mercy and kindness, protect and bless you and yours, now and forever.

No words can truly express the touching eloquence and tender pathos of the speaker or paint the scenes of that sad parting. It was a last good-bye from brother to brother.

With streaming eyes the veterans grasped the hand of their gallant leader. They retire, form in groups and speak in subdued tones. Comrade and comrade shake hands and part. Slowly they return to their bivouacs in the open field where stand the stacked arms in mute eloquence, the bayonets clasping each other as if in the last embrace of death. The battle-flags, rent with shot and shell, are now furled forever.

The Second army corps, of the Army of Northern Virginia, is no more, except as it shall ever live in history and in story, in poetry and in song.

I deem the following letter from General Lee to President Davis as a material addition to this narrative:

NEAR APPOMATTOX COURTHOUSE, April 12, 1865.

His Excellency, Jefferson Davis:

MR. PRESIDENT—It is with pain that I announce to your excellency the surrender of the Army of Northern Virginia. The operations which preceded this result will be reported in full. I will, therefore, now only state that upon arriving at Amelia C. H. on the morning of the 4th with the advance of the army on the retreat from the lines in front of Richmond and Petersburg, and not finding the supplies ordered to be placed there, nearly twenty-four hours were lost in endeavoring to collect in the country subsistence for men and horses. This delay was fatal and could not be retrieved. The troops, worried by constant fighting and marching for several days and nights, obtained neither rest nor refreshments, and on moving on the 5th on the Richmond and Danville railroad, I found at Jetersville the enemy's cavalry and learned of the approach of his infantry and the general advance of his army towards Burksville.

This deprived us of the use of the railroad and rendered it impracticable to procure from Danville the supplies ordered to meet us at points of our march.

Nothing could be obtained from the adjacent country. Our route to the Roanoke was therefore changed and the march directed upon Farmville, where supplies were ordered from Lynchburg. The change of route threw the troops over the roads pursued by artillery and wagon trains west of the railroad, which impeded our advance and embarrassed our movements.

On the morning of the 6th General Longstreet's corps reached Rice's Station, on the Lynchburg railroad. It was followed by the commands of Generals R. H. Anderson, Ewell and Gordon, with orders to close up on it as fast as the progress of the trains would permit, or as they could be directed on roads further west.

General Anderson, commanding, Picket's and B. R. Johnson's divisions become disconnected, with Mahone's division forming the rear of Longstreet. The enemy's cavalry penetrated the line of march through the intervals thus left, and attacked the wagon train moving toward Farmville. This caused serious delay in the march of the center and rear of the column, and enabled the enemy to mass upon their flank.

After successive attacks Generals Anderson's and Ewell's corps were captured or driven from their positions. The latter general with both of his division commanders, Kershaw and Custis Lee, and his brigades were taken prisoners. Gordon, who all the morning, aided by General W. H. F. Lee's cavalry, had checked the advance of the enemy on the road from Amelia Springs and protected the trains, became exposed to his combined assaults, which he bravely resisted and twice repulsed, but the cavalry, having been withdrawn to another part of the line of march and the enemy, massing heavily on his front and both flanks, renewed the attack about 6 P. M. and drove him from the field in much confusion. The army continued its march during the night and every effort was made to re-organize the divisions, which had been shattered by the day's operations. but the men, being depressed by fatigue and hunger, many threw away their arms while others followed the wagon trains and embarrassed their progress.

On the morning of the 7th, rations were issued to the troops as they passed Farmville, but the safety of the trains requiring their removal upon the approach of the enemy, all could not be supplied.

The army; reduced to two corps under Longstreet and

Gordon, moved steadily on the road to Appomattox Court House, thence its march was ordered by Campbell Court House through Pittsylvania toward Danville. The roads were wretched and the progress slow. By great efforts the head of the column reached Appomattox Court House on the evening of the 8th, and the troops were halted for rest.

The march was ordered to be resumed at one A. M. on the 9th. Fitzhugh Lee with the cavalry, supported by Gordon, was ordered to drive the enemy from his front, wheel to the left and cover the passage of the trains, while Longstreet, who from Rice's station had formed the rear guard, should close up and hold the position.

Two battalions of artillery and the ammunition wagons were directed to accompany the army; the rest of the artillery and wagons to move towards Lynchburg. In the early part of the night the enemy attacked Walker's artillery train near Appomattox station on the Lynchburg railroad and were repelled. Shortly afterwards their cavalry dashed towards the courthouse till halted by our line.

During the night there were indications of large forces massing on our left and front. Fitzhugh Lee was directed to ascertain his strength and to suspend his advance till daylight, if necessary. About five A. M. on the 9th, with Gordon on his left, he moved forward and opened the way.

A heavy force of the enemy was discovered opposite Gordon's right, which, moving in the direction of Appomattox C. H., drove back to the left of the cavalry and threatened to cut off Gordon from Longstreet, his cavalry at the same time threatening to envelop his left flank. Gordon withdrew across the Appomattox river and the cavalry advanced on the Lynchburg road, and became separated from the army. Learning the condition of affairs on the lines, where I had gone under the expectation of meeting General Grant to learn definitely the terms he proposed in a communication received from him on the 8th, in the event of the surrender of the army, I requested a suspension of hostilities until the terms could be arranged. In the interview which occurred with General Grant in compliance with my request, terms having been agreed upon, I surrended that portion of the Army of Northern Virginia which was on the field with its arms, artillery and wagon trains, the officers and men to be paroled, retaining their side arms and private effects. I deemed this course the best, under all the circumstances by which we were surrounded. On the morning of the 9th, according to the reports of the ordnance officers, there were seven thousand eight hundred and ninety-two (7,892) organized infantry with arms, with an average of seventy-five (75) rounds of ammunition per man.

The artillery, though reduced to sixty-three pieces with ninety-three rounds of ammunition, was sufficient.

These comprise all the supplies for ordnance that could be relied on in the state of Virginia.

I have no accurate report of the cavalry, but believe it did not exceed 21,00 effective men. The enemy was more than five times our numbers. If we could have forced our way one day longer, it would have been at a great sacrifice of life, and at its end I did not see how a surrender could have been avoided.

We had no subsistence for man or horse, and it could not be gathered in the country.

The supplies ordered to Pamplin's station from Lynchburg could not reach us, and the men, deprived of food and sleep for many days, were worn out and exhausted.

With great respect, I am your obedient servant.

(Signed) R. E. Lee, General,

THE SWORDS OF GRANT AND LEE.

FAME CROWNS BOTH WITH LAURELS.

Methinks tonight I catch a gleam of steel among the pines,
And yonder by the lilied streams repose the foeman's lines;
The ghostly guards who pace the ground a moment stop to see
If all is safe and still around the tents of Grant and Lee.

'Tis but a dream, no armies camp where once their bayonets shone,
And Hesper's calm and lovely lamp shines on the dead alone,
A cricket chirps on yonder rise beneath a cedar tree,
Where glinted 'neath the summer skies, the swords of Grant and Lee.

Forever sheathed those famous blades that led the eager van,
They shine no more among the glades that fringe the Rapidan;
Today their battle-work is done, go draw them forth and see
That not a stain appears upon the swords of Grant and Lee.

The gallant men who saw them flash in comradeship today,
Recall the wild, impetuous dash of valorous blue and grey,
And 'neath the flag that proudly waves above a nation free,
They oft recall the missing braves who fought with Grant and Lee.

They sleep among the tender gra s—they slumber 'neath the pines,
They're camping in the mountain-pass where crouched the serried lines;
They rest where loud tempests blow destruction in their glee—
The men who followed long ago the swords of Grant and Lee.

Their graves are lying side by side, where once they met as foes,
And where they in the wildwood died, springs up a blood-red rose;
O'er them the bee on golden wing doth flit, and in yon tree
A gentle robin seems to sing to them of Grant and Lee.

Today no strifes of sections rise, today no shadows fall
Upon our land and 'neath the skies one flag waves over all;
The Blue and Gray as comrades stand, as comrades bend the knee,
And ask God's blessings on the land that gave us Grant and Lee.

So long as southward, wide and clear, Potomac's river runs,
Their deeds will live because they were Columbia's hero sons;
So long as bend the northern pines and blooms the orange tree,
The swords will shine that led the lines of valiant Grant and Lee.

Methinks I hear a bugle blow; methinks I hear a drum,
And there, with martial step and slow, two ghostly armies come;
They are the men who met as foes, for 'tis the dead I see,
And side by side in peace repose the swords of Grant and Lee.

Above them let Old Glory wave and let each deathless star
Forever shine upon the brave who led the ranks of war.
Their fame resounds from coast to coast, from mountain tops to sea;
No other land than ours can boast the swords of Grant and Lee.

[Author unknown.—AUTHOR.]

TWO BROTHERS.

ONE IN BLUE, ONE IN GRAY.

I've wandered o'er Antietam, John,
And stood where foe met foe
Upon the field of Maryland
So many years ago.
The circling hills rise just the same
As they did on that day
When you were fighting blue, old boy,
And I was fighting gray.

The winding stream runs 'neath the bridge,
Where Burnsides won his fame;
The locust trees upon the ridge
Beyond are there the same;

The birds were singing 'mid the trees—
'Twas bullets on that day,
When you were fighting blue, old boy,
And I was fighting gray.

I saw again the Dunken church
That stood beside the wood,
Where Hooker made the famous charge
That Hill so well withstood.
'Tis scarred and marred by war and time
As we are, John, to-day,
For you were fighting blue, old boy,
And I was fighting gray.

I stood beneath the signal tree
Where I that day was laid,
And 'twas your arms, old boy, that brought
Me to this friendly shade.
Tho' leaves are gone and limbs are bare,
Its heart is true to-day
As yours was then, tho' fighting blue,
To me tho' fighting gray.

I marked the spot where Mansfield fell,
Where Richardson was slain,
With Stark and Douglas, 'mid the corn,
And Brant among the grain.
The names are sacred to us, John,
They led us in the fray,
When you were fighting Northern blue
And I the Southern gray.

I thought of Burnsides, Hooker, Meade,
Of Sedgwick, old and grave—
Of Stonewall Jackson, tried and true,
That strove the day to save.

I bared my head—they rest in peace—
  Each one has passed away;
Death musters those who wave the blue
  With those who wore the gray.

The old Pry mansion rears its walls
  Beside Antietam's stream,
And far away along the south
  I saw the tombstones gleam.
They mark each place where "Little Mac"
  And Robert Lee that day
Made proud the North, tho' wearing blue,
  The South tho' wearing grey.

Yes, John, it gave me joy to stand
  Where we once fiercely fought.
The nation now is one again,
  The lesson has been taught.
Sweet peace does fair Antietam crown,
  And we can say today:
"We're friends," tho' one was fighting blue
  And one was fighting grey.

[The author of the above is unknown, or we would take pleasure in giving it.—AUTHOR."]

CHAPTER XVIII.

W. H. Bland's Prison Life.

Baxley, Ga., December 20th, 1897.

Mr. G. W. Nichols, Jesup, Ga.:

My Dear Sir and Old Comrade—Yours to hand, asking me for my prison life, which I will try to give you. I know I cannot recollect everything that happened in the prison that might interest you or the readers of your history; but I will do the best I can, and will tell the truth. As you know, I am a poor scholar, and will have to give it to you in my own language.

I was captured at Dr. Morton's house, near Morton's ford, on the Rapidan river, on the night of the 4th of January, 1864, after we had shot away nearly all of our ammunition.

My capture happened in this way: I was at Dr. Morton's dwelling house, while you and others of our company were fighting from behind other houses.

As you well know, our skirmish line had given the Yankees a whipping, killing, wounding and capturing 400 or 500, and there were not over forty of us fighting them, and after our ammunition had exhausted, the Yankees surrounded Dr. Morton's house just at dark.

I had gone in the house and did not know that any part of our line had given way until Dr. Morton's house was entirely surrounded by the enemy. I did not see any of our boys leaving, so I was alone, and was surrounded by about fifty Union soldiers, and I just *had* to surrender. They took me to the rear in a hurry, for they were scared and in bad confusion.

When I and my guard got to the river I found that it

was bridged with round poles, and lacked a few feet of being finished on the south side of the river, and we had to make a pretty good jump to get on the bridge. I made it very well, as I was an expert jumper, so did my guard, he being sober; but some of those little cut-short Dutchmen could not make it very well, with the amount of whisky they had taken on. They could not reach the bridge, but did reach the water under the bridge, and some were too drunk to swim and some could not swim, and they drowned, for it was very dark and rainy, and their friends could not render them any assistance.

After we had crossed the river and had gone about three hundred yards from the river, we found some camp-fires. I was taken to them and kept there till the Yankees got across. After all were over, they formed in line and marched off. We went about four miles and camped.

They had a hard time in getting fire started with oak brush and chips in the rain. My guard and I sat down by an oak stump on our knap-sacks He spread his oil-cloth over us to keep off the falling rain. He was soon nodding and I thought he was asleep. I lifted the cloth off of me and raised up to run; but he woke up; so I turned over my knap-sack and sat down again quickly, to keep him from suspecting my anticipated escape. He spread the cloth over me again and I remained very quiet. He was soon nodding again and I made a second attempt, but he woke again.

By this time they had fires started and he said: "Well, Johnny, we will go to the light," and I saw no chance of making my escape.

Next day we marched about nine miles and reached their old camp. I was put in a guard house with about a dozen of their own prisoners. I being the only "Johnny Rebel" (as they called me) there, I was treated kindly. Next morning I was sent for to go to General Hayes' headquarters. While going through the camps the Yankees would say, "Hello, Johnny, when did you come over?" I would reply, "I was captured and *brought* over," for I did not want them to think that I was a deserter.

The general's headquarters were some four or five hundred yards away. When I got there the guard said: "General, here is our Johnny Reb." The general wheeled around and said: "Hello, Johnny, how do you feel today?" I replied, "I feel very well, general, how do you feel?" He said, "I am well." "Well, Johnny, do you wish to go back across the river?" I told him that I did. He says, "Oh, no, Johnny, you don't wish to go back!" "Well," says I, " all you have to do is to give me a showing to that effect, and you will see that I go back." "Well, Johnny, how are you faring on your side of the river?" I told him "I was faring very well." "Well, Johnny, what do you get to eat on your side of the river?" I replied, "bacon, flour, rice, sugar, coffee, etc." "Why, Johnny, do you draw all of that?" "Yes, sir." (Which we did, but it was scanty, especially the coffee and sugar.)

By this time he was looking in my haversack. I happened to have two day's rations for four men, and he said: "Did you draw all of this meat, Johnny?" I said "Yes, sir." "How many days is this rations for, Johnny?" I said, "two days." He turned to another general and said: "Look at the meat, general?" He replied, "Yes, I see."

He then said: "How is it, Johnny, that some of your men come over here and say that you are all on starvation?" I said, "Well, any man who will desert his country, will tell you a lie." And I further said, "As to my regiment and brigade, *we* fare very well; but as to the rest of our army, *I* can't account for."

He then said, "How is Lee's army situated?" I said, "I guess you know more about that than I do." "How much force has he got?" I says, "You know more about that than I can tell you." He turned to another general and said: "This is a fine man, general, if he *is* a Rebel." He said, "What was your loss Johnny?" I told him that I did not know. "Did you see many dead men?" I told him that I did not see any. I then asked him his losses, and he said that they lost between four and five hundred. I said, "Well, we did very well then." (I have since learned that we had two killed, one wounded and I was captured, which made a total of four.)

He told me that they all got on a drunken spree and he rushed his men over the river without orders, and that he was under arrest that day.

He told me that he rode on our skirmish line for some distance in the dark and was halted several times, but he said he told them that it was General Hayes and was allowed to go on. He said, "You have a General Hayes, which was all that saved my life."

The general then said, "Johnny, don't you want a drink of good brandy this morning?" I told him I could not refuse as I had taken a cold. He poured out a fine drink and gave it to me, and I drank it. He said, "Well, Johnny, we will have to send you to prison."

I was taken to a place that they called their "Bull Pen," about thirty miles away. Here I found six or eight more Confederate prisoners. This was on the railroad running from Fredericksburg to Alexandria and Washington. We had plenty to eat, but we came near freezing. We stayed here two days and nights and were carried to the City of Washington and put in prison in the old capitol building, which they were using for a wayside prison.

Our fare was very good for prisoners, though we were closely confined. We were in a room about eighteen feet square, which had a good fire-place, and plenty of coal and blankets. Here a Confederate prisoner from Florida killed a Confederate prisoner from Virginia while in a mad fit; but he was afterwards very sorry of the deed.

One day Mosby's cavalry made a raid on the railroad near Alexandria, Va., and caused some confusion in the City of Washington. We stayed here about four months with excellent fare; we had plenty to eat and good coffee to drink, and I weighed more than I ever did before or since. We were transferred from there to Fort Delaware. Here some Confederates made a lot of money shut up in a prison with no other tools but saws made out of case-knives, pocket-knifes, needle drills and hand-saw files, and some other small files; making bone and gutta-percha rings and putting gold and silver sets in them; and a great many other little things were made and sold by the Confederate prisoners. They traded with citizens, Yankee officers and private Yankee soldiers.

Here we fared extremely bad—in fact, we were perished very nearly to death. I would often dream of being at home at my mother's table, with a plenty of good things on it, and in my dreams I would eat and eat, but it seemed that I could never get enough. I would awaken nearly perished to death. Our rations consisted of one-fourth of a one-half pound loaf of bakers' bread. We got this twice a day. Our meat consisted of a very small, thin slice of salt pork or fresh beef, which made about one good mouthful, with one Irish potato occasionally thrown in extra.

I often gave up to perish to death. I was so nearly starved till I was reduced from 140 to 80 pounds. This caused bone-scurvy amongst a great many of the Confederate soldiers, and a great many died.

One man bet his blanket that he could eat every bit of his bread at one mouthful. He did this and won the blanket. The prisoners ate every rat they could catch. They were fine and highly relished by the prisoners, and if we could have caught a plenty of rats, we would have gotten along a great deal better than we did.

In extremely cold weather all the water we had to drink was real brackish tide water. It would not quench thirst but made us want water much worse. But we sometimes had river water brought to us in boats from up the river. We only received this brackish water when it was so cold they could not bring the other. We privates were in one department and the officers were in another. We could have no communication with them only when we could write a few lines on paper, tie it to a stone and throw it over the wall to them, when the guards were not watching us. They would often answer in the same way.

About 6,000 prisoners were there. Our guards were all old soldiers who had been used to hard service, and were mostly square gentlemen. They were kind to us and would often divide their tobacco with us and show us other acts of kindness.

I do not think we received all the government sent there for us, or intended for us to have, but I believe it was abominable rascality and speculation of some of the head managers of the prison; I am sure that, from what we heard, the officers' fare was, if possible, worse than ours.

I stayed in this prison about ten months and had the small-pox in that time. There was a department in the prison for each Southern state, and 1,000 privates were in the Georgia department.

They paroled us all, with ten Georgia officers, and marched us to the boat and put us on it.

We started about 11 o'clock A. M., on the 7th of March, 1865, to City Point, below Richmond, Va.

Six prisoners died on the boat and were buried on the banks of the James river, near City Point.

When we put our feet on Dixie's soil, how our hearts leaped with joy and our eyes filled with tears.

We were marched along through the Yankee army, which was between City Point and our army at Drewry's Bluff.

We were put on a boat and taken up the river to a landing near Richmond, Va., and marched to Camp Lee, two miles from Richmond. At Camp Lee, we drew money and clothing and stayed there four days and then received a sixty days furlough. I then started home to see my mother. I had a rough time getting home, for Sherman had torn up a great many of our railroads.

I was very poor and weak, and could walk but a short distance at a time. I arrived at home on the 27th of March, 1865. I took those at home on surprise, for they all thought that I was dead, for they had not received one bit of hearing from me in about fifteen months.

Hoping this will give you and the readers of your history of our company, regiment and brigade satisfaction, I will close. It is all true and I could tell a great deal more about my prison life, which would be true; but deeming this sufficient, I am yours very truly,

W. H. BLAND.

ROSTER OF COMPANIES

OF

THE SIXTY-FIRST GEORGIA REGIMENT.

COMPANY B.

FROM TATTNALL COUNTY, GEORGIA, FROM AUGUST, 1861, TO APRIL, 1865.

Captain A. P. McRae; promoted to major; killed at Sharpsburg, Md., September 17, 1862.

First Lieutenant D. R. A. Johnson; promoted to captain; wounded at Spotsylvania, Va., May 12, 1864; died at home.

Second Lieutenant J. M. Dus; resigned 1862.

Third Lieutenant William Partan; died in the hospital at Guinna Station, 1863.

Anderson, B.; mortally wounded at Fredericksburg December 13, 1862; died in hospital from wounds.

Brewton, B. B.; wounded at Gettysburg, Pa., July 1, 1863; yet living.

Burlong, J. T.; yet living.

Blocker, J. A.; wounded at Mary's Heights, May, 1863. yet living.

Blocker, John; wounded at Fredericksburg December 13, 1862; died from wounds.

Blocker, Cornelius; wounded at Gettysburg, Pa.; died from wounds.

Blocker, W. H.; transferred to Company K, Sixty-first Georgia Regiment.

Burkhalter, John; killed at Gettysburg July 1, 1863.

Butts, Frank; killed at Gettysburg July 1, 1863.

Bazell, W. H.; killed at Winchester, Va., September 19, 1864.

Bell, J. W.; killed at Wilderness May 5, 1864.

Bell, J. C.; died in hospital; time and place unknown.

Burk, Edward; transferred to Company K, Sixty-first Georgia Regiment; captured at Mine Run, 1863.

Curry, D. L., corporal; captured at Spotsylvania May 12, 1864.

Colson, D. C.; died at home since the war.

Cook, M. J.; died in hospital in 1862; time and place unknown.

Dinkins, Joseph; put in substitute 1862.

Dinkins, William; went in as substitute for Joseph Dinkins; killed at Fredericksburg December 13, 1862.

Dinkins, E. W.; deserted at Fredericksburg, 1862.

DeLoach, Wiley O.; wounded in Seven Days' battle, July, 1862; disabled and discharged.

Driggers, J. T; transferred to Company K, 1862.

Driggers, Zachariah; transferred to Company K, 1862.

Dubberly, W. W; killed at Fredericksburg, December 13th, 1862.

Floyd, William; killed at Gettysburg, July 1st, 1863.

Findley, Jordan; transferred to Company K, Sixty-first Georgia Regiment, 1862.

Findley, Lemuel; transferred to Company K, Sixty-first Georgia Regiment, 1862.

Gray, William F.; wounded at Warrenton, Va., 1862; captured at Spotsylvania, May 12th, 1864; yet living.

Grooms, Joseph J.; wounded at Manocacy, Md., July 9th, 1864, and captured.

Grooms, Jackson; died at Farmville Hospital, 1862.

Grooms, J. W.; died in hospital November, 1862; place unknown.

Grant, William; died with fever, 1861.

Green, David; wounded in battle Wilderness, May 5, 1864; died at home since the war.

Grace, Thomas, corporal; killed in battle, Fredericksburg, December 13th, 1862.

Henderson, Hughey; discharged, inability.

Hammock, J. M.; killed in second battle Manassas, August 29th, 1862.

Harrington, Dennis, color bearer; killed at Petersburg, 1865.

Hagan, W. I.; detailed hospital nurse; died since the war.

Hagan, S. W. W., drummer; detailed drummer, surrendered at Appomatox, April 9th, 1865; yet living.

Hagan, Joseph; died in hospital, 1863.

Hutchinson, Isaac; died in hospital, 1862.

Higgs, William; wounded in Sharpsburg, September 17th, 1862.

Jernegan, Jesse; still living.

Jarrell, John, (Snug); captured at Winchester, September 19th, 1864.

McBride, John; died in hospital in Virginia; place unknown.

McBride, A. G.; killed at Fredericksburg, December 13th, 1862.

Manning, J. T.; died at home since the war.

Martin, J. C.; captured at Mine Run, 1863.

Morris, W. P.; yet living.

Moore, C. H., sergeant; wounded in Seven-days battle before Richmond, beginning June 27, 1862; died from wounds.

Moore, W. F.; transfered to Company K, Sixty-first Georgia Regiment; wounded at Mary's Heights, May 2, 1863.

Moore, A. P., lieutenant; elected lieutenant in Company H, Sixty-first Georgia Regiment, and transferred.

Mattox, W. E.; wounded at Gaines' Mill June 27, 1862; again at Chantilly September 1, 1862; yet living.

Mattox, J. T.; wounded at Gettysburg, Pa., July 1, 1863; yet living.

Mabry, S.; died in hospital 1862.

Odum, D. H.; transferred to Company K, Sixty-first Georgia Regiment, May, 1862.

Odum, A. G.; transferred to Company K, Sixty-first Georgia Regiment.

Odum, J. H.; wounded at Gettysburg July 1, 1863.

Partin, Joseph; died in hospital; time and place unknown.

Partin, John, jr.; missing; unknown what became of him.

Partin, John, sr.; discharged—over age.

Partin, Hugh; died in hospital; time and place unknown.

Powell, Abraham; wounded at Sharpsburg, Md., September 17, 1862; again at Spotsylvania C. H., May 12, 1864; killed at home since the war.

Powell, Jackson; yet living.

Pearson, Charlie, sergeant; captured at Spotsylvania C. H., May 17, 1864.

Pittman, Julius; wounded at Sharpsburg, Md., September 17, 1862; died from wounds.

Rewis, G. E.; unknown.

Rewis, R. R.; wounded at Fredricksburg December 13, 1862; missing.

Rewis, J. J.; served through the war.

Rewis, James; faithful soldier; served through the war.

Rewis, Madison; unknown.

Reddish, P. J.; discharged—over age.

Riggs, A. B.; wounded at Gaines' Mill June 27, 1862; **died at home, 1898.**

Riggs, W. S.; wounded at Gettysburg, Pa., July 1, 1863; yet living.

Rodgers, P. W.; sergeant; wounded at Sharpsburg, Md., September 17th, 1862; killed at Fredericksburg December 13th, 1862.

Rodgers, W. W.; discharged—disability.

Strickland, H. S.; discharged—disability.

Smith, Simon; died 1862, in hospital, time and place unknown.

Shuman, Elias; died in hospital, Louisa Court House, 1862.

Sharp, H. R.; second sergeant; transferred to Company K, Sixty-first Georgia Regiment and elected first sergeant; faithful soldier; in very near all the battles; never received wound; surrendered at Appomattox; yet living.

Smith, C. W.; severely wounded at Fredericksburg December 13, 1862; lost leg; is yet living and is ordinary Tattnall county, Ga.

Smith, D. H.; discharged; mail contractor 1863; died at home.

Smith, A. A.; killed at Gettysburg July 1, 1863.

Sharp, E. F.; first sergeant; transferred to Company K, Sixty-first Georgia Regiment; elected captain; served through the war; was never seriously wounded; in nearly every battle the regiment was engaged in: commanded regiment from July 9, 1864, until January 16, 1865; received furlough home; cut off by Sherman; is yet living at St. Cloud, Florida; faithful soldier and good commander.

Sharp, J. T.; sergeant; transferred to Company K, Sixty-first Georgia Regiment.

Sharp, G. W.; missing; unknown.

Sharp, Jesse; yet living.

Surrency, W. M.; died in hospital June, 1862.

Surrency, Samuel; transferred to Company K, Sixty-first Georgia Regiment; faithful soldier.

Surrency, H. W.; captured at Winchester September 19, 1864; yet living.

Surrency, A. H.; transferred to Company K, Sixty-first Georgia Regiment; wounded at Spotsylvania C. H., May 12, 1864.

Surrency, Allen A.; transferred to Company K, Sixty-first Georgia Regiment.

Galley 68

Stafford, Joshua; transferred to Company K, Sixty-first Georgia Regiment.

Stafford, Eli; wounded at Spotsylvania C. H. May 12, 1864; yet living.

Strickland, E. D., sergeant; wounded at Fredericksburg December 13th, 1862; died at home.

Sheffield, John; transferred to Company K, Sixty-first Georgia Regiment.

Salter, William; transferred to Fiftieth Georgia Regiment.

Saturday, G. W.; captured at Spotsylvania May 12, 1864.

Stripling, A. A.; wounded at Sharpsburg, Md., September 17, 1862; died at home.

Stripling, R. W., lieutenant; captured at Spotsylvania C. H. May 12, 1864; died at home.

Stripling, Lauda, lieutenant; transferred to Company K, Sixty-first Georgia Regiment; elected lieutenant latter part of war.

Sikes, Hampton; transferred to Company K, Sixty-first Georgia Regiment; detailed in litter corps; good one; died since war.

Sapp, Jackson; missing; unknown.

Thrift, John; wounded in battle Wilderness May 5, 1864; died at home.

Thompson, R. W.; died at home.

Todd, W. W.; wounded at Sharpsburg, Md., September 17, 1862; died in hospital, Richmond, 1862.

Todd, C. D.; wounded at Fredericksburg December 13, 1862; yet living.

Tootle, James; wounded at Gettysburg July 1, 1863, and captured at Monocacy July 9, 1864.

Vincient, S. D.; wounded at Mine Run November, 1863, and captured at Spotsylvania C. H. May 12, 1864.

Varnadore, A. J.; captured at Spotsylvania C. H. May 12, 1864; died, time and place unknown, supposed in prison.

Williams, C; died on Jekyl Island, February, 1862.

Williams, R.; died in Richmond hospital, 1862.

Waters, Amos; missing; died, time and place unknown.

Waters, J. M.; transferred to Company K, Sixty-first Georgia Regiment.

Wolf, Lewis; transferred to Company K, Sixty-first Georgia Regiment.

Webb, Jackson; transferred to Company K, Sixty-first Georgia Regiment.

Yeomans, J. S.; yet living.

COMPANY C.

FROM BROOKS COUNTY, FROM SEPTEMBER 7TH, 1861, TO APRIL 9TH, 1865.

Captain James Mc Donald; elected lieutenant-colonel at organization of regiment; resigned on account of age and infirmity; died since the war.

First Lieutenant J. A. Edmonson; promoted to captain; resigned on account of infirmity; died since the war,

Second Lieutenant Daniel Mc Donald; promoted to captain; wounded at Sharpsburg, September 17th, 1862; Fredericksburg, December 13th, 1862; captured at Spotsylvania C. H., May 12th, 1864; yet living.

Third Lieutenant J. M. Harris; resigned on account of imfirmity; yet living.

First Sergeant N. M. Reddick; wounded at Fredericksburg; served through the war a faithful soldier; surrendered at Appomattox; died since the war.

Second Sergeant Remer Dukes; killed in the Valley of Virginia, 1864.

Third Sergeant John Percell; yet living in Quitman, Georgia; was detailed in charge of an engineering corps.

Fourth Sergeant E. W. Wincey; killed at South Anna, Va., in May, 1864.

Fifth Sergeant S. D. Strickland; died in hospital at Staunton, Va., 1862.

First Sergeant J. W. Dukes; yet living in Quitman county, Ga.; faithful soldier.

First Corporal G. M. Taylor; killed at Sharpsburg, on September 17th, 1862.

Second Corporal J. R. Ricks; captured at Gettysburg; yet living.

Third Corporal E. Gray; died in hospital, place unknown.

Fourth Corporal Alfred Strickland; died in hospital; faithful soldier.

Allen, Dempsy; died with smallpox.

Alderman, Henry; faithful soldier; yet living.

Alderman, Isaac; faithful soldier; died in hospital.

Alderman, William; killed at Rappahannock by a shell August, 1862.

Alderman, Thomas; killed in difficulty since the war.

Alderman, D; died at Guinea Station in 1862 in small-pox hospital.

Beaty, James L.; elected second lieutenant; good officer and soldier; living in Texas.

Beaty, Berrien; faithful soldier; yet living.

Burney, James; killed at Sharpsburg.

Burney, E.; transferred to navy in 1864; yet living.

Butler, E.; in Colquitt county, Ga.; yet living.

Browning, Neal; living in Virginia; married there during the war; yet living.

Browning, J.; died in hospital at Charleston, S. C., in 1862.

Baker, I.; faithful soldier; yet living.

Burgess, J.; faithful soldier; yet living.

Carlton, T.; faithful soldier; died in hospital

Carlton, A.; faithful soldier; died in hospital.

Carlton, Aaron; faithful soldier; died in hospital.

Colter, J.; wounded at Gettysburg; died since the war.

Colter, William; wounded at Sharspburg; killed at Tallokas, Ga., 1876.

Croft, William; wounded at Gettysburg; arm shot off; yet living.

Croft, G.; killed at Fredricksburg.

Dixon, R.; killed at Sharpsburg.

Dukes, E.; preaching in Florida; faithful soldier; yet living.

Duggan, A.; died in hospital.

Duggan, B.; yet living.

Dugger, J.; died in hospital.

Durst, J. M.; faithful soldier; yet living.

Dampier, M.; transferred; died at home.

Edwards, A.; faithful soldier; yet living.

Edmonson, S. D.; wounded at Sharpsburg; furnished substitute; yet living.

Floyd, L.; killed at Gettysburg.

Flowers, W.; discharged on account of infirmity; died since war.

Gunn, William; yet living.

Gunn, J.; deserted or killed on our return from Pennsylvania.

Gray, T.; died in hospital in 1862.

Gray, Josh; faithful soldier; yet living.

Golman, J.; faithful soldier; yet living.

Goodwin, E.; killed at Gettysburg in 1863.

Hires, D.; killed at Sharpsburg in 1862.

Hammock, J.; died in hospital in 1862.

Holloway, W.; killed at Wilderness in 1864.

Hurnden, J.; wounded at Mine Run in 1863; yet living.

Hancock, A.; wounded at Fredericksburg in 1862; yet living.

Hancock, J.; wounded at Sharpsburg; yet living.

Harris, B.; died in hospital in 1862.

Harris, J.; died in hospital in 1862.

Harris, R.; died in hospital in 1862.

Hood, Calvin; captured in 1864; was never heard from since; extra fine soldier.

Ireland, T. J.; wounded at Fredericksburg; yet living.

Ireland, William; killed at Sharpsburg.

Ingram, Sam; died in hospital in 1862.

Johnson, J. J.; furnished substitute; died since war.

Johnson, J. W., M. D.; wounded and captured at Gettysburg; yet living.

Keene, R.; faithful soldier; died since war.

Kent, G.; wounded at Gettysburg; died since war.

Lovett, J.; died in hospital in Richmond, Va., July, 1862.

Lovett, William ; died in hospital in Strasburg, Va., 1862, with pneumonia.

Lovett, Aaron ; faithful soldier ; yet living.

Lewis, M.; faithful soldier ; yet living.

Lewis, A.; wounded in battle; died in hospital; place not remembered.

Lewis, J.; wounded at Gettysburg and Wilderness; died in hospital.

Lewis, H.; died at home after being discharged for disabilities.

Little, T. E.; died at Bethesda, spine being injured by diving to the bottom of a stream; died in hospital.

McDow, F. M.; wounded at Sharpsburg with flag in hand; captured at Spotsylvania C. H. May 12, 1864, with flag; died in prison.

McMullen, H. O.; wounded in battle in 1864; lost a leg; yet living.

McMullen, W.; died in hospital after Manassas battle.

McGrow, R. A.; discharged for disabilities; yet living.

McGrow, H.; died in hospital, time and place not known.

Moore, J. T.; faithful soldier; yet living.

Miller, J.; killed at Fredericksburg December, 1862.

Mobley, William; discharged; yet living.

Newton, William; faithful soldier; died in hospital.

Newton, G. W.; faithful soldier; yet living.

Nesmith, T. R.; faithful soldier; died since war.

Nesmith, Henry; faithful soldier; died in hospital.

Rainey, B.; wounded at Gaines' Mill, 1862; disabled and discharged; yet living.

Rainey, J.; wounded at Sharpsburg, Va.; died in hospital at Strasburg, Va., 1862.

Ricks, George; faithful soldier; yet living.

Royal, I. A.; killed at Wilderness.

Royal, D. A.; elected second lieutenant; promoted to first lieutenant; wounded at Wilderness, 1864; yet living.

Reddick, Peter; died in hospital at Jekyl Island with measles in 1861.

Roberts, H.; faithful soldier; yet living.

Rentford, R. T. R.; faithful soldier; died in hospital.

Selph, G. W.; faithful soldier; yet living.

Selph, J. W.; killed at Cold Harbor.

Selph, J.; faithful soldier; yet living.

Selph, Tom; faithful soldier; yet living.

Sloan, J.; wounded at Gettysburg; elected sheriff of Colquitt county during war and resigned his office of lieutenant.

Sloan, N.; wounded and captured at Gettysburg; died in prison.

Salter, William; transferred; yet living.

Sherrod, James; wounded at Sharpsburg; yet living.

Sherrod, John; died in hospital after the battle of the Wilderness.

Strickland, S. A.; died in hospital at Whitehall, Va., 1862.

Strickland, Shade; died in hospital in 1862.

Strickland, S. S.; wounded at Sharpsburg; died since war.

Strickland, J.; faithful soldier; died since war.

Smith, Joe; killed at Fredericksburg, December, 1862.

Smith, Hill; wounded at Gettysburg and discharged; yet living.

Smith, James; leg cut off by a train at Richmond, Va., when he had started home on a furlough; died since war.

Smith, W. H. C.; wounded at Fisher's Hill in 1864; yet living.

Smith, G. W.; died in hospital, place not remembered.

Tyson, John; died in hospital, place not remembered.

Wincey, Freeman; died in hospital at Camp Bethesda, Ga., in 1862.

Wingate, L.; died in hospital, time and place not remembered.

Watkins, A. W.; wounded at Mine Run in 1863; yet living.

Weldon, John; killed at Sharpsburg, Md.

Weldon, Isaac; surrendered at Appomattox; yet living.

Yates, Wyley; captured and died in prison in 1864.

Yates, James; wounded at Malvern Hill in 1862; yet living.

Yates, Stephen; faithful soldier; died in hospital.

COMPANY D.

DEKALB GUARDS, FROM BULLOCH COUNTY, FROM SEPTEMBER 9TH, 1861, TO APRIL 9TH, 1865.

Captain Henry Tillman; resigned after the seven days' battle before Richmond; died since war.

First Lieutenant S. H. Kennedy; promoted to captain after seven days' battle; wounded at Manassas; promoted to lieutenant-colonel in January, 1865; severely wounded at Deep Run on February 6, 1865; an excellent officer and brave soldier; yet living.

Second Lieutenant J. H. Wilkinson; resigned in 1862; yet living.

Third Lieutenant J. Hoyt DeLoach; discharged in 1862; yet living.

First Sergeant J. E. C. Tillman; transferred to Company K; elected third lieutenant; yet living.

Second Sergeant W. H. Williams; promoted to adjutant; wounded at Deep Run February 6, 1865; unknown.

Third Sergeant James Mincy; elected to lieutenancy; wounded at Manassas, Gettysburg and Monocacy; yet living.

Fourth Sergeant J. L. B. Nevils; killed at Manassas.

First Corporal E. J. Martin; wounded on Three Tops mountain; a most excellent soldier; assassinated since the war.

Second Corporal William Lee; killed at Spotsylvania, C. H.

Third Corporal W. A. Woods; wounded at Fredrick City, Md.; yet living.

Fourth Corporal William Holloway; faithful soldier; captured on the last retreat before the surrender; yet living.

Alderman, J. W.; promoted to sergeant; missing at the battle of Cedar Creek, in 1864; died since the war.

Anderson, John; killed at Gettysburg.

Beasley, J. R.; wounded at Gaines' mill; came home on a furlough and never returned; yet living.

Boyet, Thomas; was in nearly all the battles and never wounded; surrendered at Appomattox; faithful soldier; yet living.

Brannen, John; promoted to lieutenant; killed at Manassas.

Bland, W. H.; captured at hospital in Frederick City, Md., in 1862, but was exchanged; was captured again at Morton's Ford in 1864; paroled March 7th, 1865; yet living.

Barrow, Isaac; killed at Fredricksburg in 1862.

Bowen, B. F.; died in hospital at Staunton, Va., in 1862.

Bird, Adam; detailed to a government bakery; yet living.

Butts, Frank; killed at Manassas in 1862.

Banks, ——; died at Brunswick or Bethesda in 1862.

Cruce, J. A. J.; killed at North Anna; promoted to sergeant in 1861.

Connell, Timothy; missing in 1863; unknown.

Collins, W. H.; faithful soldier; died since war.

Collins, Ziba J.; transferred to Company K; killed at Monocacy, Md., July 9, 1864.

Collins, G. A.; supposed to be killed at the battle of Manassas; missing.

Collins, M. V.; enlisted at the age of sixteen (company's pet); was in most of the battles; was sick and got a furlough just before the war closed; yet living.

Chenutt, Drew; detailed for a drummer and was transferred; unknown.

Collins, J. J.; wounded at Gaines' mill; died since the war.

Collins, A. J.; transferred to Company K; wounded at Gaines' Mill and Winchester; yet living.

Collins, Berrien; killed at second battle of Manassas.

Collins, R. J.; captured on the retreat from Petersburg; yet living.

Collins, Neal; died in hospital at Jekyl Island or Bethesda.

Cartee, William; discharged from hospital and returned home; died since the war.

Cartee, Ruben; died in hospital in Richmond in July, 1862.

Cartee, John; died in hospital in Richmond in July, 1862.

Cartee, Malichi; died in hospital in Richmond in July, 1862.

Davis, Henry; put in substitute and retired; died since the war.

Davis, Lemuel; yet living.

Dixon, Jasper; killed in government machine shop in 1861.

Driggers, Henry; killed in Brunswick by an assassin named Peterson in 1861.

Ellis, Joshua; wounded at Manassas; promoted to sergeant; secured a furlough and was at home at the close; still living.

Franklin, Mitchel; died in hospital at Charlottsville, Va., June, 1862.

Franklin, Hiram; promoted to lieutenant; wounded at Fredericksburg, 1862; totally disabled for service and retired; yet living.

Franklin, Remer; detailed for ambulance driver; wounded at Fort Stephens near Petersburg; surrendered at Appomatox; yet living.

Franklin, Hardy; died in Valley of Virginia, 1862.

Frawley, Daniel; missing; unknown.

Fitzsimmons, P.; missing; unknown.

Green, Charlton; detailed in government bakery; yet living.

Green, M. J.; captured at Spotsylvania, 1864; remained in prison the rest of the war; yet living.

Green, Sol.; discharged in 1861; died since the war.

Hendrix, M. B.; crippled and disabled at Bruntwick, Ga.; yet living.

Hendrix, J. J.; detailed to litter corps; severely wounded in the leg at Monocacy, Md.; captured and remained in prison till the close of the war; yet living.

Hendrix, G. F.; wounded and totally disabled for service at Manassas; yet living.

Hodges, A. W.; discharged from company; after getting well joined First Georgia Regiment and was killed at Peachtree creek, near Atlanta, Ga., July 22, 1864.

Hodges, Wesley; killed at Gaines' mill, 1862.

Hodges, S. W.; discharged in 1861; yet living.

Hodges, J. C.; promoted to sergeant; mortally wounded at Sharpsburg; brains shot out, and died eleven days afterward.

Hodges, G. W.; faithful soldier; yet living.

Holloway, Joshua; severely wounded at Sharpsburg, Md.; yet living.

Jones, Silas E.; mortally wounded at Fredericksburg and died in Richmond a few days afterwards.

Jones, T. B.; wounded in toe at Gaines' mill in 1862.

Jones, Henry; died in hospital in 1862.

Jerrell, John L.; wounded at Manassas; lost right arm; yet living.

Kicklighter, Alfred; wounded in the valley near Newtown, Virginia, in 1864; yet living.

Kicklighter, William; killed at North Anna in 1864.

Kennedy, William; died in hospital at Bethesda in 1862.

Kenneday, S. H., Jr.; killed at Manassas.

Kirkland, Joshua; killed at Gaines' mill in 1862.

Lewis, Wyley; killed at Manassas August 29, 1862.

Nichols, A. J.; killed at Gaines' mill June 27, 1862.

Nichols, G. W.; slightly wounded at Maryland Heights and Winchester; yet living.

Olliff, Henry; killed at Spotsylvania May 12, 1864.

Parrish, Daniel; wounded at Gaines' mill; totally disabled and had to retire; yet living.

Parrish, Isaiah; died at Waynesville, Ga., in 1862.

Parrish, H.; died in hospital in 1862.

Rimes, A. M.; wounded at Gaines' mill in 1862 and Morton's Ford Jan. 4, 1864.

Rushing, Harrison; killed at Gettysburg.

Scarboro, Newton; transferred to Company K and killed at Gettysburg.

Scarboro, G. W.; transferred to Company K; yet living.

Smith, John; captured (place unknown); yet living.

Smith, M. V.; wounded (place unknown) and retired; died since war.

Summerlin, Ive; in most of battles; was never hurt; surrendered at Appomattox; yet living.

Summerlin, D.; left, sick, by the roadside; never heard from again.

Turner, Jackson; killed at Manassas.

Turner, Sam; detailed to litter corps; captured at Rockville, Md., in 1864; died since war.

Underwood, Wyley; killed at Fredericksburg December 13, 1862.

Warren, Sim; got sick and retired; yet living.

Warren, Irvin; died in Richmond hospital in 1862.

Warren, Madison; severely wounded at Fredericksburg; went through the rest of the war; surrendered at Appomattox; yet living.

Warren, F. M.; wounded and totally disabled at Gaines' Mill; yet living.

Williams, R. J.; wounded at Gaines' Mill; went home on a furlough; elected captain in Forty-seventh Georgia Regiment and transferred; yet living.

Williams, S. L.; elected third lieutenant and promoted to first lieutenant; was at home on a furlough at the close of the war; died since war.

Williams, James; killed at Manassas August 29, 1862.

Waters, Wash; got sick and retired on furlough in 1864; died since war.

Waters, T. A.; wounded at Manassas; disabled and discharged; died since war.

Wilkinson, William; transferred to Company K; severely wounded (place not remembered); yet living.

Wilkson, B. W.; died since war.

Yeomans, John; killed near New Market September 24, 1864, while on retreat; shot through by a cannon ball.

Surrendered at Appomattox April 9th, 1865, armed and in line:

Remer Franklin.
Thomas Boyet.
Ive Summerlin.
Madison Warren.

Corporal William Hollaway was captured two days before the surrender.

COMPANY E.

Montgomery Shapshooters, from Montgomery County, from August, 1861, to April, 1861.

Captain C. W. McArthur; promoted to lieutenant-colonel and killed at Spotsylvania C. H., May 12, 1864.

First Lieutenant J. W. Vaughn; resigned in spring of 1862.

Second Lieutenant John J. McArthur; resigned in winter of 1861.

Third Lieutenant Thos. M. McRae; promoted to captain; killed April, 1865, on retreat from Petersburg to Appomattox C. H.

First Sergeant John L. Matthews; promoted to second lieutenant March, 1862; wounded at Sharpesburg and again at Wilderness May 5, 1864, and retired.

Second Sergeant Thos. Benton Conner; died in Charlottsville July, 1862.

Third Sergeant J. W. McRae; promoted second lieutenant 1862; died in prison, after being wounded at Gettysburg, on Johnson's Island, Lake Erie.

Fourth Sergeant H. T. Wright; wounded at Spotsylvania May 12, 1864.

Fifth Sergeant W. S. Clark; died of typhoid fever in spring of 1862 at Bethesda.

First Corporal Stephen Nash; died of typhoid fever at Bethesda, 1862.

Second Corporal W. R. Vaughn; wounded at Monocacy July 9, 1864, and taken prisoner.

Third Corporal A. R. Browning; died of typhoid fever at Bethesda in spring of 1862.

Fourth Corporal J. Joyce; died in hospital.

Adams, A. J.; died in hospital in 1862.

Adams, M. J.; wounded at Fredericksburg December 13, 1862.

Adams, R. R.; wounded at Newtown, 1864.

Burch, B.; transferred to Company K, Sixty-first Georgia Regiment.

Beagles, J. J.; transferred to Company K, Sixty-first Georgia Regiment.

Browning, G. W.; wounded at Sharpsburg.

Browning, J, A.

Browning, J. D.; died at home since the war.

Bryan, R. A.; discharged for disability.

Burkhalter, J. M.; wounded at Gettysburg and died from effect of wound.

Burkhalter, J. C.; killed at Gettysburg.

Bone, T. K.; wounded at Monocacy, July 9, 1864, and murdered since the war.

Buchannan, L.; died in hospital in 1863.

Bridges, G.; died of miningetis near Hamilton's crossing in Spring of 1863.

Bridges, C.

Clements, A. M.; died in hospital at Denville.

Clements, J. B.; wounded at Sharpsburg.

Clements, D. G.; wounded at Sharpsburg.

Clark, P. H.; wounded at Sharpsburg.

Clark, W. A. died of typhoid fever at Bethesda

Conner, W. W.; killed at Fredericksburg December 13, 1862.

Clark, J. F,; survives.

Chaney, William; killed at Fredericksburg December 13, 1862.

Conner, J. A.; woundeded at Fredericksburg and died in hospital from wound.

Conner, J. F.; died in hospital in 1863.

Calhoun, H. A.; transferred to Company K; survives.

Clark, W. F.; survives.

Galbrith, H. A.; killed at Monocacy.

Ganes, B. F., survives.

Gay, J.; transferred to Company K; survives.

Gillis, J.; died in hospital.

Hughes, M. D.; wounded at wilderness May 5th, 1864 and retired.

Hughes. J. P.; died at Bethesda.

Hampton, L. H.; discharged for disability.

Higgs, D.; discharged for disability.

Johnson, R.; died in hospital, 1863.

Johnson, P.; wounded at Sharpsburg and survives.

Lovett, H.. died in hospital, 1863.

Latimer, O. O.; transferred to Company G, and discharged for disability.

McArthur, M. D.; promoted March 5th to third lieutenant; promoted December 27th to second lieutenant.

McSwain, J.; survives.

McQuaigg, J.; killed at Fredericksburg December 13th, 1862.

McKay, W. R.; killed at Fredericksburg, December 13th, 1862.

May, J.; killed at Monocacy July 9th, 1864.

Morrison, R.; killed at Cedar Run.

Muller, S.: died of typhoid fever at Sulphur Springs, Va., September 1862.

McLeod, W. H.; died in hospital 1863.

McRae, D. N.; wounded at Sharpsburg.

Mozo, H. C.; transferred to Company K, May 1862; killed at Sharpsburg, Md.

McCrimmon, A. H.; survives.

McAllister, J. W.; wounded at Sharpsburg; again at Wilderness May 5th, 1864.

McDaniel, M.; killed accidentally while on duty May 12th. 1862.

McRae, F. W.; died at Charlottsville 1862.

McBride, W. F.; discharged for disability.

Mobley, J. J.; transferred to Company K in May 1862, and promoted to first lieutenant; wounded at Gettysburg and captured.

Nash, L. C.; survives.

Nash, J. S.; survived the war, and murdered since.

Nail, Jim; killed at Hamilton's Crossing December 13, 1862.

Nail, B.; survives.

O'Conner, J.; wounded at Second Manassas.

Peterson, M. D.; survives.

Purvis, C. C.; wounded and lost an arm at Second Manassas.

Purvis, J.; survives.

Vaughan, J.; survives.

Vaughan, R. T.; survives.

Watson, J.; survives.

Wright, J. J.; wounded at Cold Harbor; captured at Spotsylvania C. H. May 12, 1864; died since war.

Williams, F. G.; faithful color-bearer; wounded several times; survives.

RECRUITS THAT WERE ADDED TO THE ORIGINAL COMPANY.

Adams, J. W.; wounded at Fredericksburg December 13, 1862.

Adams, W. T. E.; wounded at Fredericksburg December 13, 1862.

Browning, W. A.; killed at Monocacy July 9, 1864.

Browning, W. W.; died in hospital in 1864.

Burkhalter, G. M. C.; survives.

Bridges, Thomas; survives, home on furlough at surrender.

Carmichael, Duncan; survives.

Carmichael, B. J.; wounded at Gettysburg.

Currie, Thomas; killed at Gettysburg.
Currie, Dan; unknown.
Galbraith, Henry; discharged for disability.
Galbraith, Angus; survives.
Joyce, Thomas; died in hospital in 1864.
McSwain, Hector; survives.
Morrison, M.; killed at Cold Harbor in 1864.
McArthur, A. D.; died in August, 1865.
McBryde, R. B.; survives.
Purvis, Dan; unknown.
Vaughan, J. J.; unknown.
Vaughn, Bill; wounded near Petersburg.
Watson, Alex; survives.
Wall, Archie; died in hospital in 1864.
Wright, J. B.; unknown.
Wright, A. T.; wounded at Fredericksburg.
Wooten, R. D.; missing in battle at Fredericksburg, December 13, 1862.
Wooten, Hughes; killed.
Gillis, Hugh; survives.

MR. NICHOLS—At your request, I have done the best that I could on the muster roll of Company E.

Our county authorities haven't yet made out a muster roll of all the old soldiers from this county.

With my many best wishes for your undertaking, I am, very respectfully, your friend and comrade,

JAMES J. MOBLEY.

Lumber City, Ga., Oct. 7th, 1898.

COMPANY F.

GUARDS STARKE, FROM QUITMAN COUNTY, FROM 1861 TO 1865.

Captain Peter Brannon; promoted to major in the spring of 1863; brave man; efficient officer; killed at Gettysburg, Pa., July 1st, 1863.

First Lieutenant R. T. Cochrane; promoted to captain, 1863; most excellent officer; wounded at Spotsylvania C H, May 12th, 1863; yet living, 1898.

Second Lieutenant R. A. Fountain; resigned in 1862.

Third Lieutenant Joel Crofford; promoted to first lieutenant 1863; wounded in the foot in seven days battle before Richmond, 1862; again at Mine Run, November, 1863; is yet living, but blind, at Georgetown, Ga.

Albritton, Joshua; died in hospital, 1862.

Armstrong, John; yet living.

Atwell, R. T.; captured at Gettysburg, Pa.; yet living.

Bryant, Samuel; died in hospital, 1862.

Bowers, James; severely wounded in the hip at Sharpsburg, September 17th, 1862; yet living.

Brewer, Mathew; yet living, in Coffee County, Ala.

Bowen, George W.; yet living.

Barton, Septamus; yet living.

Bell, Drew; killed in battle of Monocacy, Md., July 9th, 1864.

Bridger, Leroy; died since the war.

Bolton, Henry; wounded in the shoulder, 1862, place unknown.

Bolton, John, wounded in the arm at Fredricksburg, December 13th, 1862.

Clancey, J. W.; died in hospital, time and place unknown.

Combs, Henry T.; killed at Cold Harbor, June, 1862.

Curlee, James; wounded in the knee at Sharpsburg on September 17th, 1862; yet living.

Cooper, Oliver; wounded at Cold Harbor; died in hospital 1863.

Causey, Harrison J.; yet living.

Culpepper, John; wonnded at Cold Harbor, 1864; died in hospital.

Catchins, Leonidus; killed at Sharpsburg, Md., September 17th, 1862.

Cook, G. W.; died since the war.

Croft, Spencer; went in as substitute for W. E. Gay in 1862.

Duggan, William; yet living.

Ellis, Thomas; died in hospital in 1862.

Foster, Thomas; yet living.

Foster, George; yet living.

Forrest, Briggs; died since the war.

Forest, John; yet living.

Forest, James.

Fields, H.; died since the war.

Guilford, Henry; discharged; died since the war.

Gaffney, Thomas; detailed on pioneer corps.

Goode, James T.; appointed quarter master-sergeant; died since the war.

Graves, Frank N.; transferred from Thirty-first Georgia Regiment; appointed commissary sergeant and elected lieutenant in 1864; captured at Spotsylvania C H, May 12, 1864; yet living.

Guynn, William; killed by Delk in Pike county Georgia, while in discharge of his duty as high sheriff Delk was duly executed for his crime.

Gay, Moses; killed at Mine Run in 1863.

Gay, William E.; discharged by substitute in April 1862; yet living.

Gay William; killed at Fredericksburg December 13, 1862.

Griffin, S. F.; died since the war.

Harrison, James, second lieutenant; promoted to ordnance sergeant December, 1861, and elected second lieutenant in May, 1864, at Spotsylvania C H.

Hardee, Eldridge; killed at Sharpsburg September 17, 1862.

Hardee, Charles; died since the war.

Hogan, Thomas, sergeant; extra fine soldier; died since the war.

Hillman, Robert; sergeant, died in Richmond hospital

Hale, Owen; extra fine soldier; wounded July 9, at Monocacy, Md.; died from wounds.

Hatcher, Henry; corporal; promoted to sergeant; killed on the 19th of September, 1864, bravely carrying the flag after the color bearer had been shot down.

Harrell, P. W.; killed at Sharpesburg, Md., September 17, 1862.

Harrell, William; killed in March 1865, near Petersburg, Va.

Harrell, G. W.; yet living.

Harrell, Elisha; yet living.

Hill, H. A.; missing at Gettysburg battle; supposed to be killed.

Holloman, J. M.; died in hospital in January, 1863, near Hamilton's Crossing, Va.

Hillman, Joshua; died in hospital at Richmond, Va., 1863.

Jones, James; died in hospital; time and place unknown.

Jones, William; died since war in Arkansas.

Jones, Seaborn; discharged, 1862.

Jolly, John C.; promoted to first sergeant; wounded at Gettysburg, Pa., July, 1863, and captured; exchanged in June, 1864; wounded October 19, 1864, at Cedar Creek, shot through breast; is yet living and suffering from wound.

Gordon, William J.; corporal; wounded July 9, 1864, at Monocacy, Md., and captured; paroled October 15, 1864.

Gordon, John E.; yet living.

Kelly, Elijah; yet living.

King, Bryant; wounded at Monocacy, Md., July 9, 1864; died since war with cancer.

Lindsey, Thomas; wounded in right hand; died since the war.

Lindsey, Moses; died on march in Virginia.

Lowe, Curtis A.; killed as color bearer at Fredericksburg December 13, 1862.

Lewis, Henry G.; discharged; died since the war.

Lewis, James L.; killed at Wilderness May 5, 1864.

Lewis, Charles W.; captured at Spotsylvania C. H. May 12, 1864; died in Northen prison.

Methvin, Daniel B.; captured at Spotsylvania C. H. May 12, 1864; died in Federal prison.

Methvin, Wm. T.; discharged by substitute.

Mooney, James; missing in 1862; unknown.

Morris, Richard; wounded in foot at Gettysburg July I, 1863; died since war.

Mercer, Jessie W.; wounded in shoulder and thigh (place unknown), and received other wounds.

McKinney, Henry; wounded at Sharpsburg, Md., September 17, 1862; died from wounds at Martinsburg, W. Va.

McKinney, C. C.; killed at Sharpsburg, Md., September 17, 1862.

McEachen, James W.; wounded at Gettysburg, Pa., July 1, 1863; yet living.

Meadows, Warren; wounded in face at Gettysburg, Pa., July 1, 1863; yet living.

Moore, William F., corporal; promoted to sergeant; wounded in hip; yet living.

Moore, James M.; died in hospital in 1862.

Moore, Thomas; died in hospital at Port Republic in 1862.

Moore, John C.; killed in battle at Fredericksburg December 13, 1862.

Nesbett, Mathew; wounded in head at Fredericksburg December 13, 1862, again in battle Wilderness May 5, 1864, in side; yet living.

Nesbett, Samuel; wounded in skirmish battle in 1863; yet living.

Ogletree, Seaborn; transferred to Company G, Fifty-first Georgia Regiment, for Bennett Powers; died since war.

Otis, Henry J., first sergeant; promoted to captain-quartermaster December, 1861; died since war.

Powers, David; wounded at Mary's Heights May 4, 1863; yet living.

Powers, Bennett; exchanged with Seaborn Ogletree from Fifty-first Georgia; killed at Monocacy, Md., in 1864.

Perkins, Jeff; transferred to Third Georgia Cavalry in 1863.

Parkham, Wm. B.; missing on march to Pennsylvania, 1863.

Pye, Freeman; died in hospstal in Virginia, 1862.

Roberts, John; wounded; lost left leg in battle of Wilderness May 6, 1864; yet living.

Roberts, Absolom; killed in skirmish battle May 17, 1864.

Reynolds, Jas. H.; killed in Sharpsburg battle September 17, 1862.

Rice, Stephen H.: elected corporal, then sergeant; elected lieutenant; killed at Gettysburg July 2, 1863.
Rice, William; wounded in thigh; died since the war.
Rice, George; wounded in side; died since the war.
Ryan, Peter; wounded; lost leg; died at home.
Ryan, Patrick; enlisted for G. W. Cook in 1863; killed at Morton's ford January 4, 1864, in skirmish battle.
Ryan, Michael; wounded in side at Monocacy, Md., July 9, 1864; died at home since war.
Raines, Mascon; discharged in 1861.
Rainey, Silas; killed at Gettysburg in July, 1863.
Shields, Albert A.; killed in skirmish battle July 17, 1864.
Smith, Thomas J.; died at home in 1861.
Smith, R. R.; died in hospital at Richmond, Va., 1862.
Slaton, George; wounded at Cedar Creek October 19, 1864; yet living.
Sharp, Jarod; yet living.
Sulley, Ben; discharged in 1863.
Sharp, Shared; discharged in 1862.
Sutley, Allen; died at Hamilton's Crossing in 1862.
Suggs, George; died since war.
Tilley, Lewis B. L.; yet living.
Tye, John; corporal; killed in skirmish battle at Smithfield, Va., September, 1864.
Thomas, Hardee; captured at Spotsylvania C. H., May 12, 1964.
Welch, Robert T.; yet living.
Welch, Cap; captured at Spotsylvania C H, Va., May 12th, 1864; died in Federal prison.
Willett, Polk: yet living.
Wade, John E,; died since the war.
Wade, John M.; yet living.
Watley, Green B.; died in hospital with pneumonia in Virginia, time and place unknown.

Wiggins, Henry; killed at Fredericksburg, Va., Decem-13th, 1862.

Welch, Hezakiah; substituted W. G. Methvin; died in Virginia hospital.

Webb, ——; discharged at Fredericksburg, 1863.

Wynn, ——.

Whaley, James; yet living.

COMPANY G.

WILKES GUARDS, FROM WILKES COUNTY, FROM 1861 TO 1865.

Captain Henry F. Colley; mortally wounded at Gaines' Mill and died in Richmond a few days afterwards.

First Lieutenant Zack Kendrick, resigned it 1862.

Second Lieutenant Webster Fanning; sresigned in 1862.

Third Lieutenant C. L. Moss; mortally wounded at Sharpsburg; died in Frederick City, Md.

First Sergeant John T. Erwin; elected captain after the Seven Day's Battle around Richmond; wounded at Gettysburg and Wilderness—totally disabled.

Second Sergeant Jeff T. Walton; killed at Richmond, Va., in 1862.

Third Sergeant Samuel Thornton; died at home.

Fourth Sergeant George W. Burdett; wounded at Fredericksburg; was disabled and retired.

First Corporal T. O. Smith; died in Virginia hospital in 1862.

Second Corporal John L. Girard; wounded at Gettysburg in 1863.

Third Corporal J. F. Smith; wounded at Sharpsburg in 1862; also at Gettysburg in 1863.

Fourth Corporal G. B. Cosby; killed at Sharpsburg, Md., in 1862.

Agee, J. C.; yet living.
Amison, Willis, died since the war.
Amison, W. B.; killed at Fredericksburg in 1862.
Allgood, Peter; discharged in 1862; died since the war.
Burdette, V. E., died at home in 1862.
Bailey, George S.; killed at Sharpsburg in 1862.
Bailey, Josiah; discharged in 1862; died since the war.
Bailey, James B.; died (time and place unknown).
Bryant, W. W.; unknown.
Bryant, J. C.; wounded at Sharpsburg and captured in hospital; died with small-pox.
Bryant, W. A.; unknown.
Bell, T. W.; wounded (battle not remembered).
Booker, E. A.; enlisted at the age of 15; was in all the battles and marches; died since war.
Barrett, M. R.; yet living, in Texas.
Burkhalter, W. A.; unknown.
Colley, D. C.; promoted to first lieutenant after the battle of Sharpsburg; killed at the battle of Fredericksburg.
Colley, G.; promoted to corporal; wounded at Fredericksburg; surrendered at Appomattox; yet living.
Colley, F. G.; unknown.
Colley, Henry C.; wounded at Fredericksburg.
Cooper, J. M.; discharged while at Jekyl Island; died since war.
Cade, W. B.; died at home while on a furlough.
Danner, F. W.; promoted to sergeant; wounded at Fredericksburg; died at home while on a furlough.
Danner, J.; died in hospital (time and place unknown).
Dunaway, J. M.; unknown.
Dunaway, T. H.; unknown.
Downer, George; wounded at Fredericksburg and the Wilderness.
Downer, David; killed at Gettysburg July 1, 1863.

Dinkens, J. A.; killed at Fredericksburg, 1862.

DuPriest, Wm.; unknown.

Evans, J. W.; severely wounded at Fredericksburg; disabled and retired.

Elliott, W. N.; killed at Gettysburg July 1, 1863.

Eads, R. H.; unknown.

Edmonds, Dick; captured in Pennsylvania while out foraging.

Echolls,—; unknown.

Farmer, Josiah; killed at Fisher's Hill in 1864.

Florence, Gibson; killed at Gettysburg.

Gibson, J. H.; wounded at Fredericksburg; retired from service.

Garrard, Wm.; unknown.

Gullatt, Geo.; killed at Kernestown, near Winchester in 1864.

Gresham, Geo.; died in hospital at Winchester in 1862.

Hopkins, G. W.; detailed in litter corps; a good one too; died since war.

Hopkins, Geo. I.; died since war.

Higgins, Geo.; promoted captain of commissary department; resigned in 1863 and joined Morgan's cavalry.

Holtzclaw, Daniel; unknown.

Holtzclaw, Henry; wounded at Mine Run in 1863.

Hallowes, J. N.; promoted to sergeant-major; killed at Sharpsburg.

Hammond, Wm.; unknown.

Hester, John T.; promoted to first lieutenant after the Fredericksburg battle; extra fine officer; severely wounded at Spotsylvania; yet living.

Jackson, Wm. R.; promoted to corporal; unknown.

Lindsey, John T.; mortally wounded at Fredericksburg; died in hospital.

Latimer, O. O.; discharged in 1862 on surgeon's certificate; unknown.

Lansford, Jas. E.; died since war.
McKenny, A. L.; died in Savannah, Ga., hospital.
Marlow, Hugh; transferred to Company K.
Maxwell, Geo. M.; died since war.
Mansfield, T.; died in hospital in Georgia in 1862.
Meadows, J. W.; killed at Gettysburg July 1st, 1863.
Mullikin, Thomas J.; faithful soldier; died since war.
Mullikin, W. C.; yet living in Augusta, Ga.
McAvoy, William; promoted to first sergeant 1862; a brave, cool soldier in battle; died since the war.
Nash, Daniel; faithful soldier; yet living.
Oglesby, Ray; killed at Sharpsburg 1862.
Poss, W. R.; killed at Gaines' Mill 1862.
Poss, John A.; yet living.
Poss, W. C.; died since the war.
Power, John C.; died in hospital in Virginia.
Powers, William; unknown; wounded at Fredericksburg 1862; also at Wilderness 1864.
Roberts, John; died in hospital in Savannah, Ga. (?)
Revere, George; severely wounded at Gettysburg; retired from service.
Smallwood, Henry; detailed to drive ambulance; a good one too; yet living.
Smith, G. Burdette; promoted to second lieutenant after the battle of Fredericksburg; captured at Mine Run; remained in prison till the war closed; unknown.
Smith, George Blakely; yet living; surrendered at Appomattox.
Smith, James R.; Living in California when last heard from.
Smith, Frank; unknown.
Smith, Hawkins; discharged in 1862; died at home.
Short, John N.; wounded at second battle of Manassas; surrendered at Appomattox; unknown.
Short, Dan M.; faithful soldier; promoted to corporal.

Strozier, Gid N.; wounded at Mine Run 1863; again at Cold Harbor 1864;

Sherrer, A. Frank; died ln hospital in Virginia, 1862.

Silvie, I. M.; slightly wounded at Gaines' Mill June 27th, 1862.

Sisson, J. Calt; detailed to litter corps; a good one too; unknown.

Thurmond, William; unknown.

Turner, Judson; transferred to Company K, Sixty-first Georgia Regiment.

Turner, Luke; unknown.

Wolfe, Alex; wounded at Maries' Heights in1863; again at Fisher's Hill in 1864.

Wolfe, H. J.; faithful soldier; yet living.

Wolfe, J. N.; faithful soldier; yet living.

Woolfe, George A.; discharged and died at home.

Wellmaker, A. F., killed at Wilderness, May 5, 1864.

Wellmaker, W. L.; died in Virginia hospital in 1862.

Wellmaker, J. H.; died in Virginia hospital in 1862.

Wellmaker, F. C.; moved to Texas; unknown.

Boatwright, ——; killed at Monocacy, Md.

Frazier, J. L., promoted to third lieutenant after the battle of Fredericksburg; wounded May 12, 1864.

Surrendered at Appomattox.

Anderson, Thad; unknown.

Anderson, Z. W.; yet living in Wilkes county, Georgia.

Bradford, W. P.; died since the war.

Bunch, S. J.; yet living in Wilkes County, Georgia.

Heard, S. D.; was transferred to cavalry; died since the war.

Keough, John; died since the war.

Sanders, George W.; moved to Mississippi; unknown.

Safford, R. B.; moved to California; unknown.

Thurmond, J.; yet living in Wilkes County, Georgia.

COMPANY H.

Tattnall County Volunteers, from Tattnall County, from May 9th, 1862, to April 9th, 1865.

Captain J. B. Smith; resigned at Richmond, Va., in June, 1862; died since the war.

First Lieutenant J. M. Dasher; promoted to captain in June, 1862; returned home on account of bad health; died at home, September, 1862.

Second Lientenant M. B. Brewton; killed at second battle of Manassas.

Third Lieutenant W. J. M. Edwards; resigned in June, 1862, and returned home; still living.

First Sergeant M. M. Sikes; died in hospital in Virginia 1862.

Second Sergeant Alfred Strickland; died in hospital at Charlottsville, Va., 1862.

Third Sergeant James E. DeLoach; elected second lieutenant in August, 1862; promoted to first lieutenant August, 1862; promoted to captain the fall of 1862; severely wounded at Gettysburg; taken prisoner at Fisher's Hill, 1864; remained in prison till the close; still living.

First Corporal D. D. Sikes; died in hospital in Virginia, 1862.

Second Corporal Peter Burkhalter; killed at second battle of Manassas in August, 1862.

Third Corporal Alfred Kennedy; promoted to second sergeant in the fall of 1862; brave as a lion; was assassinated since the war by H. Futch.

Bazil, J. W.; went through war; faithful soldier; still living.

Burkhalter, Bryant; captured and died in a Northern prison.

Bacon, A. E.; died since war.

Bacon, E. L.; surrendered at Appomattox; returned home; faithful soldier; yet living.

Bacon, John ; died in hospital in 1862 or '63.

Bacon, Benj.; died in hospital in 1862 or '63.

Barnard, J. J.; died in hospital at Charlottsville, Va., 1862.

Bargarron, B. E.; one thumb shot off at Wilderness; yet living.

Causey, T. J.; faithful soldier; yet living.

Causey, Wm.; faithful soldier; yet living.

Collins, Horatio; wounded in hand; yet living.

Carpenter, C. H.; faithful soldier; yet living.

Conley, W. C.; promoted to corporal in 1862; is now a Methodist preacher.

Clifton, Wm.; promoted to second corporal; killed at second battle of Manassas, 1862.

DeLoach, J. D.; elected third lieutenant in August, 1862; promoted to second lieutenant August 29, 1862 ; promoted to first lieutenant September, 1862; taken prisoner in 1864 at Spotsylvania; held in retaliation forty days ; yet living.

DeLoach, J. A.; died in hospital at Charlottsville, 1862.

Dowdy, A. M.; killed at Gettysburg July 1, 1863.

Fiveash, Peter; died in hospital (time and place unknown).

Frix, Nimrod ; missing at Wilderness in 1864.

Godbee, W. W.; appointed first sergeant in September, 1862.

Groomes, W. W.; missing in battle in 1863; unknown.

Gayney, Wm.; killed at second battle of Manassas.

Gray, Daniel; killed at Spotsylvania C. H., 1864.

Hardeeman, P, H.; transferred to navy in 1862; yet living.

James, Josiah; died since war.

James, M. M.; transferred to navy in 1863; never returned; unknown.

Johnson, G. J.; yet living.

Kennedy, Henry; died in hospital in 1862.

Kennedy, O. W.; discharged for disability in 1862; still living.

Kennedy, Hampton; died in hospital in 1862 or 1863.

Kennedy, Rayford; discharged for disability in 1863; died since the war.

Lynn, Asberry; extra fine soldier; still living.

Lynn, J. B.; died since the war.

Lynn, R. H.; surrendered at Appomattax; died since the war.

Lynn, C. W.; extra fine soldier; still living.

Lang, Joshua; extra good soldier; still living.

Lang, William; died from wound in 1863.

Lang, Henry; died from wound in 1862.

Lang, George; died in hospital in 1862.

McKay, T. A.; fine soldier- still living.

McKay, James; killed at second battle of Massassas.

Moore, Nathaniel; killed at Sharpsburg, September, 1862.

Mikell, Edward; died in hospital in 1862.

McDildee, George; died in hospital in 1863.

McDildee, A.; faithful soldier; still living.

Oneal, E; killed at second battle of Manassas in August, 1862.

Richardson, S.; still lives.

Rogers, S. B.; fine soldier; died since the war.

Rogers, M. J.; fine soldier; still living.

Sharpe, W. W.; fine soldier; still living.

Sikes, A. J.; captured in Pennsylvania or Maryland in 1863; still living.

Strickland, Albert; died in hospial in Charlottsville, Va., 1862.

Strickland, J. M.; died in hospital in Charlottsville, Va., 1862.

Strickland, W.; discharged for disability; unknown.

Tootle, M. J.; promoted to third sergeant; lost an arm at Gettysburg; still lives.

Thomas, Stephen; still lives.

Wilkes, J. O.; fine foldier; yet living.

Williams, P. A.; fine soldier; yet living.

COMPANY I.

THOMSON GUARDS, FROM BIBB COUNTY, FROM 1861 TO 1865.

Captain James D. Vanvalkinsburg; promoted to major in 1863, and to lieutenant-colonel in 1864; killed at Monocacy, Md., July 9, 1864.

First Lieutenant C. S. Virgin; wounded at Gaines' Mill; promoted to the office of captain in July, 1863.

Second Lieutenant E. P. Lewis; killed at second battle of Manassas.

Third Lieutenant Eugene Jeffers; promoted to first lieutenant; captured at Spotsylvania C. H.; died since war.

First Sergeant S. W. Berry; missing at Gaines' Mill; supposed to have been killed.

Second Sergeant Geo. W. Sims; severely wounded in foot and leg August 30, 1862. yet living.

Third Sergeant W. R. Avant; taken prisoner at Gettysburg; died since war.

Fourth Sergeant Geo. W. Norris; lost left arm at Gettysburg.

Fifth Sergeant Jas. A. Simpson; wounded at Gaine's Mill; taken prisoner at Gettysburg.

First Corporal F. M. C. Rape; killed at Sharpsburg September 17, 1862.

Second Corporal W. P. Shaw; wounded in the hand at Cedar Mountain.

Third Corporal James R. James; wounded at Sharpsburg, Md.; elected second lieutenant; wounded at Gettysburg and Petersburg; yet living.

Fourth Corporal Joshua G. Clarke; killed at Winchester September 19, 1864.

Arnold, J. W.; taken prisoner at Spottsylvania.

Anderson, J. P.; died in prison at Elmira, N. Y., 1864.

Amerson, Charles; faithful soldier; unknown,

Arnold, S. D.; faithful soldier; unknown.

Arnold, W. B.; fine soldier; surrendered at Appomattox; unknown.

Barnett, James; lost left arm at Gettysburg; unknown.

Bone, C. N.; killed at Sharpsburg.

Berry, W. H.; detailed as teamster; died since the war.

Burkett, Robert; fine soldier; unknown.

Boothe, William; surrendered at Appomattox; died since the war.

Brannen, J. H.; died in Lynchburg hospital in 1863.

Brice, W. H.; fine soldier; unknown.

Bridger, W. R.; wounded at Sharpsburg; unknown.

Bivens, G. T.; died in Richmond hospital in 1862.

Blair, Joseph; killed at South Mountain, August 9, 1862.

Blair, B. T.; good soldier; unknown.

Blair, McKenzie; surrendered at Appomattox; unknown.

Braddock, W. A.; surrendered at Appomattox; unknown.

Brown, W. T.; surrendered at Appomattox; unknown.

Cobb, Joel; wounded at Gettysburg; died since the war.

Chapman, James P.; lost leg at Monocacy, Md., 1864; unknown.

Chapman, Giles; killed at Wilderness in 1864.

Dail, James D.; died in Staunton, Va., hospital in 1862.

Davis, J. C.; died in Winchester hospital in 1862.

Davis, W. J.; taken prisoner at Spotsylvania; unknown.

Davidson, I.; good soldier; died since the war.

Davidson, John; good soldier; unknown.

Doyle, John; discharged at Charleston, S. C., in 1862; died since the war.

Defoor, Joseph A.; faithful soldier and company's commissary; unknown.

Ford, William; killed at Gettysburg, wounded at second battle of Manassas.

Ford, Josiah; faithful soldier; unknown.

Gresham, W. J.; faithful soldier.

Gresham, W. H.; faithful soldier; unknown.

Groomes, S.; discharged in April, 1864; unknown.

Grist, Ranson; discharged; died since war.

Grist, G. N.; discharged; died since war.

Goodyear, Ben; detailed for drug clerk; surrendered at Appomattox; unknown.

Hambrick, J.; unknown.

Harrell, W. H.; discharged in 1862; unknown.

Heath, W. M.; wounded in hand (battle unknown); unknown.

Herndon, M. P.; wounded in second battle of Manassas and Wilderness; died in hospital.

Jones, H. R.; transferred to Company K; unknown.

Jones, C. G.; wounded at second battle of Manassas and Gettysburg; unknown.

Jessup, W. F.; wounded at Mine Run, 1863; unknown.

Jackson, Wm.; killed at Smithville, Va., 1864.

King, W. S., Jr.; unknown.

King, John V.; unknown.
King, J. A.; unknown.
King, A. M.; wounded in hand at Manassas; unknown.
King, W. S., Sr.; unknown.
Kelly, W. P.; taken prisoner at Spotsylvania; unknown.
Knight, J. T.; killed at Fisher's Hill in 1864.
Kilpatrick, J. I.; killed in battle (unknown).
Lancaster, L. C.; discharged at Orange C. H., 1864; unknown.
Lovett, J.; unknown.
Miller, M. V.; died in valley, 1864.
Miller, G. W.; lost a leg at Gettysburg; unknown.
Miller, A.; died id prison at Fort Delaware, 1864.
Miller, N. H.; killed at second battle of Manassas.
Miller, W. G. T.; killed in valley in 1864.
Miller, James; killed at Fredericksburg in 1862.
Mims, H. M.; detailed as ordnance sergeant; surrendered at Appomattox; unknown.
Moore, Thomas W.; discharged in 1863; unknown.
Moncrief, J. J.; detailed in litter corps and company commissary.
Morris, D. A.; fine soldier; unknown.
Owens, J. P.; fine soldier; nnknown.
Peavy, J. G.; fine soldier; unknown.
Pitts, A. F.; died in hospital at Charlottsville, 1862.
Peyton, Thomas C.; died in hospital at Charlottsville, 1862.
Peyton, John B.; detailed in ordnance department; unknown.
Poole, W. W. W.; extra fine soldier; unknown.
Ruffe, John; wounded at Fredericksburg.
Reese, Joseph; fine soldier; unknown.
Raines, Burton; killed at Gettysburg, 1863.
Raines, Cullen; killed at Gettysburg, 1863.
Roberts, Zack; died in hospital in Lynchburg, 1863.

Roberts, William; killed at Fredericksburg, 1862.
Renfroe, S.; killed in Fredericksburg, 1862.
Rape, M. C.; missing.
Reynolds, R. F.; discharged in 1862.
Scott, H. R.; unknown.
Spicer, W. H.; killed at Winchester, 1864.
Spicer, Todd; taken prisoner at Winchester; died since the war.
Smallwood, J.; killed at Cedar Creek, 1864.
Skipper, J. W.; unknown.
Seaborn, David; killed in 1863; (battle unknown).
Stafford, J. W.; fine soldier; unknown.
Shaw, J. R.; started as a musician; unknown.
Sizemore, George; wounded at Gettysburg; unkdown.
Sheton, W. L. transferred to Twentieth Georgia Regiment.
Thompson, James; transferred to cavalry; died in hospital.
Taylor, W. T., killed at Bristoe Station in 1863.
Venable, J. E.; detailed to Macon arsenal in 1862; unknown.
Wolfe, H. E.; faithful soldier; unknown.
Wilson, John; faithful soldier; unknown.
Williams, M.; surrendered at Appomattox; faithful soldier.

NAMES OF THOSE WHO SURRENDERED AT APPOMATTOX.

Arnold, M. B.; Boothe, William; Burkett, Robert;
Defoor, J. A.; Peyton, J. B.; McKinsy, Blair;
Cullin, Raines; Mimms, H. M.; Goodyear, Ben;
Williams, M.

COMPANY K.

MUSTER ROLL AND CASUALTIES OF COMPANY K, OF THE SIXTY-FIRST GEORGIA REGIMENT.

Captain E. F. Sharpe; went through the war without a wound; commanded the regiment six months; yet living.

First Lieutenant J. J. Mobley; promoted to adjutant; captured at Spotsylvania C. H.; yet living.

Second Lieutenant D. L. Gray; killed at Spotsylvania C. H.

Third Lieutenant J. E. C. Tillman; captured at Spotsylvania C. H.; yet living.

First Sergeant Henry R. Sharpe; served through the war without a wound; surrendered at Appomattox; yet living.

Second Sergeant H. A. Calhoun; captured at Spotsylvania; was kept in prison eight months; yet living.

Third Sergeant Z. J. Collins; killed at Monocacy July 9th, 1864.

First Corporal J. Stafford; fine soldier; died since the war.

Second Corporal B. H. Ryals; still living.

Third Corporal J. J. Finley; wounded, place unknown; died since the war.

Brown, H. N.; killed at Gettysburg.

Blocker, J. A.; fine soldier; yet living; unknown.

Blocker, John; killed at Sharpsburg, Md.

Burke, Edward; killed at Wilderness May 5th, 1864.

Bigles, J. J.

Butts, Frank; killed at Gettysburg.

Burch, Berry; fine soldier; still living.

Blalock, H. H.; fine soldier; yet living.

Collins, A. J.; wounded at Manassas and Winchester; yet living.
Conner, C.; killed at Wilderness May 5th, 1864.
Conner, Benjamin; died in hospital; fine soldier.
Conner, Frank; died in hospital; fine soldier.
Driggers, Z.; killed at Gettysburg.
Floyd, W. W.
Finley, S. L.; wounded at Fredericksburg December 5th; fine soldier; yet living.
Gray, G. T.; died in hospital; fine soldier.
Gay, Jacob; unknown.
Harden, O. J.; killed at Gettysburg.
Hodges, W. G.; fine soldier; yet living.
Jerrell, John; fine soldier; yet living.
Moore, W. F.; fine soldier; yet living.
Mozo, H.; killed at Sharpsburg.
Mobley, William; died in hospital at Gordonsville.
Morris, C.; unknown.
Moses, M. T.; wounded at Fredericksburg, Va., Dec. 13; yet living.
Nails, James; killed at Wilderness.
Odum, L. B.; killed on retreat in the valley.
Odum, Dan; faithful soldier; yet living.
Odum, John; killed in the valley in 1864.
Riggs, Shep; yet living.
Riggs, A. B.; wounded 27th of June, 1862; yet living.
Ryals, J. J.; died in hospital.
Sikes, H.; excellent soldier; yet living.
Smith. M. V.; killed; place unknown.
Scarboro, J. N.; killed at Gettysburg, July 1, 1863.
Scarboro, W. D.; fine soldier; got sick and retired; yet living.
Surrency, S. S.; faithfnl soldier; yet living.
Surrency, J. M.; faithful soldier; unknown.
Surrency, H. H.; faithful soldier; yet living.

Surrency, Allen; unknown.
Turner, Judson; killed near Petersburg in 1865.
Underwood, W. L.; unknown.
Wilkinson, W. R.; severely wounded twice (places unknown); yet living.
Waters, W. H.; unknown.
Watson, Alex; faithful soldier; yet living.
Wolfe, Lewis; killed at Spotsylvania May 12, 1864.
Waters, J. M.; surrendered at Appomattox.

FIELD OFFICERS.

Captain Thomas M. McRae, killed on retreat from Petersburg.
Ordnance sergeant, H. R. Mims.
Hospital steward, Benjamin Goodger.

Company A.

Sergeant, J. McDuffie,
William Branch,
H. L. Paulk,
Sergeant, R. H. Henderson.
J. Branch,
M. Hansel,
William Vickers—7.

Company B.

Musician, S. W. W. Hagin,
J. H. Odum,
William Higgs,
John Powell,
J. T. Sharp—5.

Company C.

1st Sergeant N. M. Reddick
E. W. Burton,
J. T. Moore,
C. R. Browning,
W. Lewis,
William Smith,
G. Isaac Weldon—7.

Company D.

Corporal Wm. Holloway,
Lemuel Davis,
Remer Franklin,
Madison Warren,
Thomas Boyet,
Jackson Collins,
Ivy Summerlin,
Thomas Waters—8

Company E.

Captain Thos. M. McRae, killed on the retreat from Petersburg.

Sergeant D. N. McRae,
G. M. Burkhalter,
J. L. Clark,
H. McSwain,
R. T. Vaughan,
J. Browning,
P. H. Clark,
J. McSwain,
L. C. Marsh,
J. Watson,
F. G. Williams—11.

Company F.

Serg't John E. Wade,
Corporal George F. Rice,
G. W. Bowen,
H. L. Causey,
E. E. Harrell,
John A. Jorden,
Irwin Nesbett,
Serg't John M. Wade,
S. Barton,
Levi Bridges,
B. W. Forrest,
G. W. Harrell,
Thomas Lindsey,
Samuel Nesbett,
J. Mercer—15.

Company G.

Corporal G. Colley,
A. B. Ammerson,
J. Hanson
James E. Lansford,
George Blakely Smith,
Corporal E. A. Booker,
D. B. Connor,
G. W. Hopkins,
John N. Short,
Alexander Wolf—10.

Company H.

E. L. Bacon,
R. H. Lynn—2.

COMPANY I.

W. B. Arnold,
William Booth,
J. A. DeFoor,
Cullen Raines,
Sergeant H. R. Mims,
Robert Burket,
McKinsie Blair,
John B. Peyton,
W. Williams,
Hosp'l Stwd. B. Goodger—10.

COMPANY K.

First Sergeant H. R. Sharp,
H. H. Blalock,
Sergeant J. M. Waters.
Hampton Sikes,
H. H. Sharpe—5.

Total—80.

I certify that only forty-nine of this number were armed and in line on the morning of April 9th, 1865, the day General Lee surrendered at Appomattox.

W. B. JONES, Colonel,
Commanding Sixtieth and Sixty-first Georgia Regiments.

To show the readers of this history how some of the brigades were reduced in the Army of Northern Virginia, I will give them the numbers in the ten Louisiana regiments that once formed Generals Hayes and Taylor's Louisiana brigades, which went to Virginia in 1861 about 12,000 strong.

The two brigades were consolidated before the war closed and was commanded by Colonel E. Waggaman, of the Tenth Louisiana Regiment. I feel safe in saying the world has never produced better soldiers than these noble heroes.

There were three hundred and sixty-eight rank and file surrendered in the different regiments, as follows:

The First Louisiana Regiment surrendered 18 non-commissioned officers and men.

The Second Louisiana Regiment surrendered 41 non-commissioned officers and men.

The Fifth Louisiana Regiment surrendered 18 non-commissioned officers and men.

The Sixth Louisiana Regiment surrendered 48 non-commissioned officers and men.

The Seventh Louisiana Regiment surrendered 42 non-commissioned officers and men.

The Eighth Louisiana Regiment surrendered 54 non-commissioned officers and men.

The Ninth Louisiana Regiment surrendered 64 non-commissioned officers and men.

The Tenth Louisiana Regiment surrendered 13 non-commissioned officers and men.

The Fourteenth Louisiana Regiment surrendered 25 non-commissioned officers and men.

The Fifteenth Louisiana Regiment surrendered 17 non-commissioned officers and men.

The ten different Louisiana regiments surrendered 28 commissioned officers, making a total of 368 in all.

My dear comrades, widows and children of the fallen heroes, I now feel that my work is done, and respectfully ask you all to look over the imperfections in this book. I have done the best I could to give my readers a thorough̲ly reliable history.

THE END.

A GALAXY OF SOUTHERN HEROES.

BY O. T. DOZIER, M. D., BIRMINGHAM, ALA.

Once more the genial Southern sun
 Has called the roses into bloom,
Once more the golden jessamine
 Lades all the air with sweet perfume;
Once more the little mating birds
 In every tree and bush are seen,
Once more the earth her carpet spreads
 Of softest velvet—grassy green.

Once more the dove of peace is heard
 In every valley, glen and cove;
Once more I come with rapturous heart
 To greet the comrades that I love;
And freed from hate and prejudice,
 All bitter memories laid aside,
My muse but wakes to sing the praise
 Of those who for my country died.

And anon, here and there to lay
 A chaplet on some worthy brow
Of glorious hero—yet alive—
 And, as I place it, humbly bow,
As well I should, with reverence due;
 For language is too weak to prove
How deep, how strong the wond'rous depths
 Of my unfathomed founts of love.

But would to God my struggling muse
 Could break the bonds that bind my soul,
And let my wild, impassioned thoughts,
 Like ocean's stormy billows roll,
While I so vainly now attempt
 To sing in lofty pæans grand
That meed of praise to patriots due—
 The Heroes of my native land.

With heaven's face for music scroll
  And realms of space for octave bars,
My clefs should be the sun and moon,
  My music notes the blazing stars,
And oh! I'd sing with lofty strain
  And sweep the gamut of the skies,
Till every sleeping patriot's soul
  Should wake and from his grave arise.

But oh!. how feeble, weak am I,
  Poor, humble creature of the sod,
Who deigns to touch a theme too grand
  For any being. but, that God,
Who rules the earth and realms above,
  Who speaks, and Suns and worlds obey,
He, only He, the living God
  Their meed of praise can ever pay.

What tho' I had the cyclone's force,
  The flaming lightning for my tongue,
A brain as broad as universe,
  My voice to tones of thunder strung.
I still must fall unmeasured short
  In praise of those I fain would name,
For God but made such God-like men
  To point the source from whence they came.

How many names—bright, glorious gems—
  In Southern galaxy are set,
To blaze like suns forever bright
  In fame's eternal coronet.
Behold you, first, our Washington,
  Whose hands the stars and stripes unfurled,
A Christian soldier, patriot true,
  The foremost rebel of the world.

Then see yon brilliant, fiery star,
  Proud Robert Toombs—majestic man,
Whose wild, tempestuous, flaming soul,
  Too great for human words to span,

From ut whose rugged, heaving breast,
In raging, seething tempests, rolled
Consuming flames of eloquence—
Mount Ætna, he of human mould.

And could I paint with master hand
The great Orion of the sky,
With starry belt and lifted club,
With daring mien to do or die,
What would I but hold up to view
The chief of that heroic clan
Who San Jacinto's battle won,
And name Sam Houston as the man.

But countless as the countless stars
That in the dome of heaven shine,
Each name as bright as face of Mars,
Made glorious by their deeds sublime,
And bright'ning with the passing years,
Is that great constellation grand
Who followed where our Davis led—
The heroes of our Southern land.

No lowering cloud of dark defeat
Can dim or shut their light from view,
But high above the horizon,
Where God to justice gives its due,
They shine within a firmament
As fixed as that of heaven's own
And shed a glory on the world,
The brightest earth has ever known.

Go stand upon the Cumberland,
Go view the heights of Tennessee,
Go climb to Lookout's lofty point
And gaze as far as eye can see;
On every crag and every plain,
Marked by the storm of battle blast,
Joe Johnston's name is over all,
To linger there while time shall last.

And lo! above each mountain pass,
  Each hill and vale, each cove and glen,
A glorious halo lingers yet,
  Where, meteor-like, that prince of men,
In brilliant speed and splendor swept
  Athwart the flames on battle crest,
Pat Cleburne with his flashing blade,
  The blazing comet of the west.

Now look on yon great ocean wide,
  Extending far as billows sweep,
Cut by the "Alabama's" keel,
  See there a name engraven deep—
Eternal and as lasting there
  As Neptune's star in yonder sky—
Brave Admiral Semmes, a hero grand,
  Whose name and fame can never die.

And when storm-rocked Atlanta shook
  And writhed beneath the shrieking shell,
While tempests wild around her raged
  And leaden hail in fury fell,
When light'ning's flashed and thunders rolled
  And flowed her streets with crimson flood,
Who then stood there—bright star of hope—
  But brave, defiant Ajax—Hood?

And o'er yon Old Dominion State,
  Star gemmed, her crown with glory shines,
With Southern pride I here avow
  That nowhere on this earth's confines
Can there be found another land
  Which can so many heroes claim,
And bright amid her brightest stars
  Shines glorious Stonewall Jackson's name.

And glittering like a diadem
  Above my own fair Georgia high
I see another briliant star,
  As bright as ever decked the sky,

Intrepid, brilliant Gordon, brave,
  The patriot, statesman, warrior grand,
Of Southern manhood, brightest type,
  An honor to his native land.

Nor less resplendent is the light
  Of him, old South Carolina's star,
Whose fiery soul was made by God
  To blaze amid the storms of war ;
And high on fame's eternal height,
  With all the glorious and sublime,
Wade Hampton's name, in glory set,
  Will shine while rolls the wheels of time.

And yet, oh yet with rapturous eyes
  To Alabama turn your gaze.
See o'er her proudest mountain heights
  A rising light, destined to blaze
Eternal, on Old Glory's field.
  Joe Wheeler, spared by hand of God,
Hath plucked from out our Southern seas
  Another star to glitter there—
  'Tis Cuba, Queen of Antilles.

Now see yon grand, majestic stream,
  The great mid-continental sea,
Whose course no human force can check,
  Whose current deep but flowing free,
Unswerving in its onward sweep,
  Proud Mississippi, king of streams;
See, and behold while gazing there
  A fitting type to me it seems

Of him whose grand and kingly soul—
  Too strong for tyrant bonds to quell,
Too deep for prejudice to mar,
  Too broad to curb by prison cell—
Proud, God-like man, I breathe his name
  With reverence and with deathless love—
Jeff Davis, brightest star of fame,
  May heaven rest his soul above.

But where! oh where, my wavering muse,
Where wilt thou lead me in thy flight
To find a type or simile
Of him the grandest, noblest knight
That ever sword from scabbard drew?
Not in the land Columbus gave
Canst thou a likeness for him find,
But far beyond old ocean's wave,

Where God His grandest works designed;
Go view the Alps and Pyrenees,
Then onward to the Himalays,
Where great Mount Everest, rising, sees
All other mountains far below,
His own grand form enrobed with cloud,
His royal head God crowned with snow—
Yes, go and view this mountain proud;

This great, majestic, towering king,
The grandest, highest of the world—
God's monument of strength and power,
Defying every storm that's hurled,
All lightning blows from rival foes;
Yes, go, and you this mountain see,
Then tell me if thou yet hast found
A prototype of Robert Lee?

Ah, no! ah, no! my faithful muse,
Thou further yet must wing thy flight.
Go, mount yon heaven's vaulted dome,
Explore the azure seas of night,
Go poise amid the glittering throng
Of starry pageants in the sky,
And measure thou great Alcyone,
The central sun of worlds on high.

'Round whom all suns and worlds revolve—
The first, the greatest and the best
Of all the shining heavenly spheres—
And, poising there, thy wings may rest;

For in that far celestial zone,
  There 'mid the circling pleiades see
That king of worlds, imperial orb,
  God's prototype of Robert Lee.

And now, oh now, my halting muse,
  While poising 'mid celestial heights
Of blazing suns and mighty worlds,
  Of shining moons and satelites,
I bid thee, if thou canst, to pluck
  From orbs on high celestial fire
And fling it now into my soul,
  That it may warm me and inspire

My song to higher, loftier strain
  That ever bard hath dared to sing,
For meed of praise to privates due
  Should make the very welkin ring
And call angelic convoys down
  From heaven's bright, supernal sphere,
To catch the strain and tune their harps
  To notes that they would gladly hear.

What tho' no circumstance or pomp
  Hath written down each separate name—
What tho' no granite column tells
  The individual's private fame—
What tho' on earth there's no reward
  For all their suffering, toil and strife—
Their names, thank God, in realms on high
  Are written in the "Book of Life."

Yes, tho' unmarked and hardly known,
  Almost obscured and hid from view,
Their's is a glory, none the less,
  As bright as ever heaven knew.
Yea, like the rolling, shining orbs
  That glow in yonder "milky way,"
Tho' only faint and dimly seen
  They blaze as does yon god of day.

For never since the morning stars
  Together sang with joyful song
O'er new born earth, by God-head sent
  To join the grand, triumphal throng
Of suns and worlds that onward sweep
  Around His great, majestic throne,
Was ever truer, nobler men
  Than Southern private soldiers known.

Not even that celestial host
  Who drove, with wrathful thunders dire,
The traitor, Satan, and his horde
  From heaven's courts to pits of fire,
Was more unselfish, brave and true
  Than was that grand, heroic band
Who fought beneath the stars and bars
  For God, for home and native land.

And when old earth's last round is run,
  And God commands her march to halt,
When Gabriel, adjutant on high,
  The roll shall read from yonder vault,
Where suns and worlds in ranks aligned,
  Shall stand to hear God's orders read,
May crowns the brightest God can give
  Be there for every private's head.

Index

Note: This index does not include the 61st Georgia rosters that appear on pages 28–29 and 236–283 of the original edition.
Italics signify illustrations